AMERICA FIRST

A general view of the America First rally held in Madison Square Garden on May 23, 1941, at which Charles A. Lindbergh and Senator Burton K. Wheeler of Montana were speakers.

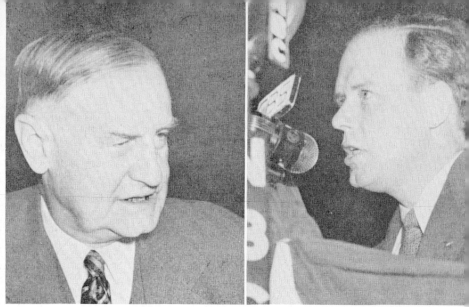

Top left: General Robert E. Wood. *Right:* Charles A. Lindbergh. *Bottom left:* R. Douglas Stuart, Jr. *Right:* Senator Burton K. Wheeler.

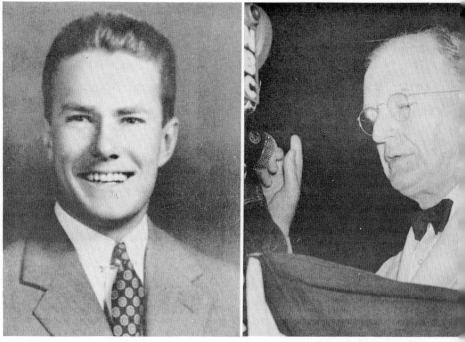

AMERICA FIRST

The Battle Against Intervention

1940-1941

by Wayne S. Cole
University of Maryland

1971

OCTAGON BOOKS
New York

Reprinted 1971

by special arrangement with Wayne S. Cole

OCTAGON BOOKS
A DIVISION OF FARRAR, STRAUS & GIROUX, INC.
19 Union Square West
New York, N. Y. 10003

LIBRARY OF CONGRESS CATALOG CARD NUMBER: 74-159174

ISBN 0-374-91800-7

Printed in U.S.A. by
NOBLE OFFSET PRINTERS, INC.
NEW YORK 3, N. Y.

To
Virginia

21957

Preface

"OUR PRINCIPLES were right. Had they been followed war could have been avoided." So ran the final statement of the America First Committee issued in December, 1941, after the official entry of the United States into World War II.

Organized to keep the United States out of the European war, the America First Committee failed completely to achieve its primary objective. The organization was not even able to defeat any major Administration "short-of-war" proposal actually put to the test in Congress.

Nevertheless, the America First Committee was the most powerful mass pressure group engaged in the struggle against the foreign policy of the Roosevelt administration in the crucial years of 1940–1941. Under its banner numerous prominent American personalities battled against a foreign policy which they believed to be contrary to the best interests of the United States. General Robert E. Wood, Colonel Charles A. Lindbergh, Senator Burton K. Wheeler, Senator Gerald P. Nye, Philip La Follette, John T. Flynn, Kathleen Norris, Lillian Gish, Chester

Bowles, General Hugh S. Johnson, and many other well known American figures used the America First Committee as a vehicle through which to oppose American entry into World War II. Even the present United States Ambassador at Large, Philip C. Jessup, aligned himself with America First in 1941. The Committee conducted a colorful, dramatic, and earnest campaign. And it continued to be a powerful, vocal, and well-organized force in the debate right down to the hour the Japanese attacked Pearl Harbor. The noninterventionist strength, which the Committee and other groups represented, definitely affected the strategy of President Franklin D. Roosevelt. More than that, persons close to Roosevelt felt that the noninterventionists had fought the President very nearly to a standstill near the end of 1941 when the Japanese attack took the decision out of American hands.

The recent "Great Debate" on American foreign policy has stimulated renewed attention in the controversy of a decade ago. Numerous historians have engaged in the fascinating task of examining the complicated course which ultimately led to American participation in World War II. Most of the books thus far published on the subject, however, have emphasized the role which the Administration leaders and their supporters played in this colorful story. There has been little serious research into the nature of the opposition to President Roosevelt's policies. The purpose of this study is to examine the personnel, views, activities, and criticisms of the America First Committee—the leading noninterventionist pressure group during the fifteen months preceding December 7, 1941.

This study is based largely upon an examination of the records of the America First Committee. I have had unrestricted access to the records of America First at the Hoover Library on War, Revolution, and Peace at Stanford University, California. This splendid collection includes the records of the America First national headquarters as well as those of numerous state and local units of the organization. In addition I have used Committee materials in the files of General Robert E. Wood, Chicago, Illinois, and R. Douglas Stuart, Jr., San Francisco, California. I have also had interviews and correspondence with many persons active in the battle against intervention.

I am indebted to the many individuals who, through letters and interviews, have supplied helpful information and suggestions. Thanks are due General Robert E. Wood and R. Douglas Stuart, Jr., for permission to use materials in their files and for their helpful conferences with me. The staffs at the Hoover Library, the University of Wisconsin Library, the University of Arkansas Library, the Des Moines Public Library, and the Library of the Wisconsin State Historical Society were most helpful. A grant from the University of Wisconsin made possible the research in Hoover Library. B. Broughton Gingell, formerly of the University of Arkansas, helped to improve the literary style of the manuscript. I am especially grateful to Professor Fred Harvey Harrington of the University of

Preface

Wisconsin for his invaluable assistance and guidance in all stages of the project. My wife, Virginia Rae Cole, assisted me with proofreading and made numerous helpful suggestions in matters of style.

Wayne S. Cole

Fayetteville, Arkansas
August 27, 1951

Contents

AMERICA FIRST

I The Genesis

ON THE "date which will live in infamy," December 7, 1941, the bursting Japanese bombs and torpedoes left three and one-half thousand dead and wounded Americans at Pearl Harbor. Much of the American fleet at Hawaii was converted into a mass of twisted shambles while military aircraft went up in flames without even getting into the air against the enemy. The same Japanese pilots who wrought this havoc also abruptly terminated the spectacular foreign policy debate which had been provoked by the outbreak of World War II. Included in the debris left by the Japanese attack was the shattered corpse of the America First Committee, the principal noninterventionist pressure group in that "Great Debate."

IN THE 1930's an already distraught Europe was successively jolted by the Italian-Ethiopian War, remilitarization of the Rhineland, the Spanish Civil War, and the German seizure of Austria and Czechoslovakia. Japanese aggression in Manchuria and China added to the general sense of insecurity. The Russo-German nonaggression pact of August 23, 1939, opened the way for the Nazi invasion of Poland on September 1, 1939. This attack precipitated the most destructive of the long succession of general European wars. The "Phony War" after the collapse of Poland proved to be only a temporary respite. In April, 1940, Adolph Hitler's forces overwhelmed Denmark and Norway. On May 10, 1940, the German armies drove into the Netherlands, Belgium, and Luxemburg. Within a few days the *Blitzkrieg* was rolling into northern France. Less than a month after the attack began, the British army in Europe was driven into the sea at Dunkerque. With France reeling from the blows of the German assault and from her own internal weakness, Italy chose to attack the unhappy nation in the south. Finally, with the Germans in control of their capital city and considerably over half of their area, the French under Marshal Petain signed an armistice with Hitler on June 22, 1940. Even before the fall of France the German *Luftwaffe* had begun its assault on the British Isles. By August and September of 1940 the Battle of Britain was well under way. At the same time the German submarines were taking a heavy toll of British shipping. The outlook for the Western democracies in Europe was indeed dismal by September, 1940.

During the 1930's the United States sought to keep out of future European wars by means of a series of Neutrality Acts. Under these acts the United States proposed to sacrifice its traditional insistence upon the freedom of the seas in time of war. These acts also provided for restrictions upon trade and economic relations with belligerent powers.

It was hoped this national self-negation would prevent the development of economic ties and military incidents which might catapult the United States into any general conflagration. With the beginning of the European war in September, 1939, Americans overwhelmingly considered Germany the aggressor and hoped for an Allied victory. But at the same time most Americans hoped the United States would not be drawn into the conflict. The Government reflected these views in November, 1939, by revising American neutrality legislation. The repeal of the arms embargo partially opened the way for the United States to become the "arsenal" for the democratic belligerents. The cash-and-carry provisions of the Neutrality Act were re-enacted to help keep the United States out of the war.

The collapse of the Western democracies in 1940 convinced many Americans that if Great Britain fell the United States would be next to feel the power of Hitler's might. Agreements with Canada and the Latin American powers were designed to strengthen hemispheric defense. Early in September, 1940, Congress passed the first peace-time compulsory military service measure in American history. The destroyer deal by which the United States traded fifty old destroyers to Great Britain in exchange for bases in the Western Hemisphere was made public on September 3, 1940. It was designed both to strengthen the British and to bolster the defense of the Western Hemisphere. By the end of the summer of 1940 an aroused Congress had appropriated thirteen billion dollars for national defense.

5

The Genesis

As a consequence of the conflicting desires of the American people with regard to the European war, the vocal elements in the American public divided into two highly heterogeneous groups. The "interventionists" in the foreign policy debate before December 7, 1941, were those who believed that it was more important for the United States to assure a British victory over the Axis than for the United States to keep out of the European war. The "isolationists" or "noninterventionists" were those who believed it was more important for the United States to keep out of the war than to assure a British victory over the Axis. Representatives of both points of view organized committees or mass pressure groups. These organizations were designed to perform two basic functions. They hoped to stimulate support for their particular point of view on foreign policy. They also sought to direct the force of this opinion so as to influence the formulation of American foreign policy. Both major contestants in this "Battle of the Committees" were composed of extremely heterogeneous elements. Each group drew support from all regions of the country; from different age, ethnic, and social groups; and from persons holding widely diverse economic and political views. They included persons who held differing views even on foreign policy questions. The motivation for the support on each side in this foreign policy debate was exceedingly complex and diverse.

ALL THE interventionists agreed that a British victory over the Axis was absolutely essential to American security and

The Genesis

welfare. But their views differed on the means for ac-
complishing this British victory. Many interventionists believed this end could be obtained if the United States
would simply render all-out aid short of war. This group
reflected the public statements of President Franklin D.
Roosevelt.[1] In the "Battle of the Committees" William
Allen White, a respected Republican newspaper editor
from Emporia, Kansas, provided leadership for Americans
with this point of view. With Clark Eichelberger and others
he led a Non-partisan Committee for Peace through the
Revision of the Neutrality Law in the fall of 1939. This
Committee vigorously supported President Roosevelt's
move to secure repeal of the arms embargo. After Congress
repealed the embargo in November, 1939, the organization
became inactive.[2] However in May, 1940, the formation
of a new Committee to Defend America by Aiding the
Allies was announced. William Allen White was national
chairman of the new organization and Clark Eichelberger
was executive director. The sponsoring committee included prominent individuals from many walks of life.[3]
Though there was no official connection, the Committee
to Defend America by Aiding the Allies was something of
an unofficial public relations organization for President
Roosevelt's foreign policies. White and other leaders of
the Committee frequently consulted with the President,
his Cabinet members and other Administration leaders.[4]
There was not always perfect agreement between the Administration and the White Committee leaders, but this
group more closely represented the views of the Adminis-

7

tration than any other major foreign policy pressure group.
There was another major element in the interventionist
camp which gained increasing strength during 1941. This
group believed that American aid short of war would not
be sufficient to enable Great Britain to defeat the Axis.
Therefore they believed it essential for the United States
to intervene in the war against the Axis as a full military
belligerent. This point of view gained increased support
even within the Committee to Defend America by Aiding
the Allies. The strength of this element was one of the
factors which led White to resign as chairman of the Committee in January, 1941.[5] Another indication of this trend
of thought within the interventionist camp was the formation of the Fight for Freedom Committee in April, 1941.
Senator Carter Glass of Virginia was honorary chairman
of this new pressure group and Bishop Henry W. Hobson,
Episcopal bishop of southern Ohio, was chairman. This
organization favored American participation in the war
against the Axis as a full belligerent.[6]

In addition to these two principal interventionist pressure groups there were many others, both local and
national, which advanced variations of the interventionist
point of view. Notable among these was Union Now led
by Clarence Streit.

THE FORCES motivating support for the noninterventionist
point of view were complex. A very small percentage of
the American people took this position because of their
pro-Nazi and pro-fascist views. Many were anti-Semitic.

Until June 22, 1941, when the German attack on the Soviet Union suddenly converted them into interventionists, the American Communists were noninterventionists. Some of the supporters of the noninterventionist position were idealistic pacifists who believed that conditions in Europe temporarily made their earlier internationalist approach to peace impracticable.[7]

Most of the noninterventionists, however, were moved more by other considerations. Support for the noninterventionist position came from parents who were horrified by the mental image of their sons mangled on a foreign battle field. Young men and women viewed this possibility with understandable revulsion. American nationalism and distrust of Europeans, aggravated by disillusionment with the results of World War I, were of major significance. Related to this was a chronic dislike for the British and the skepticism for British motives found among large segments of the American people. Noninterventionist ideas had a special appeal for certain ethnic groups in the United States including many (though by no means all) German-Americans.[8] For many the movement was identified with opposition to President Roosevelt and the Democratic Party. Some, however, were Democrats and broke with the President only on foreign policy. Many conservatives feared that American intervention might result in the loss of the American capitalistic system and bring fascism, socialism, communism, or at least more of the hated New Deal. On the other hand, many liberals feared American intervention might result in the loss of social gains already made. They wanted the nation to concentrate its energies upon solving its own domestic social and economic problems.

Like their opponents, the noninterventionists organized pressure groups to express their point of view more effectively. Of course, pro-Nazi groups like the German-American Bund advanced noninterventionist views. Numerous anti-Semitic organizations such as Father Coughlin's Christian Front and William Dudley Pelley's Silver Shirts preached versions of the noninterventionist doctrine. Before June 22, 1941, the Communists fought intervention through the American Peace Mobilization.[9] Pacifist organizations such as the National Council for the Prevention of War and the Keep America Out of War Congress threw their weight against intervention. In addition there were many local noninterventionist organizations. In this category was the Citizens Keep America Out of War Committee, in Chicago, under the leadership of Avery Brundage. However, until September, 1940, there was in the United States no national noninterventionist pressure group comparable to the Committee to Defend America by Aiding the Allies appealing for mass support. The America First Committee filled this void from September, 1940, until December 7, 1941.

THE PERSON most immediately responsible for the formation of the America First Committee was R. Douglas Stuart, Jr., the son of the first vice-president of Quaker Oats Company in Chicago. Stuart had attended Princeton University where he studied government and international relations. After his graduation in 1937 he spent several months traveling in Europe and in 1938 entered the Law School at Yale University.[10]

Stuart became disturbed by developments in American foreign relations while still a student at Princeton. In the fall of 1939 he and a fellow student sought unsuccessfully to have a major noninterventionist speaker address a meeting at Yale.[11] In the spring of 1940 Stuart and a number of other students in the Law School met informally a number of times to discuss what could be done to oppose intervention by the United States in the European war. This group had occasional meetings with such people as Professors Fred Rodell and Edwin Borchard. The group did not, however, attract great attention at the time.[12]

After final examinations were over a number of these young people decided in June, 1940, to go further with their activities. A mimeographed letter to various students and alumni from different universities brought encouraging responses.[13] The still nameless group at New Haven led by Stuart also circulated a petition to be signed by persons under thirty years of age who were willing to devote time during the summer to oppose intervention. The text of this petition indicates the foreign policy views of the members of this student group *before* they secured active support from prominent business and political leaders:

We ... believe that the United States must now concentrate all its energies on building a strong defense for this hemisphere.

11

We believe that today our American democracy can only be preserved by keeping out of war abroad.

We do not oppose sending materials to England, but we insist on continuance of "cash-and-carry", and above all, of non-intervention in Europe.

Even if Great Britain is on the verge of defeat, we demand that Congress refrain from war.[14]

In an attempt to gain the support of well-known national figures Stuart and Kingman Brewster, Jr., editor of the *Yale Daily News*, attended the Republican National Convention at Philadelphia late in June, 1940. There they consulted with many people including Senator Robert A. Taft, of Ohio, and some of his supporters. Stuart then went to Washington, D.C., where he spoke with Senators Burton K. Wheeler, Bennett Champ Clark, Robert M. La Follette, and others. Through these interviews he learned of many prominent people who might be willing to support a major noninterventionist organization. Stuart later asserted that many persons with whom he spoke mentioned General Robert E. Wood.[15]

General Wood, chairman of the board of Sears Roebuck and Company in Chicago, was a Kansas-born West Point graduate. He served in the Philippines during the insurrection and in Panama while the canal was being built. During World War I he served as Acting Quartermaster General. After the war he retired from the Army and became vice-president of Montgomery Ward and Company from 1919 to 1924. In 1924 he went to Sears Roebuck as vice-president. He became president of Sears in 1928 and has been chairman of the board since 1939.[16]

Early in the summer of 1940 General Wood had discussed with Philip La Follette, William H. Regnery, and others the problem of what should be done to combat the interventionists.[17] Regnery, president of the Western Shade Cloth Company, expressed a willingness to render considerable financial assistance if an appropriate medium could be found to oppose intervention in the European war.[18] No immediate action was taken, however.

General Wood and R. Douglas Stuart, Jr., had known each other slightly in Chicago.[19] When General Wood learned of Stuart's noninterventionist activities he wrote to commend him for his efforts.[20] Stuart found the General's letter awaiting him upon his return to New Haven from Washington, D.C. He then promptly went to Chicago and persuaded Wood to serve as temporary chairman of the proposed organization providing a satisfactory sponsoring committee could be formed. General Wood sent letters late in July, 1940, to a number of prominent Americans inviting them to serve on the sponsoring committee of the proposed noninterventionist organization.[21]

Stuart set up temporary headquarters for this "Emergency Committee to Defend America First" in the same office building as his father's Quaker Oats Company in Chicago. Through some of the early backers of the Committee they secured the assistance of three advertising agencies. General Wood, William H. Regnery, and others assured sufficient financial assistance to get the organization started.[22] In July, 1940, Stuart attended the Democratic National Convention in Chicago where he consulted

with Senator Burton K. Wheeler and others.[23] By the end
of the first week in August approximately a dozen persons
had agreed to serve on the sponsoring committee of the
proposed organization.[24]

The smooth progress of the plans for the organization
was given a severe jolt in August. On August 23, 1940,
General Wood informed his colleagues in the venture that
he had decided not to serve as chairman for the committee.
He agreed, however, to be a member of the sponsoring
committee.[25] He feared that his leadership of the organization might result in serious loss of business for Sears Roebuck and Company. Furthermore, he was not sufficiently
satisfied with the response to the invitations to serve on
the sponsoring committee.[26]

Despite this temporary loss of their chairman, Stuart,
Hanford MacNider, Jay C. Hormel, Philip La Follette,
and others proceeded with the plans for the organization.[27]
At a meeting of the national committee on August 29,
1940, it was decided to shorten the name of the organization from the "Emergency Committee to Defend America
First" to the "America First Committee." [28]

The first public announcement of the formation of the
America First Committee was made on the evening of
September 4, 1940. This first announcement listed Stuart
as national director but did not name any chairman. The
following persons were listed as members of the national
committee of America First: General Wood; William H.
Regnery; General Thomas S. Hammond, president of the
Whiting Corporation; Jay C. Hormel, president of Hormel

Meat Packing Company; Hanford MacNider, Iowa manufacturer and former national commander of the American Legion; Mrs. Janet Ayer Fairbank, author and former National Democratic committeewoman from Illinois; Edward L. Ryerson, Jr., member of the board of Inland Steel Corporation; Sterling Morton, secretary of the Morton Salt Company; Mrs. Alice Roosevelt Longworth, daughter of Theodore Roosevelt; John T. Flynn, author and economic advisor to the Senate Committee which investigated the munitions industry in 1934–1935; Edward Rickenbacker; Louis Tabor, Master of the National Grange; Bishop Wilbur E. Hammaker, head of the Methodist Church in the Denver area; Thomas N. McCarter, president of the Public Service Corporation of New Jersey; Avery Brundage, Chicago builder and president of the American Olympic Association; Dr. Albert W. Palmer, president of the Chicago Theological Seminary; Mrs. Burton K. Wheeler; Dr. George H. Whipple, joint winner of the Nobel award for medicine in 1934; Oswald Garrison Villard, former editor of *The Nation;* and Ray McKaig, head of the Grange at Boise, Idaho.[29]

This original public announcement of the America First Committee included the following statement of the Committee's Principles:

1. The United States must build an impregnable defense for America.
2. No foreign power, nor group of powers, can successfully attack a *prepared* America.
3. American democracy can be preserved only by keeping out of the European war.

4. "Aid short of war" weakens national defense at home and threatens to involve America in war abroad.[30]

The Committee also released a statement of its objectives which in effect briefly outlined the proposed activities of the organization:

1. To bring together all Americans, regardless of possible differences on other matters, who see eye-to-eye on these principles. (This does not include Nazists [*sic*], Fascists, Communists, or members of other groups that place the interest of any other nation above those of our own country.)
2. To urge Americans to keep their heads amid rising hysteria in times of crisis.
3. To provide sane national leadership for the majority of the American people who want to keep out of the European war.
4. To register this opinion with the President and with Congress.[31]

General Hugh S. Johnson led off the Committee's battle against intervention with a national radio broadcast on September 5, 1940.[32] From this small beginning the America First Committee grew into the most powerful noninterventionist organization in the United States.

2 Leadership, Organization and Finances

LEADERSHIP

GENERAL ROBERT E. WOOD served as national chairman of the America First Committee. R. Douglas Stuart, Jr., was national director, and in 1941 Mrs. Janet Ayer Fairbank and Hanford MacNider were appointed vice-chairmen. America First policies were formulated and supervised by a seven-member executive committee. A larger national committee also met to decide matters of policy. In addition, unofficial advisors, Committee staff members, and leaders of local chapters frequently influenced the course of the America First Committee.

IT WAS a severe shock when General Wood indicated on August 23, 1940, that he would not serve as chairman.[1] By September 21, 1940, he was persuaded to serve as temporary "acting chairman" but only until a satisfactory person could be found to relieve him.[2] That person was never found. Edward Rickenbacker, Verne Marshall, and Joseph P. Kennedy were among those who were approached or considered to replace General Wood.[3] Late in

March, 1941, General Wood recommended Colonel Charles A. Lindbergh as the best possible man for the position.[4] Lindbergh was not a member of the Committee but had been waging his own one-man battle against intervention since 1939. Though willing to be a member of the national committee, Colonel Lindbergh declined to be chairman of America First. He hoped the public reaction to his membership on the Committee might indicate whether it would be wise to make him chairman.[5] Lindbergh made his first major address as a member of the national committee on April 17, 1941.[6] He was thereafter the Committee's greatest drawing card at America First rallies. But Lindbergh never became chairman. During 1940 and 1941 General Wood repeatedly requested that he be permitted to step down. But he was destined to serve until the Japanese attack on Pearl Harbor terminated the Committee's existence.

General Wood was in many respects an admirable choice for chairman of America First. He was thoroughly convinced of the wisdom of a policy of nonintervention for the United States. His capacities as a leader and administrator were demonstrated by his success in the Army and at Sears Roebuck and Company. Though he had begun to criticize aspects of the President's domestic program by 1936, his record did not appear to justify classifying him as a professional Roosevelt hater.[7] Despite his heavy duties at Sears Roebuck he kept in close touch with the operation of the Committee. He spent some time at Committee headquarters nearly every day or two and was in frequent consultation with Stuart and others by telephone. No decision

18

of any significance was made without his prior approval. General Wood was sufficiently respected by the other leaders of the Committee so that he was frequently able to keep peace among them when excessive friction might have reduced the effectiveness of the organization.[8] The genuine affection which General Wood appears to have had for Stuart was of importance in the conduct of Committee affairs. Wood's status as a businessman tended to attract support for the Committee from more conservative sources than might have been desirable. But this did make it easier for the Committee to get sufficient financial backing.

The America First Committee was incorporated in Illinois on September 19, 1940, as a nonprofit organization. Under the corporation charter, management of America First was vested in a seven-member board of directors. This board of directors or executive committee was originally composed of General Wood; Stuart; General Thomas S. Hammond; William H. Regnery; Hanford MacNider; Clay Judson, a Chicago attorney; and Jay C. Hormel.[9] In the spring of 1941 Mrs. Janet Ayer Fairbank replaced Hormel on the executive committee.[10] J. Sanford Otis, a Chicago investment banker and member of the national committee, was treasurer of America First during its full history. He was not, however, included on the executive committee.[11]

The executive committee formulated and supervised America First Committee policies. It met at irregular intervals on an average of once or twice a month to decide matters of policy and finances, to elect officers and members, and to employ staff members. However, it met only three times from June 1, 1941, until December 7, 1941.[12] Many minor policy decisions were made in the following manner: Stuart or members of the headquarters staff would make a suggestion to General Wood who would then accept, modify, or reject the proposal. When a course of action had been decided upon, General Wood called the members of the executive committee and informed them of the decision.[13] Nevertheless, the executive committee had the final word on matters of policy and it made nearly all major policy decisions. At executive committee meetings MacNider, Hammond, and Regnery did not generally take aggressive or dogmatic positions. Mrs. Fairbank and Clay Judson were generally in accord and were frequently quite critical of actions by Stuart as National Director. Judson functioned as the legal authority in the executive committee while Mrs. Fairbank took special interest in the phrasing of Committee statements and principles. General Wood played the role of a respected moderator, but a moderator who was also a leader.[14]

A TOTAL of more than fifty persons were listed as members of the national committee of America First. The membership varied from time to time as new names were added and as old members resigned or were dropped.[15] The national committee met nine times to decide matters of policy but many of its members were inactive and attended no meetings. General Wood presided over both national and executive committee meetings and all executive committee members were on the national committee.[16] Consequently the small attendance at meetings by other national committee members prevented any disagreement between the policy decisions of the two organs.

In selecting members for the national committee efforts were made to secure persons who were widely known and respected in the United States. Members were sought with varied political and economic views and from different lines of endeavor.[17] At one time or another the national committee included a dozen manufacturers or businessmen, three investment bankers, two labor leaders, two officers of the Grange, three clergymen, three scientists, two aviators, half a dozen university faculty members, a movie actor, and an actress. Several members had authored books. More than a dozen had earlier served in one of the branches of the armed forces of the United States. Eight had held political or diplomatic posts. At least three were Catholics and one member in the fall of 1940 was Jewish.[18]

The contributions of individual members of the national committee varied widely. Many like Samuel Hopkins Adams, Bishop Wilbur E. Hammaker, Louis Taber, Dr. George H. Whipple, Irvin S. Cobb, Henry Ford, Dr. Albert W. Palmer, Frank O. Lowden, Mrs. Florence P. Kahn, and Edward Rickenbacker were inactive in the committee.[19]

Many, however, played positive roles in the battle against intervention. In addition to the members of the executive committee, the following national committee members influenced America First policies: Mrs. Bennett Champ Clark; John T. Flynn; Colonel Charles A. Lindbergh; Edward L. Ryerson, Jr.; William R. Castle, former State Department official; George N. Peek, former head of the Agricultural Adjustment Administration; Edwin S. Webster, Jr., New York investment banker; Chester Bowles, then an advertising executive; and Isaac A. Pennypacker, Philadelphia attorney. A considerable number were officers and leaders of state or local units of America First. These included Otto Case, chairman in the state of Washington; Mrs. Clark, chairman, and Mrs. Burton K. Wheeler, treasurer, of the Washington, D.C., chapter; Mrs. Fairbank and General Hammond, leaders of the Committee in Illinois; Flynn, chairman, Webster, secretary, and Mrs. John P. Marquand and Amos R. E. Pinchot, members of the executive committee, of the New York chapter; Pennypacker, chairman in Philadelphia; Dr. Gregory Mason, chairman in Stamford, Connecticut; and Alice Roosevelt Longworth, honorary chairman of the Cincinnati, Ohio, chapter. Among the national committee members who spoke for America First meetings and broadcasts were Colonel Lindbergh, Mrs. Clark, Flynn, Kathleen Norris, Rev. John A. O'Brien, Lillian Gish, General Wood, and Stuart. National committee members who contributed substantial sums of money to the Committee included William H. Regnery; H. L. Stuart, Chicago investment banker; Robert Young, railway magnate; General Wood;

Mrs. Ruth Hanna Simms; Sterling Morton; and Edwin S. Webster, Jr.[20]

While authority to formulate America First policy was vested in the executive and national committees, persons who were not members of these organs also exercised influence. Prominent leaders in and out of Congress were consulted for advice. Stuart relied heavily upon the advice of William Benton, vice-president of the University of Chicago, and Chester Bowles. Samuel B. Pettengill, former Democratic Congressman from Indiana, and Philip La Follette, former Governor of Wisconsin, were especially influential unofficial advisors of the Committee. Among others of significance were Senator Burton K. Wheeler, Senator Bennett Champ Clark, Senator Gerald P. Nye, Congressman Karl Mundt, and Robert M. Hutchins.[21]

Three national meetings of local chapter leaders were held to determine their views on Committee policies.[22] Chapter leaders were also consulted by mail. Even letters from local members of America First urging a particular course of action sometimes helped color Committee policy.[23] The members of the America First Committee staffs in Chicago and Washington, D.C., were particularly influential in shaping the course of America First.[24]

R. Douglas Stuart, Jr., as national director of America First had the responsibility for executing the policies formulated by the executive and national committees. Under his direction staff members organized and supervised local chapters. They supplied speakers for major rallies and prepared Committee pamphlets and advertisements. They kept the financial records of the organization and handled all of the administrative duties involved in conducting the Committee's battle against intervention. Stuart also provided general supervision over the America First research staff and lobby in Washington, D.C. It was not, therefore, surprising that Stuart (also a member of both the executive and national committees) and the principal members of the Committee staffs exercised very great influence upon America First policies.

Stuart's idealism, agreeable personality, obvious sincerity, and deep conviction that the Committee was serving the best interests of the United States were valuable assets to America First. No one more nearly gave the limit of his capacities in the Committee's battle against intervention than Stuart. Nevertheless, there were certain other factors concerning this personable young man which displeased some leaders and supporters of the organization. The greatest strike against him was his extreme youth. He was only twenty-four years old when he began to promote the organization.[25] He had had no significant administrative or public relations experience. Older persons and potential financial supporters were sometimes skeptical of the wisdom of having such a young and inexperienced person directing the affairs of the Committee.[26] Mrs. Janet Ayer Fairbank was particularly outspoken in her criticism of Stuart.[27] Some important chapter leaders complained of his conduct of Committee affairs and especially

24

of the slow response of national headquarters to its correspondence.[28]

A number of steps were taken to alleviate the misgivings
of supporters of the Committee and to provide for supervision of Stuart's work by older and more experienced persons. In correspondence with skeptical contributors they
emphasized that Stuart only had authority to carry out
policies previously formulated by the executive and national committees and approved by General Wood.[29] On
several occasions (usually when the General planned to
be out of the city) General Wood appointed an older person to serve as his personal representative in America First
headquarters. Hanford MacNider, Philip La Follette, and
Samuel B. Pettengill all served in this capacity at one
time or another during 1941.[30] Late in March, 1941, the
executive committee elected Mrs. Fairbank and Hanford
MacNider vice-chairmen of America First to try to assuage
the fears of backers of the Committee.[31] In April, 1941,
the executive committee voted to change Stuart's title
from national director to executive secretary.[32]

In actual practice, however, none of these steps significantly reduced Stuart's responsibilities or influence.
The total time spent by MacNider, La Follette, and Pettengill in America First headquarters appears to have been
less than six weeks at the most.[33] MacNider did not assume
any administrative duties as vice-chairman, and he declined re-election in the fall of 1941.[34] Mrs. Fairbank as-
sumed complete jurisdiction over the chapters in Illinois
and Iowa; she did not, however, move into the national

headquarters.[35] The change in Stuart's title had no effect.

In the fall of 1941 Stuart considered returning to Law School at Yale but decided against it and continued as director of the Committee until its demise in December, 1941.[36] Despite his youth and administrative inexperience, Stuart brought to the America First Committee a selfless idealism which is a priceless ingredient in any mass movement. His judgment on matters of policy was generally sound when measured in terms of the continued effectiveness and respectability of the Committee. And he had a capacity to learn.

ORGANIZATION

The principal efforts of the America First Committee in the fall of 1940 were concentrated on placing full-page advertisements in the newspapers of widely scattered cities and in sponsoring radio broadcasts.[37] From the beginning, however, Stuart indicated his desire to organize local units of the America First Committee throughout the nation.[38] After November 4, the Committee temporarily terminated its newspaper advertising campaign,[39] and on November 12, 1940, the national committee authorized the formation of local chapters in important centers.[40]

The plans formed for organizing local chapters of the America First Committee were essentially the same as those used by the Committee to Defend America by Aiding the Allies.[41] Each local chapter was to choose its officers and finance its own activities. Each was free to wage its own battle against intervention providing it adhered to the general principles and policies of the America First Committee. America First national headquarters was to provide guidance, supervision, and co-ordination for the efforts of local chapters. Committee headquarters also arranged for speakers at major rallies and supplied literature to chapters at cost.[42]

National leaders of the America First Committee initiated the efforts to form chapters in key cities like Chicago, New York, and Washington, D.C.[43] In some instances Committee field representatives engineered early organization in a city. But in a numerical sense the overwhelming majority of chapters were formed by persons who had written to the America First Committee expressing enthusiasm for its campaign.

The loose form of the America First organization presented the national headquarters with the problem of insuring control over local chapters. Many precautions were taken in the attempt to increase control. Each group which desired to form a chapter was required to make a signed application with references. The applicants agreed to "take no action in the name of the America First Committee which deviates from the policies laid down by the Committee." [44] A chapter manual was provided to guide new units.[45] In addition several hundred bulletins were sent during 1941 to guide, inform, and stimulate each chapter. Any advertising and printed matter other than that supplied by Committee headquarters which the chapter desired to use was to be submitted to national headquarters for prior approval.[46] Field representatives of America First also supervised local activities and ironed out specific chapter problems.[47]

Some state organizations of America First were formed to provide closer supervision and direction of chapter activities. Functioning state units were organized in Illinois, Wisconsin, New York, Washington, Colorado, and Indiana.[48] The unit in Los Angeles served Southern California while the headquarters in San Francisco served the rest of the state.[49] Efforts were also made in a few other states with varied success.[50]

In addition to regular chapters, the America First Committee made some efforts to organize special groups. A Charles A. Young Division of America First for Negroes under Perry W. Howard was organized and some local chapters formed units for Negroes.[51] Limited efforts were made to organize youth groups.[52] In some areas particularly strong opposition or inadequate leadership made the organization of full-fledged chapters impracticable. Consequently, late in 1941 efforts were initiated to organize less elaborate America First clubs to provide a small core for noninterventionist activity.[53]

The America First Committee system of chapter organization had many virtues. It took full advantage of local enthusiasm for the noninterventionist point of view. Local units served as centers to stage meetings and distribute literature to enhance noninterventionist strength. The system provided the machinery through which Congress and the President could be flooded with letters on key issues

28

at strategic times. It decentralized the financing of the battle against intervention.

Nevertheless, in operation the America First system of organization had defects which interfered with the Committee's effectiveness. The basic shortcomings of the system were twofold: First, despite precautions the understaffed, overworked, and relatively inexperienced national headquarters staff was not able to exercise adequate control over local chapters.[54] Second, it was extremely difficult to secure competent and respected chapter leaders who were willing and able to give sufficient time to the conduct of chapter affairs.[55]

These shortcomings were aggravated by the precipitancy with which the headquarters staff granted approval to many new chapter applications. Great care was taken to secure competent and respected leaders in many cities. But many new chapters were approved by America First headquarters too soon after receiving original applications to permit an adequate check on the character of the applicants.[56] This procedure sometimes resulted in the formation of effective chapters. But the consequences were not always so fortunate.[57] This headquarters procedure was not the product of disregard for the qualities of the people who were to lead local chapters. It appears, rather, to have been the result of the inexperience of the staff members, the deluge of work which overwhelmed the always shorthanded staff, and the eagerness of the Committee to organize as many chapters as possible.[58] To make matters worse, there were never enough competent Committee field representatives to handle all of the chapter problems which arose. It was a rare chapter which did not at one time or another experience an internal conflict among its leaders. Aid by competent field representatives of America First could be supplied in only the most serious of the controversies. Yet such friction within chapters reduced the effectiveness of the Committee in many localities.[59]

THE AMERICA First Committee's growth was an irregular but continual process. The greatest burst of America First organizational and membership expansion occurred, however, during the six month period from December, 1940, through May, 1941. By December 7, 1941, the America First Committee had approximately 450 chapters and subchapters though some of these were relatively inactive. In such a loose-knit and mushroom organization it was not possible to keep an accurate record of the total Committee membership. No estimate can be more than an approximation, but it is probable that the total national membership of America First was around 800,000 to 850,000. Nearly two-thirds of the membership was located within the three hundred mile radius of Chicago which includes Illinois, Wisconsin, Indiana, Michigan, and parts of Ohio, Missouri, Minnesota, and Iowa. Roughly one-fourth of the membership was located in the states of New York, Massachusetts, Pennsylvania, Connecticut, New Jersey, and Maryland. There were also strong chapters in California, Colorado, Washington, and Washington, D.C.

No America First Committee chapter was without its organizational or leadership problems. But among the better chapters in terms of leadership, size, and effectiveness of organization were the chapters in St. Louis, Missouri; Pittsburgh, Pennsylvania; Denver, Colorado; Fort Wayne, Indiana; Philadelphia, Pennsylvania; Cincinnati, Ohio; Washington, D.C.; San Diego, Los Angeles, and San Francisco, California; Chicago, Illinois; and New York.[60]

Though the Committee found adherents in every state and units were formed in most of them, the South was strikingly resistant to its organizational efforts. The America First Committee was never able to organize effective functioning chapters in Arkansas, Georgia, Kentucky, Louisiana, Mississippi, the Carolinas, Tennessee, or West Virginia.[61] Even most persons holding noninterventionist views in the South were afraid to expose themselves to the harsh public disapproval by expressing their opinions. Some who attempted to take part in America First efforts in the South were driven to the cover of silence.[62] But strong opposition was not limited to the South. It was found everywhere and was especially strong in the East.[63] Among other states where America First was unable to organize effectively were Delaware, New Hampshire, Nevada, and Wyoming.[64]

FINANCES

THE AMERICA First Committee's battle against intervention was financed almost exclusively by voluntary contributions. The initial expenses of the Committee in the fall of

1940 were underwritten largely by William H. Regnery and General Wood.[65] The executive committee determined in September, 1940, to limit individual contributions from any one person to a maximum of one thousand dollars [66] but in December, 1940, this limitation was raised to ten thousand dollars.[67] Even this limit was exceeded in a handful of instances. No contribution of more than one hundred dollars was to be accepted until an investigation of the source had been made.[68] During its existence the America First Committee national headquarters received approximately $370,000 [69] from some 25,000 contributors.[70]

Contributions to the Committee were received from every state in the nation and ranged from a few cents to sums running well into five figures. More than two-fifths of the national headquarters' income was supplied by persons who contributed one thousand dollars or more. Most of the largest contributors were businessmen. William H. Regnery, president of the Western Shade Cloth Company and a member of the America First executive committee, was the largest financial backer of the national organization. Another of the contributors of large sums was H. Smith Richardson of the Vick Chemical Company in New York City. General Wood contributed more than $10,000. Among others who contributed $4,000 or more were H. L. Stuart, Chicago investment banker; J. M. Patterson, president of the *News* of New York City; Colonel Robert R. McCormick, publisher of the *Chicago Tribune;* Robert R. Young, railroad magnate; Jeremiah Milbank, New York corporation executive; John W. Blodgett, Jr., Grand Rapids,

Michigan; Edgar J. Uihlein, Chicago; John Burnham; Page
Hufty; and Mrs. Ruth Hanna Simms. Among those who
contributed $2,000 or more to America First were Lunds-
ford Richardson of the Vick Chemical Company; Robert T.
Paine, II, a Boston lawyer; C. R. Sheaffer, of the Sheaffer
Pen Company in Fort Madison, Iowa; Sterling Morton;
Henry Gund, Jr., La Crosse, Wisconsin; B. K. Leach, St.
Louis, Missouri; Philip T. Swift, Chase M. Smith, and
Henry Babson, Chicago, Illinois; and Max C. Fleischmann.[71] Of course most individual contributions were small
sums—frequently one dollar or less. The pensioned widow
of a Civil War veteran who apologized for contributing
only twenty-five cents from her thirty-dollar-a-month
pension was not an isolated example.[72]

LOCAL CHAPTERS were largely self-supporting through
voluntary contributions. The New York chapter received
slightly more than $190,000, most of it from its 47,000 con-
tributors.[73] The St. Louis chapter received $20,000 during
its history while the receipts of the chapter at Pittsburgh,
Pennsylvania, totaled less than $8,000. In contrast most
chapters operated on far more modest budgets. The chapter at Eau Claire, Wisconsin, was fairly typical. This unit
with approximately 150 members received $229.03 during
its lifetime.[74] Most local chapters were more dependent
than the national headquarters upon the very small financial contributions.

While the leadership, organizational, and financial bases
were still being laid, the America First Committee was

faced with its first critical issue and engaged in its first major campaign. The issue involved the extension of credit aid to Great Britain, and the campaign was waged against the Lend-Lease Act.

3   The Great Arsenal of Democracy?

AN IMPORTANT basis for the America First Committee strength was the chronic dislike for Great Britain and the skepticism for British motives found among large segments of the American people. Many leaders, speakers, and members of the Committee could justly be labeled "Anglophobes." [1] Some America First chapter publications and speakers played on variations of the cliché that Britain would fight to the last drop of American blood. [2] After Lend-Lease became law an America First Bulletin asserted that the British theme song was: "There'll always be a dollar." The Bulletin listed luxury and pleasure items which it insisted the British had secured with Lend-Lease funds. [3] One chapter leader insisted that history proved that America must distrust every act of Great Britain. [4] Doubtless many of the Committee supporters agreed with him. The America First Committee's foreign policy proposals would have resulted in less total assistance than the British desired and the Committee to Defend America by Aiding the Allies favored. To that extent the America First program was perhaps intrinsically anti-British.

The America First Committee, however, exerted efforts

to reduce its vulnerability to the accusation that it was anti-British. Samuel B. Pettengill, an influential advisor on Committee policy, wrote that "the Committee ought not to be anti-British or anti-anybody. We are pro-America." [5] Professor Howard G. Swann, a speaker for America First, took a practical view of the matter. He advised against condemning England publicly "because it will win no new friends. The English haters are won to us anyway." [6] A Committee staff member gave the following advice to a chapter leader:

I would suggest that you avoid a preponderance of attack on Britain and Britain's imperialistic policy. I am sure you can readily see that if such assaults are made on Britain and Britain's policy, soon the America First Committee becomes gradually known as an anti-British organization. Our opponents are using every means of attempting to break down our first Principle of being for America first.[7]

For whatever its reasons, the America First Committee officially discouraged anti-British statements *per se*.

A BASIC issue between the America First Committee and the Committee to Defend America by Aiding the Allies lay in the relative significance to the United States which each group attached to Britain's battle against the Axis. The Committee to Defend America by Aiding the Allies held that a British victory was absolutely essential to American security and welfare. Leaders of the interventionist organizations viewed the possibility of a negotiated peace between Britain and Germany as tantamount to a

German victory. They believed such a peace would only be a temporary lull before the renewal of even more fearsome Axis aggression.[8]

Despite the large number of America First speakers and the relatively weak control over their statements, there was a fairly uniform pattern in their expressed views on Great Britain. Nearly all America First leaders voiced sympathy for the British and hoped they would not be defeated in World War II. Many of them declared that the defeat of Britain would be a serious blow to the United States and the whole world.[9]

Nevertheless, spokesmen for America First denied that Great Britain was fighting to defend democracy. They insisted that the European war was a battle for power and that Britain was fighting to preserve her empire. Some even said the war was of Britain's own making. All denied that the European war was America's war. They pointed to the recurring European conflagrations and insisted that America could not solve Europe's problems nor police the world. Though they admitted the existence of danger in the world, America First spokesmen denied that it was necessary to "buy time" by aiding Britain. They denied that Britain was America's first line of defense.[10]

America First Committee leaders did not believe Hitler could successfully invade Great Britain. Nor did they believe that Britain could defeat Hitler without the full military participation of the United States in the war. Though Lindbergh was more pessimistic, most Committee spokesmen believed the United States could defeat Germany.

But they were convinced that even a successful American intervention would be more disastrous for the United States and the whole world than a British defeat. They predicted that the American people would lose their democracy and freedom if they entered the war. Many believed American intervention would result in national bankruptcy and the collapse of the American system of capitalism and free enterprise. They feared it would result in a prolonged war which would leave both Europe and Great Britain in ruins. America First leaders denied that ideas could be destroyed by military force. On the contrary, they predicted that the chaos and destruction left by the war would result in the spread of fascism or communism in Europe.[11]

Since Committee leaders were convinced Britain could not defeat Germany without American intervention, and since they believed American intervention would be even more disastrous than a British defeat, America First leaders urged a negotiated peace in Europe. General Wood repeatedly asserted that if the United States would clearly indicate it would not enter the European war, the result would be a negotiated peace. In such a peace he believed Great Britain would be able to retain her navy and colonies while Germany would maintain economic control of Western Europe. He believed President Roosevelt or the Pope would be logical persons to initiate steps toward a negotiated peace.[12] Most America First leaders and spokesmen were in essential agreement with General Wood on the desirability of a negotiated peace.[13] Colonel Lindbergh went further and would even have preferred a negotiated peace to a British victory. He believed a complete victory by either side would "result in prostration in Europe such as we have never seen." [14] Despite these views, the America First Committee never waged a major concerted drive for a negotiated peace.[15]

America First leaders denied that American involvement in the European war was inevitable.[16] Rather than enter the war, Committee spokesmen declared that the United States should perfect its own democracy and solve its own domestic problems. Then when the war was over the United States would be in the best possible position to bind the wounds and help to restore freedom and democracy in the world.[17]

THERE WERE marked variations in the views of America First leaders regarding the extension of aid to Great Britain by the United States. In 1940–1941 there was a gradual trend in American public opinion toward increased approval of aid to the British. This trend was also evident in the America First Committee even though many of the Committee's followers continued to oppose aid to Britain. Among the Committee members who favored granting limited aid, there were differences regarding the extension of credit to the English.

Many America First spokesmen, including Colonel Lindbergh, Senator Wheeler, Senator Nye, John T. Flynn, and Philip La Follette had opposed repeal of the arms embargo in 1939.[18] The letter over General Wood's signature mailed

39

in July, 1940, to potential sponsors of the proposed organization urged: "No further extension of supplies to England beyond cash-and-carry in the belief that it would weaken our own defensive strength and lead to active American participation in war abroad." [19]

The first public statement of the America First Principles in September, 1940, expressed neither explicit opposition nor positive approval for cash-and-carry. It declared: " 'Aid short of war' weakens national defense at home and threatens to involve America in war abroad." [20] The Committee had not yet made its debut when the "destroyers-for-bases" deal was consummated. But later in the fall of 1940 the America First Committee opposed the direct transfer of equipment from American military and naval forces to Britain. Specifically it opposed the transfer of twenty-five Air Force "Flying Fortresses" to Great Britain.[21] A revised statement of the America First Principles in December, 1940, gave explicit approval of aid to Great Britain within the limits of cash-and-carry. The revised Principle declared:

The cash and carry provisions of the existing Neutrality Act are essential to American peace and security. Within the limits of the Act, Americans may properly aid Great Britain. Aid to her beyond the limitations of the present Neutrality Act would weaken our defense at home, and might well involve us in conflict. We oppose any change in the law which would permit American vessels to enter the combat zone or which would permit the American Navy to convoy merchant ships through that zone, as any such course would inevitably plunge this country into Europe's war.[22]

40

The Great Arsenal of Democracy?

The variations in views among Committee leaders and members on aid to Britain were highlighted when Colonel Lindbergh became a member of the national committee in 1941. In his first address as a member of the committee on April 17, 1941, he stated:

Some of us, including myself, believe that the sending of arms to Europe was a mistake—that it has weakened our position in America, that it has added to the bloodshed in European countries, and that it has not changed the trend of the war. Other members of this committee have supported aid to Britain, trusting in the promises of our President and our congress that such aid would actually be "short of war."

The America First Committee is open to any patriotic American citizen who opposes intervention, regardless of what his attitude on aid to Britain has been.[23]

Even those Committee members who supported granting aid agreed with General Wood that there was "a point beyond which aid to Great Britain yields us diminishing returns." [24] They all insisted that aid must not interfere with American rearmament nor lead to American involvement in the European war.[25] Virtually all agreed that direct transfer of equipment from American armed forces to Britain interfered with American rearmament. All agreed that the use of American merchant ships to transport goods to England and the use of the American Navy to convoy ships through war zones would inevitably put the United States into the conflagration.[26] An additional limitation in the minds of most Committee leaders was that American aid must be paid for by the British.[27]

The Great Arsenal of Democracy?

What policy should the United States follow when Great Britain was no longer able to pay cash for the materials she sought in the United States? This question was brought increasingly to the fore late in 1940. Due largely to pressure from Edward L. Ryerson, Jr., a member of the national committee and chairman of the board of Inland Steel Corporation, the America First executive committee after lengthy discussion voted on December 17, 1940, that it "would not actively oppose the making of loans to belligerents." [28] But despite this decision most America First leaders were by no means prepared to give positive approval for loans to Britain. No public statement of the Committee advocated loans. The revised statement of the America First Principles prepared later in December, 1940, insisted upon the continuance of cash-and-carry. [29] In public statements on the issue General Wood invariably expressed uncertainty or doubt concerning the wisdom of extending credit or loans to Great Britain. [30] The whole issue was brought to a head in the first quarter of 1941 during the crucial debate on the Administration's Lend-Lease proposal.

AT A PRESS conference on December 17, 1940, President Roosevelt described his plan "to eliminate the dollar sign" in aiding Great Britain. [31] In his Fireside Chat on December 29, 1940, the President vividly portrayed the disastrous consequences to American security if Great Britain fell or agreed to a negotiated peace. He called upon Americans to unite to make the United States "the great arsenal of

42

democracy." [32] In his message on January 6, 1941, President Roosevelt urged Congress to pass legislation to implement his lend-lease idea.

General Wood described President Roosevelt's Fireside Chat as "virtually a personal declaration of war on Germany." He stated that:

We think the American people wanted to hear the President say clearly and without equivocation that we should continue to give all possible help to Britain but not to the point of involving ourselves in war abroad. They did not hear him say it. . . . It is time the Administration made it perfectly clear that the American people, in aiding Britain, will stop before the methods that mean war. . . . The most serious decision in the President's talk is his flat rejection of the idea of a negotiated peace. Thus the President has taken upon himself a large share of the responsibility for a continuation of the war. [33]

On January 11, 1941, General Wood announced that the America First Committee would fight the Lend-Lease Bill "with all the vigor it can exert." He declared that "the President is not asking for a blank check, he wants a blank check book with the power to write away your manpower, our laws and our liberties." The Committee wired demands for "full, separate and open hearings" on the bill. General Wood urged Americans to flood Washington with protests against the measure. [34] The America First national committee on January 14, 1941, voted officially to oppose H. R. 1776 and approved general plans for its campaign. [35]

Hanford MacNider and William R. Castle represented the America First Committee in testifying against the Lend-Lease Bill before the House Foreign Affairs Committee. In his testimony Hanford MacNider said he would like to see the dictators and aggressors defeated. To attain this objective he favored selling "such weapons as we can spare" to the nations fighting aggressors. However, he did not believe "we should give away our own defenses." He predicted that passage of Lend-Lease "would mean the beginning of the end of the Republic with consequent disaster not only to the American people but to free men everywhere." He insisted the measure would eventually put the United States into the war.[36] William R. Castle called Lend-Lease a war measure "which signs away our freedom, creates a dictatorship, does not enable us to help Britain more than we are doing now except insofar as it permits the President to ignore such laws as he pleases and thus make war." [37]

General Wood himself testified against Lend-Lease before the Senate Foreign Relations Committee. He based his opposition to the measure principally upon the absence of any specific limits to the powers which it would give to the President. He declared there was nothing in the measure which would prevent the President from sending American merchant ships to war zones or American troops to Europe. He even insisted that under the provisions of the bill it might be possible for Great Britain to use the United States Navy or Air Force. He was convinced the objectives of the Lend-Lease Bill could be obtained through legislation granting *specific* authority. He urged that assistance be limited in terms of time, countries to be aided, and the amount of money to be spent. He favored aid to Britain providing she exhausted her resources in America before loans or gifts were granted. General Wood expressed the fear that the United States might become involved in the war within ninety days if the bill was passed.[38]

Hanford MacNider also represented America First in the Senate hearings on Lend-Lease. Colonel Charles A. Lindbergh, who testified before the Senate and House committees, was not a member of the America First Committee at the time. John T. Flynn in a written statement to the Senate Foreign Relations Committee insisted that Great Britain had nearly four and one-half billion in dollar assets in the United States to meet its war purchases. This was in sharp contrast to the testimony of Secretary of the Treasury Morgenthau who had asserted that British assets in the United States were virtually exhausted.[39]

The America First Committee provided speakers for innumerable meetings, radio programs, debates, and forums. Committee speakers were urged to refer to Lend-Lease as the "War Bill." [40] The historian Harry Elmer Barnes declared at an America First meeting that the Lend-Lease Bill would give the President more power than Hitler had had in 1935.[41] Supporters of Lend-Lease denied that President Roosevelt would ever use all of the powers which conceivably could be exercised under the bill. Senator Nye then asked at an America First meeting why such broad powers should be granted if there was no intention to use them.[42] The most publicized noninterventionist comment on Lend-Lease was made by Senator Burton K.

Wheeler. He asserted that the Lend-Lease program was "the New Deal's triple 'A' foreign policy—it will plow under every fourth American boy." President Roosevelt indignantly retorted that he regarded Senator Wheeler's statement "as the most untruthful, as the most dastardly, unpatriotic thing that has ever been said. Quote me on that. That really is the rottenest thing that has been said in public life in my generation." [43] The Committee mailed transcriptions of speeches by Hanford MacNider, Alfred Landon, and Senators Taft, Wheeler, Shipstead, and Walsh to nearly every radio station in the United States. [44] Hundreds of thousands of pieces of literature were distributed to rally opposition to the Lend-Lease Bill. An analysis of H. R. 1776 prepared by the America First Committee was reprinted in the *Congressional Record* and all the Hearst newspapers. Posters were distributed and even chain letters were used. America First research personnel in Washington assisted noninterventionist Congressmen and Senators and prepared speeches which were delivered on the floor of the Senate. [45]

Appeals were made to arouse special groups against Lend-Lease. Dozens of rural weekly newspapers carried accounts of the America First battle against Lend-Lease. [46] Noninterventionist literature was sent to forty thousand farmers, to fifteen thousand educational leaders, to the entire Catholic clergy, and to Elks lodges all over the country. [47]

During the Committee's battle against the Lend-Lease Bill new America First chapters were organized virtually every day in different parts of the nation. These units were promptly mobilized to combat the measure. Thousands of letters, telegrams, and bulletins were sent by America First national headquarters to direct the efforts of these local chapters. If a Congressman appeared amenable to pressure and was not receiving sufficient mail opposing Lend-Lease, Committee headquarters requested chapters to flood his desk with mail.[48] If too much mail was being received by a Congressman or Senator whose opposition to Lend-Lease was already assured, chapters were advised to direct their efforts elsewhere.[49] On February 21, 1941, a meeting of chapter chairmen was held in Washington, D.C., to discuss plans for the final drive to defeat the "war dictatorship bill." [50]

The Chicago America First chapter waged the most spectacular of the chapter campaigns against Lend-Lease. It urged all persons who opposed the bill to write or telephone the chapter headquarters. The response to this suggestion (aided by much publicity in the *Chicago Tribune*) exceeded even the expectations of the chapter leaders. For example, on January 14, 1941, 28,000 messages poured into the chapter headquarters. Fifty volunteer workers were required to handle the avalanche. Postmen dumped bags of mail on the floor every few minutes. Messenger boys delivered batches of telegrams and long lines waited to sign petitions. The telephones rang continually. So great was the influx of protests against Lend-Lease that it became necessary to find larger accommodations for the chapter headquarters.[51] The names of those who protested

47

against Lend-Lease were placed on petitions and mailed to the Congressmen and Senators who represented those individuals. By the end of the first week of February the leaders of the Chicago chapter estimated that a total of 628,000 names from all parts of Illinois had been placed on anti-Lend-Lease petitions.[52] All original letters were sent to Senator Scott W. Lucas who favored the Lend-Lease Bill.[53] The speakers' bureau of the Chicago chapter announced that its thirty speakers were swamped with calls to address meetings.[54] The chapter distributed at least 100,000 handbills attacking Lend-Lease.[55] It also supported a resolution in the Illinois state legislature which urged the defeat of the Lend-Lease Bill.[56]

The America First Committee assisted and co-operated with other organizations in the effort to defeat Lend-Lease. A total of at least two thousand dollars was supplied to three leading pacifist organizations to aid their efforts. America First leaders also secured funds to enable the Ministers No War Committee under Harry Emerson Fosdick to send noninterventionist literature to 93,000 Protestant ministers.[57] Funds were also supplied to George W. Robnett's Church League of America to urge ministers to oppose Lend-Lease.[58]

Even when the battle seemed completely lost the America First Committee continued its efforts. At the end of February the Committee gave its support to the Ellender Amendment which would have prohibited the sending of American troops outside the Western Hemisphere. This did not mean that America First was giving up its efforts to defeat the entire bill but it wanted to be certain that if the measure passed this limitation would be included.[59]

The *Chicago Tribune* published the following information to illustrate the magnitude of the Committee's effort:

Since September it has printed and distributed 1,500,000 folders and pamphlets, 500,000 automobile stickers, 750,000 America First buttons, and 15,000 large posters for public buildings.

It has answered 100,000 separate requests for information and posted more than 750,000 pieces of mail.

More than 700,000 signatures demanding defeat of the dictator bill were gathered by the Chicago chapter alone. This unit has also tabulated 328,000 protest telephone calls.

The America First legislative office in Washington provided a running analysis of the dictator bill and its amendments for Senators, representatives, and chapter officials. A weekly news letter was mailed to 1,250 speakers.

More than 2,600 transcriptions of radio addresses by noted speakers were sent to radio stations. Thousands of mass meetings thruout the nation were held. A movie, "America First," was shown by hundreds of chapters.[60]

These figures represent the total campaign of America First from the time of its inception, but the greater part of the activity cited was directed against Lend-Lease. Neither America First headquarters nor the *Chicago Tribune* was likely to be guilty of underestimating the Committee's efforts, but these figures do suggest the striking scope of the campaign.

The America First Committee's battle against the Lend-Lease Bill proved to be of no avail. Even in the East-Central states, where the Committee's strength was greatest, popular support for Lend-Lease increased from 39 per cent on

February 11, to 50 per cent by March 1, 1941.[61] The Committee failed completely to prevent its passage in Congress. The measure was signed by President Roosevelt on March 11, 1941. Nevertheless, this campaign, unsuccessful though it was, helped establish the America First Committee as the leading noninterventionist organization in the United States.

With Lend-Lease a *fait accompli* the America First leaders determined to make certain that this aid would really be short of war. The Lend-Lease Act resolved the problem of financing and allocating aid to Great Britain. But there still remained the serious problem of assuring that the goods actually reached England and were not sent to the bottom of the ocean by German submarines. America First leaders feared the President might use the American Navy to convoy ships to England and that incidents would result to propel the United States into the war. Consequently, the Committee directed its main efforts during the three months following the enactment of Lend-Lease in opposing the use of the American Navy for convoy duty.[62]

This issue of America's role in getting goods to England remained. But the Lend-Lease Act did eliminate one major question from the foreign policy debate. To that extent its enactment made it easier for the America First Committee to endeavor to place the foreign policy debate on the simple issue of war or peace.

4   War or Peace?

DURING 1941 America First Committee leaders tried to take the debate off of the issue of aid to Britain "short-of-war." They made concerted efforts to place the debate on the simple issue of whether the United States should or should not become a full belligerent in the European war. As early as September, 1940, Clay Judson, a member of the executive committee, wrote that "the question is between war and peace, and all other arguments are of importance only as they relate to that major issue." [1] A basic tenet in the America First Committee's opposition to Lend-Lease was its fear that the measure would put the United States into the European war. After Lend-Lease was passed in March, 1941, many America First leaders were convinced the only remaining issue for the Committee was the issue of war or peace. General Wood, Stuart, Mrs. Fairbank, Judson, W. H. Regnery, J. C. Hormel, W. R. Castle, and many other America First leaders expressed this general point of view. [2]

The effort to conduct the debate on the issue of war or peace grew out of the genuine convictions of Committee leaders that all other issues were subordinate to this main consideration—particularly after Lend-Lease became law. In addition to the convictions of America First leaders, however, there were at least three practical strategic ways in which the campaign on the issue of war or peace enhanced the Committee's effectiveness. In the first place, it capitalized upon the opposition of approximately 80 per cent of the American people to entry into the war and provided a basis for opposition to the Administration's steps short of war. In the second place, this issue provided the only program upon which the Committee's heterogeneous membership was in complete accord. And finally, it gave the America First Committee an opportunity to convert its negative and defensive position into a positive and aggressive campaign. Each of these strategic bases for the Committee's war-peace campaign is of sufficient importance to justify analysis.

Both sides in the foreign policy debate in 1941 claimed to represent a majority of the American people. The interventionists cited the re-election of Roosevelt for a third term in 1940 as evidence of popular approval of the President's policies. They could point to public opinion polls which indicated that a majority of Americans had approved each major proposal advanced by the Administration to aid the British short of war.[3] Since 1940 a clear majority had believed it more important to aid Britain in her effort to defeat Germany than it was for the United States to keep out of the war.[4] The interventionists, therefore, urged America First leaders to stop their noninterventionist agitation and unite behind the Administration in the nation's time of peril.[5]

Most America First leaders were convinced after the passage of Lend-Lease that the strong popular approval for aiding Britain made it neither practical nor politically expedient to conduct the campaign on that front. But Committee leaders vociferously claimed to represent a majority of the American people. Like Philip La Follette they viewed the 1940 presidential election as a " 'fixed fight'. . . where the President and Wendell Willkie vied with one another in protesting their love of peace, only to team up on the road to war once the ballots were counted." [6] They could point to public opinion polls which showed that approximately 80 per cent of the people opposed American entry into the war. According to these polls, at no time before Pearl Harbor did a majority of the American people favor a declaration of war on the Axis.[7]

Committee leaders feared that in spite of public opposition to entering the war the Administration's steps short of war would place the United States in a position which would make intervention inevitable. They feared that Lend-Lease, patrols, the "shoot-on-sight" policy, and repeal of the vital provisions of the Neutrality Act would result in incidents which would plunge the United States into the European conflagration.[8]

Many America First leaders became convinced that the Administration and the interventionists actually *hoped* steps short of war would lead to American intervention. General Thomas S. Hammond said the Committee to De-

53

fend America by Aiding the Allies sought to prepare the American public for a declaration of war.[9] General Wood said: "The 'short-of-war' phrase was a cloak to mask the real intentions of the backers of the committee. It is now advocating our actual entry into the war." [10] The fears of many America First leaders concerning the intentions of the Administration were given credence by the interventionist columnists Alsop and Kintner. In June, 1941, these columnists wrote that the President was determined "to force the Germans to fire the first shot." They also maintained that "the President and the men around him privately hope the [Atlantic] patrol will produce an incident." [11]

During the last half of 1941 America First spokesmen increasingly denounced the "subterfuge" by which interventionists allegedly were leading America to war while professing to be working to keep the nation out of war. Committee leaders contended the interventionist minority was attempting to drag the unwilling majority into war by deceitfully misleading Americans concerning their real intentions. In a radio address on August 1, 1941, Stuart declared: "The willful few who cry for war . . . . can never have their way while majority rule prevails . . . . The only thing these fighters for democracy have to fear is democracy itself." [12] A few days later Charles A. Lindbergh expressed a similar view:

The same groups who call on us to defend democracy and freedom abroad, demand that we kill democracy and freedom at home by forcing four-fifths of our people into war against their

54

will. The one-fifth who are for war call the four-fifths who are against war the "fifth column." . . . They know that the people of this country will not vote for war, and they therefore plan on involving us through subterfuge. . . . Since this country will not enter war willingly, they plan on creating incidents and situations which will force us into it.[13]

Speaking before a meeting of America First chapter leaders on November 1, 1941, Philip La Follette said:

Two years ago the President and the War Party launched us on a course of action labelled "steps short of war" to "keep us out of war." That was the most cunning of the many deceitful phrases employed in the propaganda campaign to get us into this war. . . . The sin of the War Party is not that they advocate war. The sin is that their only answer to the menace of Hitlerism in Europe is step by step to create Hitlerism in the United States. Every step taken in the past two years has been put over on us by the same fraudulent methods practiced by the European dictators.[14]

Essentially this same point of view was expressed in speeches by many other America First leaders. When the interventionists denounced the America First Committee for causing disunity in a time of national crisis, Senator Wheeler retorted that "the war mongers talk of unity— what they mean is that the 83 per cent of the people should join the 17 per cent, anxious to take part in the bloody conflicts which rage in Europe and Asia." [15]

It was sound strategy to wage the Committee's campaign on grounds which gave it the theoretical support of four-fifths of the American people. It was also sound strategy for the America First Committee to conduct its campaign on grounds which provided the greatest possible unity within the organization for its battle against intervention. The composition of America First was nearly as complex and diverse as that of the nation as a whole. Almost any positive program which the Committee might advance would alienate some of its followers. Virtually the only point on which there was complete agreement was that the United States should not enter the European war.[16] Conducting the campaign on the issue of war or peace would enable the America First Committee to utilize its strength with a minimum of disaffection.

Throughout its history the America First Committee was plagued by a seeming necessity for assuming negative roles in opposing Administration measures. The Committee opposed Lend-Lease. It opposed convoys. It opposed sending draftees outside of the Western Hemisphere. It opposed the "shoot-on-sight" policy. And it opposed repeal of the vital provisions of the Neutrality Act. The methods used to campaign on the issue of war or peace, however, enabled America First to wage positive battles for positive measures.

How did the America First Committee specifically propose to conduct its campaign? The pacifist organizations had long supported measures to enable the people to vote on the question of war or peace. After Lend-Lease was passed, the Keep America Out of War Congress, the National Council for the Prevention of War, and other peace groups campaigned for an advisory referendum on war or peace. These groups had the co-operation of Senators Nye, Wheeler, La Follette, and others and they sought the support of the powerful America First Committee.[17]

The America First executive committee in February, 1941, discussed the feasibility of supporting the Ludlow Amendment but decided to concentrate its energies against Lend-Lease.[18] In March, 1941, the executive committee considered a "Peace-War" vote suggested by William Benton but no real action was taken.[19] From March through May, 1941, the Committee was preoccupied with opposing the use of the American Navy for convoy duty and with staging rallies and speaking tours across the nation.

By June, 1941, the fear that the Administration might seek Congressional authorization for convoying had passed. The question of draft extension had not yet been raised. Debate on repeal of the Neutrality Act did not begin until the fall. Consequently, the summer months provided a lull in the battle against intervention favorable for consideration of an advisory referendum. On June 18, 1941, General Wood said he wished it might be possible "to settle this matter thru a simple referendum on the question of peace or war." General Hammond, Mrs. Fairbank, Regnery, and other Committee leaders concurred in this view.[20]

On June 23, 1941, the executive committee voted to add a sixth America First Principle. This Principle declared: "The America First Committee advocates a national advisory referendum on the issue of peace or war." This was not to be a constitutional amendment nor was it to bind the hands of Congress or the President. America First proposed a concurrent resolution by Congress authorizing a purely advisory vote by the people on the issue of war or peace. A Gallup poll in June, 1941, indicated that 56 per cent of the American people approved such a referendum.[21] There does not appear to have been any real expectation among most Committee and Congressional leaders that the measure would pass or even be voted upon in Congress. They approved the policy in part because they could think of no better way to wage a positive campaign on the issue of war or peace. Support for a national advisory referendum would provide local chapters with a positive goal and definite activities during the summer lull. Committee leaders believed the campaign would help keep the issue of war or peace before the American people. It was also hoped that the agitation for the referendum might put the Administration on the defensive on the issue of war or peace. Conceivably it could have put the interventionists in the embarrassing position of opposing a democratic procedure.[22]

The executive committee withheld public announcement of the decision until it had made arrangements with Congressmen and Senators for the introduction and support of the resolution.[23] Congressmen Oliver of Maine and Knute Hill of Washington agreed to introduce a resolution in the House of Representatives.[24] Senators Nye, La Follette, Wheeler, and three others had already introduced a similar measure in the Senate. On June 30, 1941, the newspapers carried accounts of the America First Committee's decision.[25] Chapters were deluged with challenging bulletins urging them to flood Washington with mail supporting the referendum.[26] In his radio address on July 7, 1941, General Wood suggested that the referendum should ask what the American people favored regarding American intervention to aid Britain. He suggested that it should ask what action the United States should take in case of attack on the Western Hemisphere. General Wood also proposed a question concerning repeal of the Neutrality Act.[27]

The burst of America First energy in support of a national advisory referendum was, however, short-lived and ineffective. Chapters did not respond to the challenge as they did in fighting Lend-Lease or the repeal of the Neutrality Act. Activity was limited largely to June and July, 1941. The campaign may have helped relieve the summer lull in chapter activities. However, it did not effectively put the foreign policy debate on the issue of war or peace. By August, 1941, the Committee again had Administration proposals with which to cope. The question was raised again in November, 1941, after the repeal of the Neutrality Act but Stuart said neither the members of Congress nor chapter members believed there was any possibility of securing passage of the legislation. The national committee this time decided not to support the proposal.[28]

Though the efforts to secure passage of a Congressional resolution authorizing an advisory referendum were unsuccessful, the America First Committee itself financed referendums in specific areas. The Committee induced Congressmen Hamilton Fish of New York, Knute Hill of

Washington, Harry Sauthoff of Wisconsin, and Paul Shafer of Michigan to sponsor referendums on war or peace in their districts. These referendums asked whether the United States should or should not enter the European war. In each case the America First Committee financed the venture though this was given no publicity in the newspapers. The questions were mailed to the constituents under the Congressmen's franks. Each of the polls showed exactly what the America First Committee expected them to show. They indicated that approximately 80 per cent of the voters in these districts opposed entering the European war. The referendum in Hamilton Fish's district was particularly interesting since it indicated that the voters in President Roosevelt's own district opposed intervention by nine to one.[29] America First considered conducting a referendum in North Carolina under the sponsorship of Senator Robert R. Reynolds. Senator Reynolds, however, advised against it because he was convinced it would result in an embarrassing pro-war vote.[30]

Life magazine conducted a survey in Neosho, Missouri which indicated that the people of the community believed the United States should aid Britain even at the risk of American intervention. The America First Committee, however, financed a survey in the same community which showed that 70 per cent of the people in Neosho opposed American entry into the war.[31] The *Chicago Tribune* and the New York *Daily News,* both of which sympathized with America First, sponsored referendums among the voters of Illinois and New York. The results in New York were seven to three against intervention while in Illinois the ratio was four to one.[32]

R. Douglas Stuart, Jr. was skeptical of the validity of the Gallup poll findings on foreign policy questions. He was convinced the questions were "loaded" to give results favorable to the interventionist point of view. The America First Committee, therefore, provided the funds to enable a committee under Robert M. Hutchins, president of the University of Chicago, to conduct an independent public opinion poll.[33] The results of this survey indicated that the public overwhelmingly believed Congress should be the source of any action likely to involve the United States in war. It also indicated that two-thirds of those with opinions opposed use of American armed forces in bases in Africa, the Azores, or the Cape Verde Islands. Nearly 80 per cent opposed American entry into the war as a full belligerent. But approximately two-thirds opposed any offer by the United States to mediate between England and Germany. A clear majority would have been willing to go to war if the Western Hemisphere were attacked.[34]

In the fall of 1941 America First sought to have the issue of war or peace submitted for a definite vote in Congress. Hanford MacNider and Jay C. Hormel both urged the Committee to sponsor such a move.[35] MacNider appears to have opposed democratic referendums on war or peace because he believed they were contrary to American traditions of representative government.[36] This criticism obviously could not be leveled at the proposal for submitting the issue of war or peace directly to Congress. Samuel B.

Pettengill, an influential America First advisor, was disturbed by the increase of executive authority at the expense of the legislature. Early in October, 1941, he strongly urged America First to ask the President to submit the issue of war or peace to Congress. The America First Committee was under particularly severe attack in the fall of 1941, and this plan offered opportunities for reducing the Committee's vulnerability to criticism. Under this plan America First would be advocating an accepted constitutional procedure at a time when the Committee was being criticized for being "subversive" and "un-American." Interventionists had insisted that noninterventionist agitation was unpatriotic because, in their opinion, the United States was already in the war. If the President refused to have a war resolution submitted, or if Congress voted against war, there would appear to have been less justification for denouncing America First on that basis.[37]

On October 20, 1941, the America First national committee discussed the plan. At the suggestion of Stuart, the national committee approved a seventh America First Principle. This Principle proclaimed:

The Constitution of the United States vests the sole power to declare war in Congress. Until Congress has exercised that power, it is not only the privilege but the duty of every citizen to express to his Representatives his views on the question of peace or war—in order that this grave issue may be decided in accordance with the will of the people and the best traditions of American democracy.

The national committee voted that an open letter should be sent to President Roosevelt urging submission of a war resolution to Congress. General Wood agreed to consult with Senator Wheeler and other Congressmen before sending the letter. The text was based upon a draft prepared by Pettengill and revised by Mrs. Fairbank, Judson, and Richard A. Moore, assistant national director of America First.[38] This open letter over the signature of General Wood was sent to President Roosevelt on October 22, 1941. This letter asserted:

The America First Committee, in the interest of peace, honor and constitutional government, respectfully asks that you cause to be submitted to Congress a resolution for the declaration of a state of war between the United States and the German Reich.

Each step thus far taken in the international situation has been upon the solemn assurance that it was for the purpose of preserving peace. Actually we have been led to the brink of a devastating war, with the inevitable loss of human lives and destruction of our national economy and way of life. This subterfuge must end. We must now squarely face the real issue, war or peace. . . . The America First Committee . . . will oppose with vigor the passage of a war resolution. Nevertheless we are convinced that the question must be settled now and in the way and by the authority required by the Constitution. If Congress votes for a declaration of war, the constitutional voice of the American people will have spoken and this Committee and all other patriotic Americans will respect that decision.

If, on the other hand, Congress, in its wisdom, votes down a declaration of war, the Administration must respect that decision and take no further step toward our involvement.[39]

Secretary of War Henry L. Stimson and other advisors had been urging the President to follow just such a course. But according to Robert E. Sherwood, the proposal by General Wood further convinced President Roosevelt that he would be defeated in such a vote.[40] Congress was not asked to declare a state of war until after the Japanese had attacked Pearl Harbor.

CRITICS OF the America First Committee ridiculed its emphasis upon the 80 per cent who opposed entering the war. They ridiculed the Committee's attempts to put the debate on the simple issue of war or peace. A release from the Committee to Defend America by Aiding the Allies insisted that the war-peace issue was a false issue for the following reason:

If there really were a simple issue between war and peace, we may be sure that virtually 100 per cent of the American people would favor peace.

Unless Hitler is defeated we will not have either peace or national security, a fact which the vast majority of our people have recognized and which has been the basis of our present national policy. So the real issue is whether we shall support this national policy, or whether we shall reverse it and then fight a Battle of America against Germany alone. . . . Only a small minority of the 80 per cent whom the Isolationists claim are against "war" would now favor reversing our national policy and permitting Hitler to defeat Britain.

This release cited a public opinion poll to show that a majority of the American people favored going to war if it were necessary to defeat Germany and Italy. It also cited a poll indicating that Americans favored checking Japan even at the risk of war.[41]

Stuart refused to believe that these polls fairly measured the views of the American people on the nation's foreign policy. He was convinced that Americans wanted to stay out of war more than they desired a British victory over Germany.[42] Whatever validity his views may or may not have had, they were *not* verified by the Hutchins committee poll which America First financed.[43]

In terms of measured public opinion, the issue of war or peace provided the only base upon which the America First Committee had a theoretical chance for victory in the battle against intervention. Americans were overwhelmingly sympathetic with the British and desired an Axis defeat. The public opinion polls consistently indicated that Americans favored aiding Britain even at the risk of war. According to the polls a majority believed it was more important to defeat Germany than it was to keep out of the war. The American people drew back only when confronted with the specific question of whether the United States should declare war and enter the conflagration as a full belligerent. In emphasizing the issue of war or peace the America First Committee was attempting to conduct the foreign policy debate on a much simpler basis than the views of most Americans actually justified. The support which the majority of Americans gave to each of the Administration's short of war proposals virtually assured the defeat of America First in each of these campaigns. Moreover, President Roosevelt was a master political strategist. He was an extremely capable judge of the strength of his legislative and popular support. President Roosevelt sought Congressional authorization only for those measures for which he could reasonably anticipate the support of a majority in Congress and in the nation.

War or Peace?

He could be relied upon to choose no grounds which would give the noninterventionists a serious chance to defeat him.[44]

The America First Committee's strategy of emphasizing the issue of war or peace was not completely unsuccessful. It may have helped delay "short of war" moves which Committee leaders believed were steps toward war. Moreover, by keeping the emphasis upon the issue of war or peace in its campaigns against Administration proposals, the Committee was able to make orderly retreats after each specific defeat without being forced to surrender completely. It could then re-form its lines on new grounds and continue its battle against intervention. To this extent the Committee's strategy was successful. By the end of November, 1941, President Roosevelt had the authority to do almost everything to aid Britain against Germany except send the American Army and Air Force into the battle. He could supply Britain with goods on a Lend-Lease basis. His "shoot-on-sight" policy was virtually an undeclared naval war on the Axis fleets in the western Atlantic. With the repeal of the vital provisions of the Neutrality Act, armed American merchant ships could carry goods directly to England. But still neither the American people nor, in all probability, the United States Congress was prepared for an actual declaration of war. If the Japanese had not attacked on December 7, 1941, and if the German submarines had successfully avoided sinking American ships carrying and convoying goods for England, it is conceivable that

America First might have won its battle against intervention.[45]

Nevertheless, the America First Committee was never able to focus public attention exclusively on the simple issue of war or peace. The possible consequences to the United States of an Axis victory seriously disturbed most Americans. A majority was convinced Germany had to be defeated even if that required American intervention in the war. Despite the America First Committee's efforts, the foreign policy debate in 1941 was conducted primarily upon grounds chosen by the President—not simply on the issue of war or peace.

Furthermore, the noninterventionist strength, which the America First Committee represented, actually made President Roosevelt and many of his advisors even *less* willing to place the debate squarely on the issue of war or peace.[46] The President's general attitude with regard to the European war was established before the America First Committee was formed.[47] But the efforts of the Committee in marshaling and focusing noninterventionist strength probably helped to make him unwilling to discard his tried and tested "short of war" approach in foreign policy.

Strategically and statistically the America First Committee's opportunity to win the battle against intervention lay in getting the debate on the narrow issue of war or peace. Its inability to do so and the Japanese attack on Pearl Harbor insured the defeat of the America First Committee.

But the Committee was not without its own re-enforcements. The Nazi decision to attack the Soviet Union on June 22, 1941, gave America First leaders renewed hope that their battle against intervention might succeed.

5   Capitalism, Communism and Catholicism

THE NONINTERVENTIONIST movement as a whole drew support from both economic liberals and conservatives. Many writers have tended to assume that there was a high correlation between conservative and noninterventionist views. Basil Rauch wrote that: "The great mass of isolationists were simply conservative, and the main body of isolationist propaganda was designed to fortify the conservative temper." [1] On the other hand, the conservative *Saturday Evening Post* asserted that: "Socialism and national planning are inevitably isolationist in the long run." [2] Actually there were liberals and conservatives on both sides of the foreign policy debate in 1941.

Many interventionists held views which could properly be classified as Left of Center. The interventionists included many New Dealers and liberal Democrats. The Administration leadership and the Democratic Party discipline undoubtedly helped keep some hesitant liberals in the interventionist fold. Many liberals in academic circles were interventionists. Labor was divided much like the nation as a whole, but a majority of organized labor favored aiding Britain and believed it was more important to defeat Germany than to keep out of the war.[3] After the Germans attacked the Soviet Union, American Communists were suddenly converted into interventionists.[4]

But the interventionists also drew strong support from conservatives. The traditionally conservative South was easily the most interventionist major region in the nation.[5] Some Republicans and many prominent businessmen supported the Administration's foreign policy. Labor leaders contributed to the Committee to Defend America by Aiding the Allies, but so did J. P. Morgan and Henry Luce.[6]

The noninterventionists also received much conservative support. Pro-Nazis and pro-fascists on the extreme Right were noninterventionists. Most conservative old-line Republicans and New Deal haters opposed the President's foreign policy. The conservative Middle West was the nation's most strongly noninterventionist region. The reactionary *Chicago Tribune* was a vituperative opponent of the Administration's foreign policy.

Nevertheless, there were many noninterventionists to the Left of Center. Some liberal Democrats and New Deal supporters like Senator Burton K. Wheeler were noninterventionists. Philip La Follette, Robert M. La Follette and other former Progressives fought the Administration's foreign policy. Some labor leaders such as John L. Lewis and Kathryn Lewis were on the noninterventionist side.[7] Many Socialists and liberals like Norman Thomas and Stuart Chase were noninterventionists. The *Progressive* and the Socialist *Call* both supported the nonintervention-

·ist position. Until June 22, 1941, the Communists opposed American entry into the war. It is not, therefore, correct to assume the identity of economic conservatism and "isolationism" in 1940–1941.

Noninterventionists, however, tended to group them-selves into foreign policy pressure groups which were more homogeneous in terms of their economic views than the movement as a whole. The American Communists and fel-low travelers supported the American Peace Mobilization before they were converted into interventionists. Many liberals and Socialists with noninterventionist predilections were attracted to the Keep America Out of War Congress.[8] The No Foreign War Committee and the Citizens Keep America Out of War Committee had the support of many conservatives. Extreme Rightists worked through the German-American Bund and similar organizations.

Where did the America First Committee fit into this distribution of noninterventionist pressure groups? The leadership and financial backing of the Committee came predominantly from the conservative wing of the non-interventionist movement. America First leaders sought to exclude Communists, Nazis, and fascists from the organiza-tion. The membership of the Committee included repre-sentatives of more diverse social and economic views than most other major noninterventionist organizations. Its strength and effectiveness attracted the support and co-operation of many who did not agree with the economic views of its leaders. Nevertheless, most executive and na-tional committee members of America First represented varied shades of conservatism on domestic and economic issues.

The core of the America First Committee leadership and financial backing was provided by businessmen. Five of the eight persons who served on the executive committee (Wood, Regnery, MacNider, Hammond, and Hormel) were heads of business corporations. Stuart was the son of a big business executive.

General Robert E. Wood's support of the early New Deal had been well publicized. He had approved the Securities and Exchange Commission, the Agricultural Adjustment Administration, Social Security, and the housing program. He disliked the price fixing aspects of the National Recovery Administration. Though a firm believer in capitalism, he did not believe "the charge of socialism, communism, or regimentation should be hurled at every new proposal or reform." General Wood was proud of the "Savings and Profit Sharing Pension Plan" for employees of Sears Roebuck. He believed business should have a sense of social responsibility. Nevertheless, he had begun to break with the President's domestic policy even before the 1936 election. General Wood favored tax revision "to liberate capital for creative purpose." While chairman of America First he was also a director of the National Association of Manufacturers. According to Stuart, General Wood rejected an invitation in the fall of 1940 to be president of the National Association of Manufacturers. Sears Roebuck and Company by 1938 had no union agreements and did not recognize a closed shop. At that time no more than 2 per cent of its employees were organized.[9] In 1946 General Wood was one of the leaders and financial backers of American Action Incorporated. This organization was designed to counteract the Congress of Industrial Organization's Political Action Committee.[10] In 1948 he joined other conservatives in supporting General Douglas MacArthur for President of the United States.[11] A columnist, Robert S. Allen, wrote in 1950, that General Wood had contributed considerable sums to the reactionary National Economic Council headed by Merwin K. Hart.[12] Despite his approval of certain reforms, General Wood was definitely a conservative.

Most of the others on the America First executive committee held similar economic ideas. General Thomas S. Hammond was an outspoken defender of the American system of free enterprise.[13] William H. Regnery later contributed to American Action Incorporated and Hart's National Economic Council.[14] The fact that Hanford MacNider's competitors' employees were organized and his own were not resulted in labor difficulties in 1941.[15] Mrs. Fairbank, a Democrat, opposed the election of Roosevelt in 1936 before there were foreign policy bases for her opposition.[16] Stuart, however, appears to have had liberal ideas and supported President Roosevelt's New Deal program.[17]

A large number of the associations of these executive committee members were with other businessmen and other conservatives. The contacts with businessmen were valuable in enabling America First to secure sufficient funds

73

to conduct its battle against intervention on a major scale. But they also enhanced the general business and conservative character of the Committee's leadership and backing.

The America First national committee included eight or nine business executives in addition to those on the executive committee. Three national committee members were investment bankers. Even some of the national committee members and advisors who had been identified with liberalism or liberal movements gave some evidence of an essential conservatism. General Hugh S. Johnson and George N. Peek had been leading administrators in President Roosevelt's New Deal. They served, however, during the early conservative phase and were dropped as the New Deal became more liberal.[18] John T. Flynn had been a writer for the liberal *New Republic* and was chairman of the Keep America Out of War Congress, but his writings since World War II have been extremely conservative or reactionary.[19] Philip La Follette had been identified with American liberalism but the supporters which he rallied for the short-lived "MacArthur for President" boom in 1948 were remarkably conservative.[20]

This same general pattern is seen in the financing of America First. Approximately two-thirds of the national headquarters income was provided by persons contributing one hundred dollars or more. Eight businessmen supplied a total of over one hundred thousand dollars to the national headquarters.[21] Examples of conservatives and businessmen among the Committee's followers and contributors could be cited at great length.

The conservative flavor of America First made liberals reluctant to use it as a vehicle for opposing intervention. Stuart, therefore, actively sought the support of liberals and was not wholly unsuccessful. Oswald Garrison Villard, former editor of the *Nation,* was on the national committee briefly in 1940.[22] Chester Bowles, later head of the Office of Price Administration, was a national committee member. Sidney Hertzberg, an editor of the liberal noninterventionist *Uncensored,* was publicity director of America First for a few months.[23] The America First Research Bureau in Washington, D.C., was staffed largely by liberals drawn from the older pacifist organizations.[24]

All too frequently, however, the results of Stuart's efforts to add liberals to the America First roster were discouraging. Philip La Follette spoke at America First meetings and advised on Committee policy but declined to become a national committee member. Charles A. Beard, the historian, was invited at least twice to join the national committee. He did write a public endorsement of America First, but he declined to be a member.[25] Stuart Chase, a liberal writer, was invited three times to be a national committee member. A pamphlet written by Chase was distributed by America First, but he would not become a member.[26] Norman Thomas, head of the Socialist Party, was also invited to be a member. He spoke at meetings sponsored by America First and made broadcasts and college speaking tours which were financed, at least in part, by funds secured through the Committee. But he never became a member.[27]

The America First Committee sought to balance the businessmen in the organization with intellectuals and academicians. The national committee included Professors Anton J. Carlson of the University of Chicago, George H. Whipple of the University of Rochester, Gregory Mason of New York University, Albert W. Palmer of the Chicago Theological Seminary, and Clarence Manion and the Reverend John A. O'Brien of Notre Dame University. Some of these were fully as conservative as the businessmen in America First.[28] Professors Edwin Borchard of Yale, and Philip C. Jessup of Columbia, President Henry Noble McCracken of Vassar, President Alan Valentine of the University of Rochester, President Robert M. Hutchins of the University of Chicago, and others declined invitations to be on the national committee. However, these and other university faculty members spoke at Committee meetings, were sponsors or leaders of local chapters, or aided America First in other ways.[29] Professor Maynard Krueger of the University of Chicago, former Socialist candidate for vice-president of the United States, spoke at America First meetings [30] as did the historian, Harry Elmer Barnes.[31]

The America First Committee sought the support of organized labor but its efforts met with meager success. John L. Lewis, Alexander Whitney, and David Robertson all declined invitations to be members of the national committee.[32] Kathryn Lewis, a labor executive and daughter of John L. Lewis, was a member of the national committee for a year. At her request the Committee insisted that the union label be on all printed America First literature.[33] William L. Hutchinson, vice-president of the American Federation of Labor, became a national committee member in the fall of 1941.[34] The effort of America First headquarters to form a national America First labor division early in 1941 was terminated before anything was accomplished.[35] No further moves of this sort were initiated by Committee headquarters. The Chicago and New York chapters and a few others formed labor units. The chairman of the labor division of the Chicago chapter boasted by February 25, 1941, that nineteen labor unions with 300,000 workers had endorsed the Committee Principles in the area.[36] But when the chapter sponsored a workingmen's rally against Lend-Lease the attendance was only a fraction of that anticipated.[37]

The liberal Keep America Out of War Congress and the National Council for the Prevention of War were held in much higher regard by organized labor than America First. These organizations had well established contacts with labor groups. The America First Committee, therefore, sought to stimulate labor opposition to war by extending limited financial assistance for the work of these organizations in labor circles.[38] This policy utilized the best facilities available to rally labor against intervention. But it had the defect of further identifying liberal and labor noninterventionist elements with these organizations rather than with America First.

The efforts to marshal organized farm support for America First were hardly more successful. Louis J. Taber, Master of the National Grange; Ray McKaig of the Grange in

Idaho; and George N. Peek, former head of the first Agricultural Adjustment Administration, were all on the America First national committee. Early in 1941 America First
placed articles in dozens of rural weekly newspapers.[39]
Some local chapters sponsored booths at county fairs [40]
and two successful "grass roots" meetings were held to
appeal for rural support.[41] But a mailing to nearly forty
thousand farm leaders in every county of the nation
brought only slightly more than four hundred responses
and a little more than three hundred dollars in contributions.[42] The Committee's efforts to work through local units
of the Grange were ineffective.[43]

Despite its efforts, the America First Committee had
only limited success among liberals and organized labor
and farm groups. Representatives of these groups who
co-operated with America First often did so with hesitancy
and misgivings.

The limited support which the America First Committee
received from liberals and farm and labor leaders was
slightly more evident during the first half of its history
than later. For example, the liberal Kathryn Lewis resigned from the Committee in October, 1941. She was
replaced by William L. Hutchinson, a far more conservative labor leader. Oswald Garrison Villard resigned from
the Committee in October, 1940. Sidney Hertzberg resigned in March, 1941. Norman Thomas no longer spoke
at America First meetings after Lindbergh's speech at
Des Moines in September, 1941.[44] Senator Robert M.
La Follette made his only radio address for America First

in the fall of 1940.[45] Harry Elmer Barnes apparently spoke at Committee meetings largely during the first half of its history.[46] During 1941 Congressman Hamilton Fish of New York and former Senator Rush Holt of West Virginia began to speak regularly for America First.[47] Lindbergh became a member in April, 1941, and he had a particularly strong appeal among many Right wing groups.[48] Late in 1941 one of the most active speakers for the Committee was Laura Ingalls who was convicted after Pearl Harbor for failure to register as a German agent.[49]

The magnitude of this change should not be over-emphasized. The group of persons who actually exercised significant influence on Committee policy remained relatively unchanged. Two conservatives were dropped from the national committee before the end of 1940 and other conservatives resigned during 1941.[50] Nevertheless, these changes do indicate a limited shift to the Right. This trend was partially due to the severe criticism to which the Committee, its leaders, and its spokesmen were subjected. These attacks discouraged liberals and persons who were unwilling to risk their future careers by being publicly at the front of the Committee's battle against intervention.

BOTH INTERVENTIONISTS and noninterventionists in 1940–1941 predicted that the failure to follow the particular foreign policy which they espoused would result in dire consequences for the American economy. Pamphlets released by the Committee to Defend America by Aiding the Allies predicted that an Axis victory would mean the loss

79

of American social gains and the enslavement of labor. They said a German victory would result in the loss of all American trade outside of the Western Hemisphere. The Committee to Defend America by Aiding the Allies predicted that the United States could not compete successfully with Germany in Latin America because of the Nazi forced labor and barter systems. It predicted a Nazi victory would result in the destruction of individual freedom and free enterprise in the United States.[51] Walter Lippmann believed that the chances for the survival of the American businessman after a British defeat or a negotiated peace would be "very poor indeed." He feared the United States would be compelled to use measures far more "radical" than those in the New Deal to withstand Nazi economic competition.[52]

The America First Committee did not include the endorsement of any domestic policy in its Principles. There were some supporters who believed the Committee should advocate a positive economic program for the development of American prosperity as an alternative to war.[53] General Wood, Stuart, and most other Committee leaders, however, contended that America First should limit its efforts strictly to opposing intervention. They held that the Committee's membership was so heterogeneous that support for any other objectives would cause disunity and reduce its effectiveness in the battle against intervention.[54] Nevertheless, the America First Committee did appeal for support by predicting the relative effects upon the American economy of intervention and nonintervention. The foreign policy views of Committee leaders reflected their economic views.

Most America First leaders were convinced Germany could not successfully invade Great Britain. But even if England fell they believed the United States with its free labor and capitalistic system could successfully compete with German slave labor and National Socialism in world trade. They were convinced that Europe and Asia would need American products more than the United States would need their products. General Wood said if necessary the United States could adopt some of the Nazi trade practices to compete more successfully in world trade. He believed this could be done without endangering the American economic system. Some Committee leaders pointed out that foreign trade constituted only a small fraction of the total American commerce. John T. Flynn estimated that the cost of the war to the United States if she intervened would equal the total value of American foreign trade for the next four hundred years. America First leaders, therefore, believed even if an Axis victory reduced foreign trade, it would be less harmful to the American economy than intervention in the war. They believed substitutes and synthetic products could be developed to compensate for materials which might not be available because of Axis controls.[55]

America First leaders held that Communism, Nazism, and fascism arose out of internal economic distress. They insisted that the best way to prevent fascism in the United States was to prevent poverty, depression, and unemployment at home rather than by waging war abroad.[56] Nevertheless, virtually all America First leaders vigorously opposed the sort of economic planning to solve domestic problems which Norman Thomas, Stuart Chase, or Charles A. Beard favored.

America First leaders predicted that American intervention in the war would result in the loss of labor's social and economic gains and the collapse of the American system of free enterprise.[57] In a radio address John T. Flynn expressed the fears of many America First leaders concerning the consequences of intervention upon the American economy:

Every man and woman and child ... will have to pay the incalculable costs of this mad adventure. We will spend a hundred billion dollars—and borrow it—on top of the billions we still owe for the last war and the billions we still owe for the depression.

Taxes will consume your earnings and cripple your business. Vast government loans will impose a paralyzing interest charge of from three to four billions a year—and forever. A gigantic pension system for the new veterans will be reared on top of the veterans' aid burdens of the last war. The prospect of certain inflation will bring all private investment to a stop and end by sweeping away the accumulations of every man's industry and savings.

A great army of bureaucrats will help to manage every man's affairs. They will swarm over your banks, your shops, your stores. They will tell you what materials to use and for what, where to buy them and at what price. They will tell you what you can make, where you can sell it and for what. You will spend half your time seeking permits, getting visas, answering questions, making reports and satisfying the thousand and one demands of the supervisors. They will tax you until your profits vanish and, if any remain, they will squeeze them out of you in the form of force loans.

The gains of labor, the long, painfully acquired right of the worker in his job and his union will be swept away. His labor problems will be settled for him by a man in uniform. And when the war is over these armies of bureaucrats will never be demobilized. And neither will the armies of soldiers. We will have struck down the present economic system with a death blow and these millions of soldiers and civil servants on the public payroll will have become an economic necessity in a society in which private enterprise is dead or dying. . . . Our economic system will be broken. Our financial burdens will be insupportable. The great war boom will have burst. The streets will be filled with idle men and women. And the once independent farmer will become a government charge. . . . And amidst these disorders we will have the perfect climate for some promising Hitler on the American model to rise to power with promises of abundance and recovery. The peace, the security, the liberties of a whole generation will be destroyed. And we, who set out once again on a fool's errand to remodel the world and bring democracy to peoples who do not want it, especially at our hands, and to save the crumbling fragments of democracy in other lands, will see it pass out of our own country. This is what you are talking about when you talk so glibly about that terrible thing "war." [58]

The desire to preserve the American capitalistic system was an important basis for opposition to intervention in the war in the minds of many Committee leaders. They expressed the fear that American intervention would result in the spread of communism, socialism, or fascism in Europe and even in the United States. General Wood predicted that American intervention would probably result in "the end of capitalism all over the world." [59] In the summer of 1941 he wrote: "Personally I feel that this question of our entrance into the war means whether our system of free enterprise is going to exist or not. If we go into the war, I am convinced that it will not." [60] In seeking large financial contributions Stuart wrote: "It involves the question of whether private ownership of property is to survive, or whether we are to go totalitarian ourselves. It is fairly certain that capitalism cannot survive American participation in this war." [61] The Certificate of Incorporation of the New York chapter declared a purpose of the organization was to support "a more vigorous and creative system of free enterprise with the abounding opportunity which this offers to replace the present creeping paralysis of the defeatism of state socialism." [62] While most America First leaders expressed strong dislike for both fascism and communism, many of them believed communism was even worse than fascism or National Socialism.[63]

Communists in the United States opposed intervention in the European war until Russia became a victim of Nazi aggression. Nevertheless, even before the Russo-German War the Communists repeatedly denounced the America First Committee and its leaders. The Communist publications, *New Masses* and *Daily Worker,* attacked the Committee as representing a group of capitalists opposed to the interventionist Morgan interests. They insisted that the Committee's imperialism differed only in details from that of the interventionists. They specifically accused the Committee leaders of having imperialistic ambitions in Latin America.[64]

84

Capitalism, Communism, and Catholicism

The German attack on the Soviet Union on June 22, 1941, immediately converted American Communists into interventionists.[65] This Nazi attack also gave renewed hope to America First Committee leaders that their battle against intervention might yet succeed. The America First executive committee released a statement on June 23, 1941, which declared:

The entry of Communist Russia into the war certainly should settle once and for all the intervention issue here at home. The war party can hardly ask the people of America to take up arms behind the red flag of Stalin. With the ruthless forces of dictatorship and aggression now clearly aligned on both sides the proper course for the United States becomes even clearer. We must continue to build our own defenses and take no part in this incongruous European conflict. . . . In the name of the four freedoms are we now to undertake a program of all-out aid to Russia? [66]

Committee spokesmen ridiculed the idea of fighting on the side of "bloody Joe." [67] John T. Flynn asked if the United States was going to fight "to make Europe safe for Communism." [68] Charles A. Lindbergh declared: "I would a hundred times rather see my country ally herself with England, or even with Germany with all her faults, than with the cruelty, the godlessness, and the barbarism that exist in Soviet Russia." [69] Senator Bennett Champ Clark at an America First meeting asked if anyone could "conceive of American boys being sent to their deaths singing 'Onward Christian Soldiers' under the bloody emblem of the Hammer and Sickle." [70] Clearly, the America First Committee leaders hoped the United States would now sit back and let Nazism and Communism battle to their deaths.

President Roosevelt's decision not to apply the Neutrality Act to the Russo-German War was severely attacked by the America First Committee. Shipping war goods to Russia via Vladivostock would be an unnecessary risk of American lives. Such shipping might lead to an incident which would bring the United States into the war.[71] The Committee also strongly opposed the extension of Lend-Lease aid to the Soviet Union.[72]

In General Wood's opinion the Russo-German War made it even less necessary to intervene to aid Britain since she was no longer fighting alone.[73] John T. Flynn pointed to England's failure to invade the continent even after Russia had joined her in fighting Germany. He insisted that England wanted the United States to do her fighting for her.[74]

The Russo-German War also gave the America First Committee an opportunity to attack her opponents in the battle of the committees. America First had been accused of having Communist support.[75] Now Committee leaders accused the interventionist organizations of having the support of enemies of the American way of life.[76]

The America First Committee appealed for the support of Catholics in opposing intervention on the side of Communist Russia. It cited an encyclical in which Pope Pius XI said: "Communism is intrinsically wrong, and no one who would save Christian civilization may collaborate with it in any undertaking whatsoever." [77] Committee advertisements and publications denounced the religious persecution and the "massacre" of clergymen in the Soviet Union.[78] William P. Leonard, chairman of the Brooklyn America First chapter, organized a Catholic Laymen's Committee for Peace. The America First national headquarters supplied funds to enable this organization to take a poll of Catholic clergymen. More than 90 per cent of the clergymen who responded to this poll opposed American entry into the war and opposed extending aid to the Soviet Union.[79]

As the Nazis drove deeper into Russian territory many began to fear that the Soviet Union would fall just as the rest of the Continental powers had fallen. Ernest K. Lindley suggested in his column that the United States should secure defensive bases in Siberia for protection against such a possibility. The America First Committee cited distances, geography, climate, and American defense installations to attack this idea.[80] A Committee pamphlet asserted that even if Hitler conquered the Soviet Union and controlled its resources and those of Europe, he would still be dependent upon the Western Hemisphere for many vital resources and food supplies. It held that "the enlarged German economy may be weakened rather than strengthened." [81]

But despite their dislike for Communism and the Soviet Union, the overwhelming majority of Americans hoped Russia would defeat Germany. The Russo-German War did not significantly change the attitude of the American people regarding aid to Britain.[82] American fears concerning Axis military aggression were not assuaged. The interventionists continued their campaign with even greater vigor. Soon there were new issues to be debated in the battle of the committees. Late in the summer of 1941 the question of draft extension precipitated a debate on the defense requirements of the United States.

6   Military Defense

THE AMERICA First Committee was not a pacifist organization. Its first public statement barred pacifists from membership.[1] It was hoped this policy would make the Committee less vulnerable to criticism.[2]

Nevertheless, during its full history the America First Committee received the support of pacifists and co-operated with pacifist organizations. At least two pacifists, Oswald Garrison Villard and Albert W. Palmer, were on the first list of national committee members.[3] The announced policy of barring pacifists from membership was reversed during September, 1940.[4] John T. Flynn, a national committee member and head of America First in New York, was chairman of the Keep America Out of War Congress. This organization included several pacifist organizations though not all of its members were pacifists.[5] Kathleen Norris, also a member of the national committee, was a member of the Women's International League for Peace and Freedom.[6] The first director of the national headquarters' speaking bureau professed to be a pacifist.[7] Ruth Sarles, Sidney Hertzberg, and Kendrick Lee, America

First staff members in Chicago and Washington, D.C., had been active in pacifist organizations. Many workers in local America First chapters were members of pacifist groups.[8]

The America First Committee co-operated informally with reputable pacifist organizations such as the National Council for the Prevention of War, the Keep America Out of War Congress, the Youth Committee Against War, the Women's International League for Peace and Freedom, and the Ministers No War Committee. Early in 1941 America First supplied funds to these organizations to aid their campaigns.[9] Sidney Hertzberg, while employed by America First, sought to co-ordinate the Committee's efforts with those of pacifist organizations.[10] Ruth Sarles, the Committee's lobbyist and research director in Washington, D.C., during 1941, consulted with leaders of pacifist organizations.[11] Frederick J. Libby, the dean of American pacifists, conferred with America First leaders on matters of policy in the battle against intervention.[12] The Committee's decision to endorse an advisory referendum was partially due to the influence of pacifist leaders.[13] There was a certain amount of division of labor among the organizations. The major pacifist organizations concentrated much effort among liberal, labor, and farm groups where the more conservative America First Committee was less effective.[14]

Nevertheless, America First was not a pacifist organization. Both Palmer and Villard resigned from the national committee in the fall of 1940 because of its endorsement of strong military defenses.[15] Norman Thomas who spoke at America First meetings emphasized in correspondence that he differed with the Committee in his opposition to "armament economics." [16]

Six of the seven men who served on the executive committee had had military training or experience. Brigadier General Wood was a West Point graduate. He served in the Army from his graduation in 1900 until 1915 and again during World War I. Major General Thomas S. Hammond served with the Rainbow Division in France during World War I. He was in the Illinois National Guard until his retirement in 1940. Hanford MacNider served with the Iowa National Guard on the Mexican border in 1916–1917 and retired from active duty in the Army in 1919 as a Lieutenant Colonel. Between them, Wood, Hammond, and Mac-Nider were awarded decorations by four different nations. MacNider also wore the Purple Heart. Clay Judson was a Captain in the Tank Corps during the Argonne offensive in World War I. He also served in the army of occupation. Jay C. Hormel served as a First Lieutenant during World War I.[17] Stuart had a Reserve Officers Training Corps commission.[18]

Many national committee members had had military experience. General Hugh S. Johnson served in the Army from 1903 to 1919. He had been largely responsible for setting up and administering the selective service system in World War I. Charles A. Lindbergh was a Colonel in the Air Corps Reserve until criticism by President Roosevelt caused him to resign in 1941. Edward Rickenbacker was America's most famous air ace in World War I. Alford

91

J. Williams was a flying officer in the Navy from 1917 to 1930 and was later in the Marine Corps Reserve. Anton J. Carlson, J. Sanford Otis, Lessing J. Rosenwald, and Edward L. Ryerson, Jr., of the national committee all served in the American armed forces during World War I. Amos R. E. Pinchot and Frank O. Lowden served during the Spanish American War.[19]

Some local America First chapters formed veterans divisions to organize veterans of past wars against intervention.[20] During the first part of its history the America First Committee had a few supporters who were on active duty in the armed forces.[21] There was not, however, any concerted effort made to appeal for support from servicemen. In July, 1941, Secretary of War Henry L. Stimson accused Senator Burton K. Wheeler of allowing his Congressional frank to be used by America First to circularize servicemen. Stimson expressed the opinion that this came "very near the line of subversive activities against the United States, if not treason." Senator Wheeler admitted that a million cards had been mailed by America First under his frank. He insisted, however, that they had been sent to a commercial mailing list and not with the intent to circularize servicemen. Stimson, therefore, issued an apology and said his statement had been based upon "incomplete evidence." [22] After this incident, Committee headquarters directed its chapters to remove from their mailing lists "all names of members on active service with the United States armed forces." [23] The Committee sought to follow this policy during the rest of its history.[24]

In November, 1941, Colonel Early E. W. Duncan, commanding officer at Lowry Field, declared the America First headquarters in Denver "out-of-bounds" for the men under his command. He took this action because he believed they "might be instilled with thoughts and ideas harmful to morale." He also threatened to make churches out-of-bounds whose pastors "preach against true Americanism." According to the chairman of America First in Colorado, some soldiers had visited the Committee's office but no efforts had been made to propagandize them.[25]

THE QUESTION of building America's national defenses was not, in itself, at the core of the foreign policy debate in 1940–1941. Nearly all Americans believed the United States should build strong military defenses.[26] Americans had varied ideas regarding the size and character of the military machine essential for national security. But there was no significant disagreement concerning the general necessity for adequate national armed forces. Both interventionists and noninterventionists urged the building of national defenses,[27] but both sides tended to shunt the question to a secondary position in their statements and campaigns. Interventionists gave relatively more emphasis to the importance of aiding Britain than to the necessity for building America's own national forces. The noninterventionists were more interested in preventing American intervention in the war than in urging the development of American armed forces. The general approval of provision for American national defense was one factor in putting the question in a secondary role, but it was also the product of the basic premises in the respective briefs of the contestants in the battle of the committees.

The interventionists were convinced that Great Britain was America's first line of defense. They believed aid to Britain would give the United States time to prepare its own forces. They also held that aid sufficient to enable England to defeat Germany would make it less necessary for the United States to maintain a large military force of her own. They contended that Hitler would not be satisfied until he controlled the whole world—including the Western Hemisphere. Consequently, if Britain fell America would be the next to feel the power of Hitler's might. Interventionists contended that destruction or capture of the British fleet by Germany would make the combined Axis fleets much larger than the American Navy. Even if Hitler never attacked America, they feared the United States would have to maintain huge defense forces to guard against the possibility. These forces would place an excessive burden upon the American economy and democratic form of government.[28]

The leaders of the America First Committee denied that Great Britain was America's first line of defense. Most of them did not believe Britain would be crushed. However, even if Hitler were completely victorious over England, they did not believe he would attempt an invasion of the Western Hemisphere. They did not base this stand upon any faith in Hitler's promises. They believed the difficulty of the task would deter even the fanatic Hitler from attempting it. General Wood said the German people would be tired of fighting after the British defeat and would desire butter instead of guns. Committee leaders believed it would take Hitler many years to consolidate his gains in Europe and England—if he were ever able to do so. He would also have to rebuild his military forces after the destructive campaign against England before any attack on America could be launched. They did not believe Hitler could seize the British fleet intact even if England fell. If Germany gained control of the remains of a defeated British fleet, Committee leaders believed most of it would first have been sunk or damaged.[29]

In the unlikely event that Hitler was able to defeat Great Britain, capture the British Navy intact, consolidate his conquests, induce the German people to support an attack on the Western Hemisphere, and prepare his armed forces for this attack, the America First leaders were convinced he would not be successful. The America First Principles declared: "The United States must build an impregnable defense for America. With such a defense no foreign power, or group of powers, can successfully attack us." [30] America First leaders accused the interventionists of being defeatists who lacked faith in America's ability to defend itself in the Western Hemisphere. They ridiculed the interventionists for wanting to hide behind Britain's skirts. Interventionists cited Hitler's conquests of Poland, Denmark, Norway, Netherlands, Luxemburg, Belgium, and France to illustrate the ruthless effectiveness of the Nazi *Blitzkrieg*. America First leaders, however, emphasized that most of

95

these were tiny, powerless countries on the German borders. The total population of all these countries was less than that of the United States. Even France was small in population, area, and industrial capacity compared with the United States. And France, too, was right under the mouths of the German guns. Committee leaders pointed to Hitler's inability to invade Britain across the twenty-mile English Channel. They insisted it would be infinitely more difficult for him to invade the United States across the three thousand miles of Atlantic Ocean.[31] Lindbergh contended that the airplane improved America's defensive position. He said any enemy fleet could be attacked by air long before it could reach American shores.[32] America First leaders conceded that isolated planes might be able to drop bombs in the United States but they denied that Germany had planes at that time capable of conducting round-trip mass bombing raids from Europe. They also denied that America could be defeated by air attacks alone, however concentrated.[33] Lindbergh realized that future scientific developments in atomic and rocket energy might alter America's defensive position. He insisted, however, that "no generation can entirely safeguard the future for those that follow. They must meet their own problems as those problems arise." [34]

The interventionists said the relatively short distance from Dakar in Africa to Brazil was a convenient route for a German invasion. President Roosevelt dramatically stated that it was only five hours by air from Dakar to Brazil. General Wood, however, retorted that "it is only a few minutes from a dozen airfields in occupied France to London, and the Nazis have not yet crossed the Channel." [35] Flynn pointed out that if Hitler successfully landed troops in Brazil he still would be further away from the United States than he was in Germany. Thousands of miles of inhospitable jungle and mountains would lie between him and the United States.[36]

If Hitler attempted to invade the Western Hemisphere he would have to supply his army with the huge masses of material essential to modern warfare. In the opinion of Committee leaders he would not have sufficient shipping facilities to transport successfully these materials in the face of American attacks.[37]

The America First Committee believed no combination of foreign powers could successfully attack a prepared America. Committee leaders repeatedly urged provision for the military defense of America. But what area did they believe the United States should defend? A few America First leaders believed the United States should only provide for the defense of North America, the Caribbean, and northern South America.[38] Even General Wood was not certain the United States could successfully defend South America below the equator.[39] Nevertheless, most America First spokesmen believed the United States should fight if any part of North or South America were attacked.[40] Lindbergh urged co-operation with other American nations in planning hemispheric defense.[41] General Wood, at that time a director of the United Fruit Company, expressed a view reminiscent of Theodore Roosevelt:

97

And while I think we should try in every way to maintain the friendship of our neighbors to the South, I think we should also make it clearly understood that no government in Mexico, Central America and the Caribbean South American countries will be tolerated unless it is friendly to the United States and that, if necessary, we are prepared to use force to attain that object.[42]

America First leaders believed the United States should establish bases to enhance the effectiveness of its defenses. The Committee challenged the wisdom of transferring fifty destroyers, but the bases secured in the destroyer deal of 1940 were deemed desirable in America's defense program.[43] Lindbergh criticized the government's failure to construct adequate bases in the Pacific. He said the United States should either have fortified the Philippines or evacuated them.[44] President Roosevelt's decision to occupy Greenland in April, 1941, did not meet with opposition from the America First Committee. Lindbergh said the United States should fight if Greenland were invaded.[45] However, the decision to occupy Iceland, announced in July, 1941, elicited a protest from America First. An America First pamphlet insisted that Iceland was not essential to hemispheric defense; that it was actually closer to Europe. It expressed the fear that the Administration would next want bases in Ireland, Norway, or Scotland to protect Iceland.[46] In November, 1941, a meeting of America First chapter leaders in Washington, D.C., adopted a resolution calling upon President Roosevelt to withdraw American troops from Iceland.[47] General Wood did not believe bases in the Azores, the Cape Verde Islands, or the Canaries were necessary for defense of the Western Hemisphere.[48]

What defense measures did America First leaders endorse or oppose? The Committee did not outline specific recommendations for American armed forces. Those leaders who held distinct views, however, generally favored a relatively small (approximately 500,000 men), professional, highly mechanized and mobile army re-enforced by a modern air force. They believed such a force could be moved quickly to any spot to repel invaders.[49] Colonel Lindbergh endorsed a two-ocean navy.[50] Committee leaders believed an effective force could have been constructed more rapidly and efficiently than it was.[51]

The America First Committee opposed aid to Britain which would interfere with the building of American defenses.[52] It criticized the transfer of military goods from the American armed forces to Great Britain. The destroyer deal and the transfer of Flying Fortresses were attacked on this basis.[53]

Some America First leaders believed an adequate defense force could be built at less cost than had been expended by the United States.[54] A national headquarters bulletin suggested the slogan: "National Defense at any Expense but Keep Our Boys at Home." [55] A leader of the chapter at Columbus, Ohio, however, criticized the slogan as approving "warmongering activities and ruinous expenditures made in the name of 'defense'." [56] The New York chapter refused to use the slogan because of the "great financial waste in much that is being done in the name of national defense." [57]

Senator Wheeler opposed the Selective Service Bill in 1940, but Colonel Lindbergh gave his approval.[58] The America First Committee itself was not formed until just before the measure was passed and consequently did not take a position on the question.[59]

In July and August, 1941, two specific issues concerning selective service were raised. The original act in 1940 had prohibited the use of selectees outside of the Western Hemisphere. It also provided that selectees should serve a twelve-month period. In the summer of 1941 the Administration urged revision of the law to enable the President to use selectees and National Guardsmen outside of the Western Hemisphere. The Administration also desired Congressional authorization to retain selectees longer than one year.

The America First Committee flatly opposed authorizing the President to send selectees and National Guardsmen outside of the Western Hemisphere. General Wood issued a statement early in July, 1941, in which he labeled the proposal, "the Administration's bald request for a new A.E.F." He held that the proposal would have the effect of giving the President power "to wage undeclared war in whatever part of the world he may choose." He called it a "fraud upon America's one million draftees" since they entered the service with the understanding that they would not serve overseas.[60] An America First Research Bureau bulletin denied that the authority was necessary for defense purposes. It contended that the measure was "designed to give the President power to put the country into war." [61] The proposal was finally withdrawn after Congressional leaders assured the President that it could not be passed.[62] The America First Committee opposed a Congressional declaration of a national emergency. It feared such a declaration, among other things, would enable the President to use selectees outside the Western Hemisphere.[63]

At General Wood's insistence, the America First Committee did not take an official stand on draft extension. It was reasoned that this was a military matter not directly concerned with the problem of American intervention in the European war. Committee leaders feared opposition to draft extension would make the organization more vulnerable to the accusation that it opposed building American defenses.[64]

Despite the official "neutrality" of the America First Committee, the efforts of its followers were predominantly directed against draft extension. The Committee's friends in Congress fought against the measure.[65] General Thomas S. Hammond testified against the proposal before the Senate Military Affairs Committee. Though he testified as an individual rather than as a representative of America First, Committee headquarters assisted in making arrangements for him to appear.[66] The America First Research Bureau released bulletins attacking draft extension. The Bureau denied General George C. Marshall's contention that failure to pass the measure would leave only a "skeleton" army. It said no selectees would be released until November, 1941, and less than twenty thousand would be mustered

101

out by the end of 1941. These in turn would be replaced by new selectees. The Bureau concluded that "there seems no justification for the proposed Resolutions, unless military ventures into foreign lands are planned." [67] Both General Hammond and the Research Bureau said the measure would break faith with selectees who went in expecting to serve only one year. They urged providing inducements to encourage enlistments.[68] Individual members of America First were encouraged to write to their Congressmen and Senators expressing their personal views on the proposal.[69] Stuart sent telegrams to all chapter chairmen informing them that the vote in the House of Representatives was expected to be very close.[70] America First chapters in Chicago, Boston, Pittsburgh, and Berkeley, among others, actively worked to defeat draft extension.[71] The powerful New York chapter under John T. Flynn threw its whole weight against draft extension.[72]

The draft extension measure was passed in the House of Representatives by a margin of only one vote. It is conceivable that all-out America First opposition might have defeated the measure. Nevertheless, this vote was a forceful demonstration of noninterventionist strength. Stuart wrote:

The vote on draft extension in the House was the most encouraging thing that has happened in many a moon. It turned out perfectly. If the bill had been defeated by one vote, the interventionist press throughout the country would have gone wild condemning Congress for sabotaging national defense. It would have served as an excuse for the President for more executive action toward war.

102

As it turned out, the vote was a sharp rebuff to the Administration and a warning that Congress will not stand for war. The confidence and morale on the part of members of Congress who share our point of view is infinitely higher than it has been in the past nine months.[73]

The America First Committee was officially "neutral," but the energy of numerous leaders and followers was directed against draft extension. No Committee leaders positively worked in support of the measure. The Committee did not marshal its forces against the measure as it did against Lend-Lease and repeal of the Neutrality Act. But in practice it was far from "neutral." It is significant that an America First headquarters bulletin cited the closeness of the vote on draft extension as evidence of the Committee's effectiveness.[74] During its full history America First endorsed the building of adequate military defenses. But the Committee at no time made any concerted drive for the accomplishment of that end.

7 The Nazi Transmission Belt?

INTERVENTIONISTS insisted that consciously or un-consciously the America First Committee served as a rally-ing point for fascists and a channel for Nazi propaganda. During the first four months of its history the Committee was less frequently harassed by such accusations than it was during 1941. The Committee's campaign in 1940 was conducted in a dignified manner by means of correspond-ence, newspaper advertisements, and radio broadcasts. The elections in November, 1940, helped divert potential critics away from America First. Some newspaper edito-rials in 1940 discouraged name-calling and recriminations on both sides in the foreign policy debate.[1] General Robert E. Wood and William Allen White set commendable stand-ards in their early statements and correspondence.[2] But 1940 proved to be merely a lull before the storm. During 1941 recriminations and name-calling increasingly became the fashion in the foreign policy debate.

America First leaders were by no means devoid of re-sponsibility for the ultimate character of the debate. Late in 1940 General Thomas S. Hammond, Clay Judson, and other Committee spokesmen accused the White Committee of leading America toward war.[3] The assault by America First spokesmen was one factor which led William Allen White to emphasize publicly his opposition to convoys, repeal of the Johnson and Neutrality Acts, and entry into the war. The reaction to his statement led White to resign as chairman of the Committee to Defend America by Aiding the Allies early in 1941.[4]

Interventionists, however, had a decided advantage in a "mud-throwing" contest. American sympathies for the British made Anglophiles more respectable than Anglophobes. America First had the disadvantage of having Nazis, Communists, and anti-Semites venting similar foreign policy views. The battle against Lend-Lease early in 1941 established the America First Committee as the leading noninterventionist organization. This had a dual effect upon the Committee. It encouraged most noninterventionists, including "undesirables" to look to America First as the most effective vehicle through which to oppose intervention. It also led interventionists to concentrate their attacks upon the Committee. These attacks reached such an intensity during the last third of 1941 that the America First Committee's effectiveness was seriously undermined. These attacks, even when shielded by a front organization, largely emanated from interventionist sources. They spared no one, however flawless his reputation may have been. Any person who played a prominent role in the Committee's battle against intervention made his character, his belief in democracy, and his qualifications to speak on foreign policy matters subject to suspect by interventionists.

Criticism of America First came from many sources. Individuals wrote critical letters to the Committee. Communists attacked America First both before and after the Germans invaded the Soviet Union. Innumerable speakers and writers found occasion to attack the organization. The Committee to Defend America by Aiding the Allies and the Fight for Freedom Committee repeatedly assailed America First. Administration leaders added their voices to the chorus. Some of the most outspoken, persistent, and disturbing attacks emanated from Friends of Democracy, Inc. An American Legion Americanism Committee prepared a convincing indictment of America First in California. Several authors wrote books after American entry into World War II which forcefully stated the case against America First.

One defender of democracy wrote to tell Committee leaders that they were "a bunch of traitors and should be in a Concentration Camp." [5] Some letters recommended that America First members "should be run out of the Country" [6] or "should take the first ship for Berlin." [7] One gentleman asserted that "there are no patriotic Americans in your organization; it is composed of people who want to see Hitler win this war and make slaves out of Americans, the same as other countries." [8] The following paragraph suggests the extremes to which some letters to Committee headquarters went:

You Maggots from the Slums of Genoa & Berlin, you half Baked *imitation of Americans,* Go wiggle back into the manure of your old world ideas.

106

Hang your Swatsika Banner around your Neck, and butt your brainless heads against the Bulwork of American ideals which you pretend to support.[9]

The Communists in the United States were always among the Committee's assailants. Before Germany invaded the Soviet Union the Communists accused America First leaders of being imperialists.[10] After June 22, 1941, when Communists advocated American entry into the war, Communist leader William Z. Foster declared that "the 5th column is rapidly developing under the America First Committee and *The Chicago Tribune* to a point where it will menace the American republic." He labeled General Wood and Colonel Lindbergh "conscious Fascists who want to come to an agreement with Hitler at any cost, abolish the communist party and labor unions." [11]

Many columnists and editorial writers leveled their guns on the America First Committee. Dorothy Thompson said the Committee stood for "a kind of Vichy Fascism." [12] Walter Winchell said it should be called the "America Last Outfit." He insisted that the audience at an America First rally in New York addressed by Lindbergh consisted "mainly of members of the German-American Bund and various other groups which sympathize with or admire Hitler and Mussolini." [13] *Time* and *Life* magazines commented on the similarity between the salute to the flag, as given by Wheeler and Lindbergh, and the fascist salute.[14] The novelist Kathleen Norris was less vulnerable to political attacks than most national committee members but when she spoke at an America First rally in New York, a writer in the interventionist *PM* described her as follows: "Mrs. Kathleen Norris took it all in her stride, which was ample. Her bearing was what passes for motherliness. Her exploitation of the emotion of grief for the dead, in her speech, is a trick the Nazis perform superbly too." [15]

Early in 1941 Ernest W. Gibson, Jr., chairman of the Committee to Defend America by Aiding the Allies, said Lord Haw Haw and Goebbels endorsed America First.[16] An article by the Committee to Defend America by Aiding the Allies declared:

We believe the leaders of the America First Committee when they say that they want no financial support from subversive elements. We believe that the America First leaders would prefer that persons of un-American ideals stayed away from America First rallies. But that is not the point.

The point is that un-American organizations have made appeals for contributions of money to America First. Un-American elements crowd America First rallies. They applaud America First speakers. They boo the President of the United States. They do not boo Hitler or Mussolini or Stalin. . . . Some of them belong to the Nazi Bund, which is pro-Hitler. . . . What Hitler, Mussolini, Stalin and their friends in this country applaud cannot be good for America.[17]

Bishop Henry W. Hobson, chairman of the Fight for Freedom Committee advanced the opinion that America First had become the first fascist party in the history of the United States.[18]

Secretary of the Interior Harold L. Ickes said the America First Committee should be renamed "the America Next" Committee. Ickes called General Wood and Colonel Lindbergh Nazi fellow travelers.[19] President Roosevelt may also be listed among the Committee's assailants. In his Fireside Chat on December 29, 1940, without naming America First, he attacked the "appeasers" who believed the United States should support a negotiated peace.[20] During the Lend-Lease debate a virtual feud developed between the President and Senator Wheeler.[21] At a press conference in April, 1941, President Roosevelt compared Lindbergh to Clement L. Vallandigham, a leading Copperhead during the Civil War.[22]

Friends of Democracy, Inc., was described as "a non-partisan, non-sectarian, non-profit, anti-totalitarian propaganda agency." It was formed by Leon M. Birkhead, a Unitarian minister, in Kansas City, Missouri, in 1937. The branch formed in New York City in 1939 became its main office. Birkhead believed fascism was a greater threat to America than Communism. He attacked both extreme Rightists and Leftists, but directed nine-tenths of his attacks on Rightists. Friends of Democracy professed to take no foreign policy position, but Birkhead himself was an interventionist [23] and spoke at meetings of the Fight for Freedom Committee.[24] Rex Stout, who became chairman of Friends of Democracy, was a sponsor of Fight for Freedom.[25]

Birkhead accused America First of having the support "of all the Communists and Fascists" in November, 1940, before the Committee had even begun to organize chapters or hold major rallies.[26] After the Lend-Lease debate, Friends of Democracy, Inc., issued a pamphlet entitled, *The America First Committee—The Nazi Transmission Belt.* This pamphlet maintained:

109

The America First Committee . . . is a Nazi front! It is a transmission belt by means of which the apostles of Nazism are spreading their antidemocratic ideas into millions of American homes!

This is not to say that the America First Committee is a Nazi organization. On the contrary, the great majority of its officers and members are patriotic Americans who sincerely believe that this nation should pursue a policy of isolationism and appeasement.

But that is exactly what Adolf Hitler and his disciples in the United States believe, and they are using—or misusing— the America First Committee to spread those ideas.

We do not question the integrity of the leadership and membership of the America First Committee nor the sincerity of its program. But we do seriously question the wisdom of the policymakers and the soundness of a policy which has the unqualified approval of Adolf Hitler, Benito Mussolini and their agents in the United States.

The pamphlet showed the similarity between statements of Senators Wheeler and Nye and those of Hitler. It named un-American organizations whose members attended an America First rally in New York City. The pamphlet quoted a broadcast from Berlin which "placed the official Nazi seal of approval upon the America First Committee." The pamphlet concluded that America First "should reorganize on a basis which does not lend itself to misuse as a Nazi transmission belt." [27] It made no recommendations as to how this could be accomplished without changing the Committee's foreign policy views or restricting its activities. In issuing the pamphlet Birkhead said: "The America First Committee is run by very naive, simpleminded people who don't understand that Hitler is the

110

cleverest propagandist who ever came down the pike. . . . I don't know a person in the AFC who is capable of coming up against Nazi propaganda effectively." [28] Friends of Democracy also issued a brochure later in 1941 designed to show that Lindbergh had been following the Nazi propaganda line.[29]

In the fall of 1941 a district Americanism Committee of the American Legion in California released a pamphlet entitled, *Subversive Activities in the America First Committee in California.*[30] The chairman of this Americanism Committee, Ben Beery, was active in the Committee to Defend America by Aiding the Allies.[31] This report described the activities of nearly a score of persons who were said to be active leaders of subversive activities in California. It maintained that all of these persons were also active in the America First Committee in California. This report declared:

There is every indication that they have joined the America First movement for the express purpose of presenting their subversive propaganda to those sincere isolationists who have been attracted to meetings of America First.

The result of this taking over of America First meetings by the subversivists has been a gradual but complete switching of the organization's policy from one that merely encourages the theory of defense through isolation, to a policy of sponsoring the indiscriminate spread of hatred, confusion, dissension, defeatism, and various other elements of the propaganda line set down by the Nazi government for its agents in the United States.

The American Legion National Convention at Omaha in 1943 passed a resolution which referred to America First

111

as "disseminating propaganda inimical to the United States." [32]

After Pearl Harbor several writers published books and articles attacking America First. A book by Michael Sayers and Albert E. Kahn maintained that regardless of the sincerity and good intentions of America First national leaders, Axis agents made use of the Committee. Thus the leaders "became the dupes of the enemies of the United States." [33] The most widely publicized book attacking America First was *Under Cover* by John Roy Carlson. Carlson, whose real name was Avedis Derounian, worked for three years as an "undercover man in the Nazi-fascist underworld." He became a chief investigator for Friends of Democracy, Inc., in 1940.[34] He concluded that America First was the "spearhead of an American fascist movement" and the "voice of American fascism." [35] Henry Hoke wrote two small books which took a similar position.[36] Friends of Democracy supplied information for the preparation of each of these books.

In addition to verbal attacks, the America First Committee and its leaders were the victims of discrimination and pressure. In Miami, Florida; Atlanta, Georgia; Oklahoma City; Portland, Oregon; and Pittsburgh and Philadelphia, Pennsylvania; the Committee found it difficult or impossible to secure public buildings or parks in which to hold mass meetings.[37] The city council of Charlotte, North Carolina, expressed its feelings by changing the name of Lindbergh Drive to Avon Avenue.[38] Economic pressure was brought to bear on some Committee supporters. A few lost jobs or found it difficult to secure new ones because of their noninterventionist activities.[39]

WHAT WAS the response in the America First Committee to these attacks? Committee leaders expected to be called "hard names." [40] But they did not expect the barrage of criticism which actually ensued.[41] The extremely critical letters received by national headquarters were stamped, "Crank-Ignore." In replying to many other critical letters Stuart wrote: "We regret very much that you are not in accord with our policies but feel that although our approach is different our ultimate aim is the same, namely, the preservation of American Democracy." [42] Unsuccessful efforts were made to shackle Walter Winchell and H. V. Kaltenborn by approaching their radio sponsors.[43] In February, 1941, Philip La Follette made a radio broadcast to answer an attack on General Wood by the columnist Dorothy Thompson. In his address he also compared Abraham Lincoln's "with malice toward none" statement with two recent addresses by President Roosevelt. La Follette said:

In his utterances [the] President ordered the "go" sign for an open campaign to silence opposition to his dangerous foreign policy. He urged a campaign of "shaming" opposition to silence, and even bluntly made the unveiled threat of force to suppress those who did not agree. Both of the President's speeches were peppered with words like "slacker", "troublemaker", "appeaser", and the like. . . . Instead of smearing or wrecking, let us encourage and build character, in ourselves and others. Argue—

113

hit as hard as you please *on the issues,* but refuse to villify individuals simply because they do not agree. That kind of people will make our democracy stronger. The other kind might destroy it.[44]

The Friends of Democracy pamphlet created a storm among America First leaders. John T. Flynn labeled the charges "the most shocking" of "all the outrageous smears" against America First.[45] Clay Judson in a letter to General Wood voiced the feelings of most Committee leaders:

Great Britain wants us in this war. Germany, of course, wants us to stay out. Our Committee believes that its policy should not be affected one way or the other by what other nations want, but that American interests demand that we stay out. If on that one point our objective happens to be the same as the German objective, it may be unfortunate, but it cannot logically be claimed to indicate any pro-Nazi tendencies. I presume that the writers of the ... pamphlet would have to call Christ a Nazi if Hitler happened to quote the Bible.[46]

Sterling Morton observed that he had "heard no one argue that the transcontinental railroads should suspend freight operations merely because undesirable characters occasionally 'ride the rods' of their trains!" [47] Flynn announced that nine of the eleven sponsors of Friends of Democracy who responded to America First queries did not approve attacks on the Committee and its leaders. These sponsors had not seen the brochure before it was released. Birkhead said this poll "missed the point" since the pamphlet did not accuse America First leaders of being pro-Nazi. Its thesis was that the Committee was being "used and exploited" by pro-fascists.[48] Anton J. Carlson was a member

114

of the sponsoring committee of both Friends of Democracy and America First. He resigned from Friends of Democracy in a scorching letter to Birkhead.[49]

Some America First leaders individually struck back at Friends of Democracy. Some believed America First national headquarters should publicly answer Birkhead's charges. Though there were differences of opinion, the executive committee decided a reply would call attention to the attack and play into Birkhead's hands.[50] General Wood again raised the question when Birkhead made another of his periodic charges in April, 1941. Nearly all of the Committee leaders consulted opposed having America First make a public reply.[51] Individual leaders of the Committee occasionally made public answers to specific charges. But during its full history the America First national headquarters gave major critics the silent treatment. This applied to attacks by Friends of Democracy, Inc., and the Fight for Freedom Committee.[52]

The constant barrage of criticism to which America First was subjected stimulated its speakers increasingly to berate its assailants. The term "warmonger" was used repeatedly in addresses by many America First speakers. They accused interventionists of tricking and deceiving the American people while dragging them unwillingly into an unnecessary war. Many speakers at America First meetings spent more time attacking the interventionists than in positively stating the noninterventionist point of view. The result was often a display of "mud-slinging" equal to that indulged in by the opponents of America First.[53]

115

After June 22, 1941, the America First Committee used the interventionist technique to attack the interventionists for Communist support. America First reported that Communists attended meetings of the Committee to Defend America by Aiding the Allies and the Fight for Freedom Committee. It said the audiences cheered mention of Stalin and the Soviet Union. According to America First, the Communist publications, *New Masses* and *Daily Worker,* were distributed at meetings of the interventionist organizations.[54]

The attacks on the America First Committee led some of its active supporters to drop out of the campaign. It made it relatively more difficult to induce additional reputable persons to aid the Committee's battle against intervention.

From its inception, national leaders of America First tried to reduce to a minimum the Committee's vulnerability to criticism. The barrage of attacks on America First caused its leaders to intensify these efforts. Some like Edwin S. Webster, Jr., secretary of the New York chapter and later a national committee member, believed America First should not be too particular concerning the groups with which it co-operated.[55] Stuart, Chester Bowles, Sidney Hertzberg, John T. Flynn, General Wood, and most other Committee leaders, however, disagreed with Webster. They believed America First should be kept independent of any organizations or individuals likely to bring discredit on the Committee or reduce its effectiveness.[56] The conduct of Committee affairs in practice fell short of the ideal

116

set up in America First policies. Some local chapters were more lax in accepting members and co-operating with undesirable groups than the national headquarters desired. Even the national leadership compromised concerning the followers of Father Charles E. Coughlin. But most America First leaders (both local and national) tried to keep the Committee's skirts clear of subversive groups and individuals.

Stuart and Wood invited respected persons to serve on the executive and national committees. They sought reputable persons to lead local chapters—especially in major urban centers.[57] Fascists, Nazis, and Communists were declared ineligible for membership.[58] Avery Brundage was dropped from the national committee in October, 1940, because he had been accused of having pro-Nazi sympathies.[59] The executive committee agreed to accept no contribution of more than one hundred dollars until an investigation of the source had been made.[60] A four thousand dollar contribution from an anonymous donor was not accepted until assurances were obtained from the transmitting firm that the contributor was an American citizen without pro-fascist or pro-Communist views.[61] Some smaller contributions accompanied by letters expressing pro-Nazi or extreme anti-Roosevelt or anti-Semitic views were refused.[62]

In January, 1941, General Hammond wrote to the Federal Bureau of Investigation in Chicago and to Congressman Martin Dies inviting them to check the Committee's membership lists. It was hoped in this manner to prevent any subversive elements from working into the America First Committee.[63] Robert L. Bliss, America First director of organization, repeated this invitation to the Federal Bureau of Investigation in March, 1941, but the Chicago agent of the Bureau declined to check the Committee's files.[64] In June, 1941, however, an agent of the Federal Bureau of Investigation did check the files of the national headquarters and the Chicago chapter. He checked against a list of persons connected with the German-American National Alliance, but according to General Hammond they apparently found none of them in the America First contributor files.[65] Later in 1941 General Wood said America First would welcome an investigation by the House Committee on Un-American Activities.[66] When the Dies Committee finally began an investigation of America First in November, 1941, General Wood gave their representatives full access to America First files without any formal subpoena.[67]

The Flanders Hall Publishing Company, registered with the State Department as a German agent, published a book by Congressman Stephen A. Day of Illinois as a "Flanders Hall–America First Book." Both General Wood and Flynn wrote to the publisher, S. H. Hauck, protesting the use of the phrase, "America First." Hauck denied any intention of implying that the book was sponsored by the America First Committee and agreed not to use the phrase again on any publications.[68]

America First also tried to keep pro-fascists, pro-Nazis, and extreme Rightists out of the local chapters.

118

Stuart refused to authorize the reactionary Merwin K. Hart to organize the New York chapter.[69] John T. Flynn, chairman in New York, energetically fought to keep pro-fascists out of the chapter. On May 1, 1941, the German-American Bund publication, *Free American and Deutscher und Weckruf Beobachter,* urged its readers to join the America First Committee. The next day Flynn wrote to the editor that America First not only did not solicit their support but that Bundists were not eligible for membership. Flynn's letter was published, at his request, in a later issue of the *Free American.*[70] At an America First rally later in May, 1941, Flynn denounced Joseph McWilliams and his followers in the fascist American Destiny Party who were at the rally. Flynn announced that fascists, Bundists, and Communists were not wanted as members.[71] John Roy Carlson, who had been a volunteer worker in the New York chapter of America First, was asked to stay away from the Committee because he was known to be a follower of McWilliams.[72] Many other efforts were made to prevent questionable persons from working through the chapter or its sub-chapters.[73]

On the recommendation of representatives of B'nai B'rith, a Jewish fraternal organization, America First ousted leaders of several units in San Francisco who were members of William Dudley Pelley's fascist-like Silver Shirts.[74] Dellmore Lessard, chairman of America First in Portland, Oregon, accepted a twenty-dollar contribution from the German-American War Veterans Association. This transaction was publicized and denounced by the American

Legion and was brought to the attention of General Wood by representatives of B'nai B'rith. Consequently, America First national headquarters took action which led to the refund of the contribution and to the ultimate resignation of Lessard.[75] Frederic A. Chase, Executive Secretary of America First in Southern California, checked on all chapter officers of the area in the files of the Los Angeles Police Department.[76] Leaders of many other America First chapters took positive steps to prevent pro-Nazis and other undesirables from working through their units.[77]

NEVERTHELESS, the question raised by the interventionists remains to be answered. Was the America First Committee, despite the efforts of its leaders, a "Nazi transmission belt"?

There is much evidence to buttress the thesis of the interventionists. It was obviously in Germany's interest to prevent American entry into the war on the side of Britain. All of her propaganda agents and agencies in the United States opposed American entry into the war. There were striking similarities between the foreign policy views of the America First Committee and Axis propaganda in the United States. For example, *Facts in Review,* the leading German propaganda publication in the United States, quoted Marshal Goering as saying that there were no planes in Germany which, when loaded with bombs, could fly to America and return. Goering continued:

America simply cannot be invaded by air or sea. That is particularly true if her armaments and national defense are appropriate to or commensurate with the country's size, popula-

120

tion, resources and industrial production, not to mention the spirit of the people. . . .

If American defenses are what they should be, particularly if America's air force is properly developed, built up, organized and strategically based, America can defy any group of powers. No one would be so idiotic as to attempt an invasion.[78]

These words might easily have been uttered by virtually any one of the leading America First spokesmen.

German propaganda commended the America First Committee. A Nazi short wave broadcast in January, 1941, called America First "truly American and truly patriotic." [79] Hitler, himself, in one speech cited the testimony of General Wood to prove Britain's responsibility for "the present developments." [80]

One of the more active speakers for the America First Committee in the closing months of the campaign was Laura Ingalls. She was convicted in 1942 for failure to register as a German agent. Baron von Gienanth, Gestapo chief in the United States, had told Miss Ingalls: "The best thing you can do for our cause is to continue to promote the America First Committee." [81] Frank B. Burch, convicted on the same charge, was a sponsor of the Akron, Ohio, chapter of America First.[82] Ralph Townsend, convicted after Pearl Harbor for failure to register as a Japanese agent, spoke at at least two local meetings of America First on the West Coast.[83]

The German-American National Alliance, a Bund-like organization in Chicago, as early as September, 1940, urged its followers to assist America First.[84] It distributed a leaflet urging that contributions be sent to the America First

Committee.[85] Flynn's letter repudiating the support of the German-American Bund was printed in the *Free American* but at the same time the editor of the publication evidenced sympathy for the Committee.[86] Many other unsavory organizations including Pelley's Silver Shirts and the Ku Klux Klan endorsed America First.[87] There were many reports which indicate that pro-Nazis attended America First rallies.[88] Undoubtedly many of them made contributions at these rallies or by mail. Lawrence Dennis, an intellectual leader of American fascism, contributed ten dollars to America First national headquarters and the contribution was accepted.[89] He had even closer relations with some important workers in the New York chapter.[90] America First also received support from German-Americans who were not pro-Nazi.[91] Several units of the Steuben Society of America made contributions to America First, most of which were accepted.[92]

The examination of the America First files by representatives of the Dies Committee did not culminate in any published report. However, a Federal District grand jury in Washington, D.C., in September, 1941, began hearings in an investigation of foreign propaganda in the United States. These hearings revealed that George Hill, secretary of Congressman Hamilton Fish, had "served as handyman of a propaganda ring" managed by the German agent, George Sylvester Viereck. Through his contacts with Hill, Viereck had speeches by noninterventionist Congressmen and other materials inserted into the *Congressional Record*. Reprints of these items were then purchased by Prescott

Dennett and distributed through his Islands for War Debts
and Make Europe Pay Committees. These organizations
were backed and financed by Viereck who was on the payroll of the German government. The materials were sent
out in franked envelopes or were bundled and sent to various parts of the country where they were then mailed under
the Congressional frank. Both Hill and Viereck were subsequently convicted as a consequence of their roles in this
clandestine arrangement.[93]

America First had utilized the services of George Hill
in mailing the cards for the "war-peace" polls in the districts of four Congressmen.[94] Further, several bags of un-
used franked envelopes were taken from Dennett's office
and deposited at the headquarters of the Washington
America First chapter in September, 1941. This material
was immediately subpoenaed and turned over for use in
the grand jury hearings.[95]

On July 21, 1942, the Washington grand jury indicted
twenty-eight persons for plotting "to interfere with, impair
and influence the loyalty, morale and discipline" of the
armed forces. This indictment also listed various publications and organizations which had been used by those
indicted to spread their propaganda. The America First
Committee was listed as one of these organizations.[96]

The efforts of Nazis and pro-fascists to work through
the America First Committee should not be minimized.
Neither, however, should they be magnified out of their
proper proportions. The interventionists, by emphasizing
the most unsavory of the Committee's supporters, by exag-

gerating the importance of pro-fascist individuals to the organization, and by making positively false accusations, created a badly distorted picture of America First. This distortion has been widely accepted as an accurate picture of the Committee.

Laura Ingalls began speaking at meetings sponsored by America First chapters at least as early as June, 1941.[97] She first spoke under the auspices of America First national headquarters in November, 1941. Committee headquarters had heard that she tended to be extreme in her statements and were worried enough to secure reports on her performances from chapter officers. These reports were almost uniformly enthusiastic. Laura Ingalls spoke many times under national auspices during November and the first week in December, 1941.[98] Her part in the Committee's campaign is a serious blot on its record. But she worked through America First less than half of its history. She addressed none of the largest America First rallies. For every meeting addressed by this German agent during the Committee's history, patriotic America First speakers addressed dozens.

Frank B. Burch was not an officer in the Akron chapter and he was not one of the signers of the chapter application. He made no financial contribution to America First national headquarters. As a member of the chapter's sponsoring committee he was only one among forty-seven.[99]

Sayers and Kahn described Ralph Townsend as "a leading speaker for the America First Committee." [100] However, he never spoke under the auspices of the national

124

headquarters. The Committee files contain evidence of only two meetings sponsored by local chapters in California which he addressed.[101] Committee leaders appear to have had no knowledge of the foreign connections of Ingalls, Townsend and Burch.[102]

L. M. Birkhead claimed that Edward James Smythe, pro-fascist leader of the Protestant War Veterans, spoke at an America First rally in Philadelphia in 1940.[103] The newly formed speakers' bureau of America First national headquarters did make arrangements for him to speak in Philadelphia. But the meeting was canceled at the last minute. When Stuart learned of Smythe's views he was removed from the Committee's speakers list. At no time did he address an America First meeting under the auspices of national headquarters.[104]

There were pro-fascists who attended America First rallies. But the reporting of the character of America First audiences varied according to the prejudices of the observer. This can be illustrated by the accounts of an America First rally in New York on May 23, 1941. Lindbergh was the principal speaker, and John T. Flynn presided over the meeting. John Roy Carlson described Flynn's denunciation of Joseph McWilliams at the rally but declared that *"the Coughlinite mob burst into applause for Joe!!!"* According to Carlson it took Flynn several minutes to quiet the applause. He said there was a "weak, unconvincing round of boos" against McWilliams.[105] However, a writer in the interventionist *PM* reported: "The bulk of the Garden throng seemed sympathetic to Flynn's attack on Mc-

Williams. There was only a smattering of applause for the Yorkville Fuehrer." This writer, however, said that many Coughlinites attended the rally.[106] Writing concerning undesirables at this same meeting, Edwin S. Webster, Jr., secretary of the New York chapter, asserted: "Although certain of the people mentioned were probably at our rally they were in the very small minority. No press tickets or tickets of any sort are given to the people in question. It has been remarked frequently by people coming to our rallies that they have seldom seen such a fine looking crowd of Americans." [107] The exact truth cannot be determined with certainty. But the most critical reports were not necessarily the most accurate.

Henry Hoke wrote: "It could be proved . . . that a large part of the funds for supporting the America First movement came from German sources or from Americans who were favorable to the Nazi cause." [108] Despite its efforts, the Committee and some of its chapters did receive contributions from individuals holding pro-Nazi and pro-German views.[109] But there is no evidence in the America First files to indicate that the Committee would have found it necessary to reduce significantly the scope of its activities even if it had been completely successful in barring *all* funds from pro-fascist individuals.[110] Most of the major published attacks on the America First Committee by interventionists contained similar errors or distortions.

The America First Committee availed itself of the opportunity to use the franks of friendly Congressmen and Senators to mail reprints from the *Record*. Among others,

Senator Wheeler, Congressman James C. Oliver, and Congressman Stephen A. Day loaned their franks to America First. Congressmen were legally permitted to send their own speeches and other excerpts from the *Congressional Record* postage free. It was also legal for bulk packages of franked articles to be sent by a Congressman to "one addressee" who could then address and remail them. These practices had been almost universally indulged in by Congressmen of all parties. In the 1940 campaigns both the Republican and Democratic National Committees sent huge masses of material under the Congressional frank.[111]

The office manager of the Washington, D.C., chapter denied that the chapter had ever ordered reprints of speeches from Hamilton Fish's office.[112] However, Hill's facilities for supplying reprints were known to America First officials.[113] In addition to paying Hill to handle the mailings for the "war-peace" polls, the America First Committee and a few of its chapters made some purchases of reprints from Hill. But there is no evidence in the Committee files to indicate positively that any significant portion of the *Congressional Record* reprints distributed by America First were purchased from Hill.[114] There is no evidence to indicate that America First leaders knew of the ties of Hill with Viereck at the time. Obviously it was not intended that agents in the pay of a foreign government should be able to use the frank to distribute materials which were in line with its propaganda policies. Nevertheless, the practices which the America First Committee followed in the use of the Congressional frank appear to have been both legal and in accord with common practice.

Neither the first Washington grand jury indictment nor the superseding indictment on January 4, 1943, ever culminated in trial. A third and final indictment was returned on January 3, 1944. The charge was changed in an attempt to distinguish between "sincere isolationists" and "American Quislings." Thirty persons were indicted on a charge of conspiracy *with the German Government* to undermine the morale of the United States armed forces. One of the new names added to the list was Garland L. Alderman, who had been chairman of the America First chapter at Pontiac, Michigan. But the America First Committee itself was not listed in this final indictment. This was the only indictment which was brought to trial and it ended in a mistrial when the judge died.[115]

More experienced administrators might have been able to make the Committee less vulnerable to criticism. But it is doubtful if any noninterventionist mass pressure group capable of effectively challenging the Committee to Defend America by Aiding the Allies could have successfully avoided the sort of attacks which descended upon America First. Birkhead said he did not oppose "Quakers and other high-minded pacifists and anti-war groups." [116] But such groups were not powerful enough to combat effectively the major interventionist organizations. In a letter to Senator Wheeler, Henry Hoke indicated this essential interventionist basis for his attacks. After denouncing Wheeler's use of his Congressional frank, Hoke wrote:

You and Senator Nye could become two of the biggest men in our history . . . by calmly reviewing the facts . . . by admitting without thought of personal pride or ambition that you were misguided or misinformed . . . and by using your prestige and new found faith in the United States to help mould this country to the single dominant purpose of defeating the scourge of lust and power which is Hitler's Voice of Destruction.[117]

If Wheeler and Nye had become interventionists, it is doubtful if Hoke would have subjected their use of the frank to such microscopic scrutiny. An officer in the re-organized America First chapter in Portland, Oregon, expressed the conviction that "the opposition wished to maintain Mr. Lessard in his chairmanship solely for the reason of maintaining themselves in a position to 'Shoot at America First'." [118] Whether his hypothesis in this specific instance was valid or not, there is little doubt that the interventionists welcomed every opportunity to discredit the Committee. The noninterventionists, for their part, were delighted when they could find some basis for discrediting the interventionists. The battle of the committees was a fight to the finish with very few holds barred. It was the fate of the America First Committee to be on the side which was more vulnerable to effective attacks in 1941.

The following of the America First Committee consisted of highly heterogeneous elements and among the worst of these were the pro-fascists. The magnitude of the pro-Nazi support was probably greater than an examination of its files would reveal, but the Committee leaders earnestly sought to prevent these elements from working through their organization. And their efforts were more successful than most of its critics would concede. There is remarkably little evidence of explicit pro-Axis sentiment in the many thousands of letters in the Committee's files. Evidence of one tenet of the fascist line, however, was more frequently encountered. That tenet was anti-Semitism.

8   Anti-Semitism and America First

A PARTICULARLY repugnant characteristic of National Socialism in Germany and of Nazi propaganda in the United States was its extreme anti-Semitism. Virtually all anti-Semitic leaders and organizations in the United States after the rise of Hitler were influenced by Nazi ideas and propaganda. Like the Nazis, the highly publicized anti-Semitic organizations in the United States before World War II favored a noninterventionist foreign policy for America. Extreme anti-Semites viewed Communism as a Jewish conspiracy to overthrow American institutions.[1] It is, therefore, probable that the German attack on the Soviet Union made anti-Semites feel even more comfortable in the noninterventionist camp. The cruel Nazi persecution of German Jews probably led more American Jews to support the interventionist than the noninterventionist position.[2] This stimulated criticism of Jews by many noninterventionists. It cannot be concluded that all persons who held anti-Semitic views were pro-Nazi or that there were no anti-Semitic interventionists. But anti-Semitism was sprinkled widely through noninterventionist ranks.

The America First Committee tried to avoid the stigma of anti-Semitism. Through General Wood's influence, Lessing J. Rosenwald, a Jewish director of Sears Roebuck and Company, became an America First national committee member in September, 1940. However, Henry Ford was made a member of the national committee at the same time. Stuart deliberately released the announcement of these two new members simultaneously. He hoped in this way to demonstrate that persons with different views were able to put aside differences and unite under America First to oppose intervention.[3] His idea, however, backfired. Ford had conducted an anti-Semitic campaign through his *Dearborn Independent* from 1920 to 1922 and in 1924–1925. This campaign included the publishing of the fraudulent Protocols of the Elders of Zion. Ford publicly denied that he was anti-Semitic in 1927 but his name continued to be identified with anti-Semitism in the minds of many. His association with America First brought the charge of anti-Semitism upon the Committee and increased the difficulty of getting Jewish support for the organization.[4] Ford's presence and the consequent pressure led Rosenwald to resign from the national committee early in December, 1940. The America First executive committee, therefore, voted to drop Ford from the national committee. According to the minutes of this meeting, the action was taken because Ford had "been unable to give any time or attention to the work of the Committee, and because the Committee could not be sure that from time to time Mr.

132

Ford's views were consistent with the official views of the Committee." Stuart hoped the move might induce Rosenwald to reconsider his resignation but in this he was to be disappointed.[5] Despite his anti-Semitic reputation, Ford probably would not have been dropped if he had been willing to make a sizeable financial contribution to the Committee.[6]

This incident further convinced America First leaders of the necessity for extreme caution to avoid the charge of anti-Semitism. Prominent Jews were invited to serve on the national committee [7] but none of these invitations was accepted after Rosenwald resigned. Jews were welcomed as members and were included on the national headquarters staff, Research Bureau, and the staffs and sponsoring committees of some local chapters.[8] An America First form letter late in 1940 emphasized that the Committee did "not countenance anti-Semitism." [9] Many contributions accompanied by anti-Semitic letters were returned.[10] National officers were cautious in their relations with *Scribner's Commentator* and *The Herald* at Lake Geneva, Wisconsin, because of their anti-Semitism.[11] The editors of the extremely anti-Semitic *Publicity* and *X-Ray* were requested not to send copies of their publications to America First chapters.[12]

The Committee tried to prevent anti-Semites from addressing America First meetings. Donald Shea of the National Gentile League and other anti-Semitic organizations addressed an America First unit in Chicago. When

133

this was discovered by national headquarters, Mrs. Fairbank instructed local chairmen in Illinois not to permit him to address their chapters.[13] The Salt Lake City chapter invited former Congressman Jacob Thorkelson, an outspoken anti-Semite, to speak at a local meeting. The national headquarters learned of this too late to stop the meeting but the chapter was informed that Thorkelson was not acceptable as an America First speaker because of his anti-Semitism.[14] Several chapter leaders were specifically instructed to have nothing to do with Gerald L. K. Smith's Committee of One Million.[15] Edward James Smythe was removed from the speakers' list when his anti-Semitic views were discovered.[16] At the suggestion of B'nai B'rith, some members of the anti-Semitic Silver Shirts were ousted from America First in San Francisco. Information from B'nai B'rith also led the Committee to replace Dellmore Lessard as chairman in Portland, Oregon.[17] Many extreme anti-Semites denounced America First for its failure to attack the Jews. Others accused the Committee of being a Jewish organization.[18]

The America First Committee was cautious in its policy toward the followers of Father Charles E. Coughlin. Coughlin and the publication *Social Justice* had begun to attack the Jews by 1938. They fervently espoused a noninterventionist foreign policy for the United States. The greatest Coughlinite Christian Front strength was in Eastern cities such as New York and Boston.[19] The Washington America First chapter barred followers of Coughlin from its membership.[20] John T. Flynn sought to keep Christian Fronters out of the New York chapter.[21] The Committee's Eastern organization director, Joseph R. Boldt, Jr., outlined the America First policy as follows:

The Coughlinite situation has always been a difficult one for us. It has been our policy to not permit any Coughlin organization leaders to be in a position of leadership or direction in our local chapters. Of course, you cannot prevent their becoming members or working to get other members. The important thing is to handle the situation so that they do not in any way identify the chapter with the Coughlin movement per se. By all means do not permit copies of "Social Justice" to be sold at your meetings. While you perhaps cannot legally prevent this from being done on sidewalks outside the auditorium, you may be able to do it by direct request to the people who are intelligent enough to understand the situation. It is of particular importance that none of these supporters be permitted to inject anti-Semitism into the work of the chapter. We have the support of many Jewish people, and will not abide intolerance as a part of this movement.

Robert L. Bliss as national director of organization was even more outspoken. He wrote that America First had "no sympathy at all with Father Coughlin, his paper or anything it contains with relation to his movement." [23]

The Coughlin *Social Justice* was disturbed by this coolness. It particularly criticized the "pro-Marxists" whom it accused of trying to split America First into fragments.[24] Flynn tried unsuccessfully to prevent the Reverend Edward Lodge Curran of the Christian Front from offering the invocation at a chapter meeting. Consequently Curran tried (but failed) to have Flynn ousted as chairman of America First in New York.[25] A crisis occurred in July, 1941, when *Social Justice* reported that General Wood had told a person distributing the publication outside an America First meeting to go away. *Social Justice* quoted Wood as saying: "We don't want you people at America First meetings. You people confuse the issue." [26] This editorial caused many followers of Father Coughlin to protest and resign from America First chapters.[27] The membership of the chapter at Pontiac, Michigan, was reported to have resigned en masse in protest.[28]

Despite the efforts to reduce the Committee's vulnerability to the charge of anti-Semitism, many supporters of America First held anti-Semitic views. Not all national and local America First leaders were cool or hostile toward followers of Father Coughlin.[29] Even Stuart early in 1941 denied that the Committee rejected their support.[30] General Wood saw no harm in accepting contributions from Robert M. Harriss who had been a broker for Father Coughlin.[31] Wood also had friendly relations with the Reverend Edward Lodge Curran.[32]

From the beginning of the Committee's history *Social Justice* commended America First and urged support for the organization.[33] In June, 1941, *Social Justice* declared: "Let all groups, as well as all individuals who support the *America First Committee*, submerge, momentarily at least, their motivating objectives to the one grand object of keeping this country out of war. No other interest should engage our common mind." [34] Even its editorial concerning Wood's reputed denunciation of Coughlinites did not explicitly urge followers of Father Coughlin not to support America First.[35]

136

The number of protests to America First aroused by this editorial suggested the magnitude of Coughlinite support for America First in the East. Concerning followers of Father Coughlin the chairman of the America First chapter at Worcester, Massachusetts, wrote that "this committee cannot afford to lose the support of these loyal workers." [36] The secretary of the Akron, Ohio, chapter said their ranks included "many devout readers of the *Social Justice*." [37] The vice-chairman of the Boston chapter said "many followers of Father Coughlin have joined as individuals. They have been able supporters and hard workers." [38] Another leader of the Boston chapter wrote that the Coughlinites were among the chapter's "best friends." [39] Each of these chapter officers protested against General Wood's stand as reported in *Social Justice*.

The America First headquarters staff denied that *Social Justice* had correctly reported the incident. In answering letters from irate supporters of Father Coughlin, headquarters staff members wrote: "America First welcomes the support of members of all faiths; Catholic, Protestant, or Jewish. It remains strictly independent of all organizations. It accepts no support from Nazis, Communists, anti-Semites, or others whose political affiliations make impossible true loyalty to the Constitution." [40] On July 28, 1941, *Social Justice* printed a letter in which General Wood declared: "I have not rejected the Christian Social Justice movement. I welcome their support in our common objective—preventing this country from getting into the war." It also published a letter from Mrs. Burton K. Wheeler which expressed similar sentiments.[41] This America First policy enabled the Committee to retain the support of many Coughlinites. But it also resulted in the resignation of the liberal Dorothy Dunbar Bromley from the sponsoring committee of the New York chapter.[42] The strength of the Coughlin element in some Eastern chapters may have been so great that its loss would have weakened the Committee. Some insisted that there were "good" and "bad" Coughlin followers and that not all readers of *Social Justice* were anti-Semitic.[43] A group of the less desirable Coughlinites was ousted from the Pittsburgh chapter in the fall of 1941.[44] But by following this conciliatory course in the summer of 1941, the Committee missed an opportunity to make itself less vulnerable to the charge of anti-Semitism. It also made it more difficult to rid the Committee of those who were less desirable as judged by the announced standards for membership in America First.

Some leaders of local America First chapters held clearly anti-Semitic views. The chairman of America First in Terre Haute, Indiana, was convinced that "Jews or their appointees are now in possession of our Government" and were causing the "panic and wars that ruin everybody." [45] A leader of a Kansas chapter labeled the New Deal the "Jew Deal." She wrote that Churchill was half-Jew and that the English government was "a Jewish Government." She insisted that "Roosevelt and his wife are Jewish and this goes for 90% of his Administration." She "also learned that many Jews are inside the America First organization." [46] The leader of a Florida chapter expressed the opinion that "the Jews and the organizations such as B'nai B'rith are primarily responsible for our being advanced so far along the path to war. . . . Under Mr. Roosevelt's administration . . . the nine-million Jews are directing the affairs of the entire one hundred and thirty million." [47] Garland L. Alderman, chairman of the Pontiac, Michigan, chapter wrote:

I am not anti-Semitic but as most of our business men in Pontiac are Jews they won't cooperate. *Every single* one of them preach war. . . . I am trying to check anti-semitism and tell our members we have no use for it but my personal opinion and I tell no one this but you that if anti-Semetism [sic] comes it will be brought on by the Warburgs, Ickes, Morgantaus [sic], Frankfurters, Sol Blooms, Barauchs, Winchells, and people like the congressman who just died. [48]

He was convinced America First should not "insult" people like Joseph McWilliams, Gerald L. K. Smith, Father Coughlin, William Dudley Pelley, or their followers. [49] There were also other less striking instances of anti-Semitism among chapter leaders. [50] In the worst instances America First headquarters warned the chapter leaders not to attack the Jews and re-emphasized that the Committee was not anti-Semitic. [51] But none of the chapter leaders mentioned above were removed from their positions of leadership. In San Francisco the ousted Silver Shirts continued to attend America First meetings. [52]

Not all contributions accompanied by anti-Semitic letters were returned. [53] Some speakers at local America First meetings held anti-Semitic views.[54] Even some national leaders and spokesmen of America First were accused of anti-Semitism.[55]

Despite its precautions, the America First Committee did co-operate to a certain extent with the publishers of *Scribner's Commentator* and the *Herald*. The staffs of these publications gave some assistance to national headquarters and a few local chapters with the mailing of noninterventionist literature.[56] General Wood and other Committee leaders authorized the publication of speeches in the magazine.[57] Some chapters distributed copies of the publications.[58]

A move in the Senate in August and September, 1941, to investigate war propaganda in motion pictures gave new vitality to the charge of anti-Semitism against noninterventionists. Early in 1941 Stuart wrote that "films that have nothing to do with the European war are now loaded with lies and ideas which bring about an interventionist reaction." [59] America First found it next to impossible to secure support from movie actors and actresses. At the same time interventionists gained strong support in Hollywood.[60] On August 1, 1941, Senators Gerald P. Nye and Bennett Champ Clark called for a Senate investigation of war propaganda in motion pictures. The matter was referred to the Committee on Interstate Commerce headed by Burton K. Wheeler who promptly appointed a subcommittee to conduct hearings.[61]

Though this "investigation" was not sponsored by America First, it did receive the Committee's support and assistance. John T. Flynn aided the Senators by directing a private investigation of war propaganda. The funds for his work were supplied, at least in part, by one of the major financial backers of America First.[62] General Wood also corresponded with Senator Wheeler on the subject.[63] America First national headquarters sent bulletins to local chapters urging them to inform the subcommittee of "every instance of 'war propaganda' observed in the motion pictures." [64]

Jews controlled considerably more than half of the motion picture industry.[65] Senator Nye and the others denied that their hearings were anti-Semitic.[66] Nevertheless, the counsel for the motion picture industry, Wendell L. Willkie, effectively made the hearings more embarrassing for the noninterventionist Senators than for the movie industry. His charge that the hearings were anti-Semitic probably encouraged the early adjournment of the hearings in the fall of 1941. They were never renewed.[67] The subcommittee hearings did not change the character of motion pictures. But they did further identify leading America First spokesmen with anti-Semitism in the minds of many.

ON SEPTEMBER 11, 1941, Charles A. Lindbergh delivered an address at an American First rally at Des Moines, Iowa, which brought the whole question of anti-Semitism in the Committee to a head. Before December 7, 1941, Lindbergh, more than any other person, was the personification of isolationism for the mass of the American people. No other major noninterventionist speaker aroused such enthusiastic support or was subjected to such vehement denunciations as Lindbergh. His colorful career had made him something of a hero to millions of Americans. He was by far the most sought-after America First speaker after he became a national committee member in April, 1941. Nearly all chapters from the very smallest to the largest wanted Lindbergh to address their meetings. National headquarters promised first consideration for a "Lindbergh rally" to the chapter winning a contest to gain new members. Individual chapters flooded Committee headquarters with letters and telegrams in concerted drives to get the Lone Eagle for a major rally.[68] And with good cause. No other America First speaker was able to attract audiences equal in size to those which flocked to hear Lindbergh. He invariably addressed overflow crowds. The attendance at some of his rallies exceeded thirty thousand people. At these meetings he received tremendous ovations lasting several minutes. These rallies always resulted in a sharp increase in the sponsoring chapter's membership.[69]

But from the date of his first speech on American foreign policy in September, 1939, until he was silenced by the attack on Pearl Harbor, Lindbergh was subjected to a torrent of criticism. He had been the target for most of the "standard" criticisms countless times before the America First Committee had even been formed. The epithets used in attacking him ranged from the rather mild "ignorant" and "blind," through "coward," to "number one fifth columnist" and "Nazi." [70] Robert E. Sherwood said Lindbergh was "a Nazi with a Nazi's Olympian contempt for all democratic processes—the rights of freedom of speech and worship, the right to select and criticize our own government and the right of labor to strike." [71] Secretary of the Interior Harold L. Ickes called Lindbergh a "peripatetic appeaser who would abjectly surrender his sword even before it is demanded." [72] He was repeatedly criticized for accepting a medal from Marshal Goering in 1938.[73] Indeed, Stuart had serious misgivings about inviting Lindbergh to join America First because he was convinced it would bring a deluge of attacks upon the Committee.[74] Lindbergh denied that he wanted a German victory. He said he believed it would be a tragedy to the whole world if Britain were defeated. But he made himself vulnerable to criticism by refusing to denounce Nazism, by saying that Britain had already lost the war, and by expressing a preference for a negotiated peace over a British victory.[75] Lindbergh had a particularly strong appeal among the anti-Semitic, Coughlinite, and pro-fascist groups.[76] The criticism of Lindbergh continued after he joined America First. It reached such an intensity following his Des Moines speech that his influence as a leading and unifying force in noninterventionist ranks was seriously impaired.

In his earlier speeches, Lindbergh had repeatedly attacked the "powerful elements in America" which he believed were attempting to lead the United States into the war. However, he had generally not specifically identified these persons or groups.[77] In his Des Moines speech, Charles A. Lindbergh identified the groups which he believed were "responsible for changing our national policy

143

from one of neutrality and independence to one of en-
tanglement in European affairs." He declared: "The three
most important groups who have been pressing this country toward war are the British, the Jewish and the Roosevelt administration. Behind these groups, but of lesser importance, are a number of capitalists, Anglophiles, and intellectuals who believe that their future, and the future of
mankind, depends upon the domination of the British Empire . . . . these war agitators comprise only a small minority
of our people; but they control a tremendous influence."
In elaborating upon the Jewish influence Lindbergh said:

It is not difficult to understand why Jewish people desire the
overthrow of Nazi Germany. The persecution they suffered in
Germany would be sufficient to make bitter enemies of any
race. No person with a sense of the dignity of mankind can
condone the persecution the Jewish race suffered in Germany.
But no person of honesty and vision can look on their pro-war
policy here today without seeing the dangers involved in such
a policy, both for us and for them.

Instead of agitating for war the Jewish groups in this country should be opposing it in every possible way, for they will
be among the first to feel its consequences. Tolerance is a vir-
tue that depends upon peace and strength. History shows that
it cannot survive war and devastation. A few farsighted Jewish
people realize this and stand opposed to intervention. But the
majority still do not. Their greatest danger to this country lies
in their large ownership and influence in our motion pictures,
our press, our radio, and our government.

He expressed the opinion that if any one of these three
major groups stopped "agitating for war" there would be
little danger of American intervention. He concluded that
these groups had succeeded in bringing the United States

144

to the brink of war and now needed only to create "sufficient 'incidents'" to bring the United States into the actual shooting war.[78]

It would be difficult to exaggerate the magnitude of the explosion which was set off by this speech. Not only did the regular "full-time" critics of the Committee loose their fury upon the speech, but new voices from every quarter were added to the deluge. Even many leaders and supporters of America First and other noninterventionist organizations disapproved of the speech. Undoubtedly much of this uproar was due to genuine disapproval of Lindbergh's key statement regarding the Jews. Many may have denounced the speech publicly to protect themselves from any possible charge of anti-Semitism. But there can be no doubt that interventionists exploited this incident in an attempt to discredit and weaken the campaign against intervention in the European war.

Newspapers and periodicals were almost unanimous in their denunciation of the speech. In most newspapers President Roosevelt's "Shoot-on-Sight" speech the same evening stole the headlines.[79] But Lindbergh's speech managed to get an ample amount of publicity without them. The *Des Moines Register* editorialized that, "it may have been courageous for Colonel Lindbergh to say what was in his mind, but it was so lacking in appreciation of consequences—putting the best interpretation on it—that it disqualifies him for any pretensions of leadership of this republic in policy-making." This editorial continued by saying that the speech was "so intemperate, so unfair, so dangerous in its implications that it cannot but turn many spadefuls in the digging of the grave of his influence in this crisis." [80] The *New York Herald Tribune* flailed the speech's anti-Semitism while the *Kansas City Journal* declared that "Lindbergh's interest in Hitlerism is now thinly concealed." These sentiments were echoed in newspapers all over the nation.[81] Some writers promptly pointed out that the Jewish people probably controlled less than their share of the daily newspapers and the magazines.[82] *New Masses* and *Daily Worker* were notably outspoken in their denunciations of Lindbergh's speech.[83]

The Committee to Defend America by Aiding the Allies and the Fight for Freedom Committee denounced the speech and called on America First to repudiate Lindbergh. F. H. Peter Cusick, national executive secretary of the Fight for Freedom Committee, pointed out that though interventionist sentiment was strongest in the South and Southwest, these sections had the smallest Jewish population.[84] Fight for Freedom also distributed a pamphlet entitled *America's Answer to Lindbergh* which quoted speakers and writers all over the nation who attacked the Des Moines speech.[85] A similar pamphlet was distributed by the Council Against Intolerance in America.[86] In Austin, Texas, the lower house of the state legislature passed a resolution informing Lindbergh that he was not welcome on any speaking tour he might plan in the state.[87]

Prominent national political leaders added the weight of their voices to the indictment. Wendell Willkie said the speech was "the most un-American talk made in my

146

time by any person of national reputation." Governor
Thomas E. Dewey of New York referred to it as "an inex-
cusable abuse of the right of freedom of speech." [88] Though
President Roosevelt made no comment, White House
Secretary Stephen T. Early said he thought there was a
"striking similarity" between Lindbergh's speech and "the
outpourings of Berlin in the last few days." [89]

Denunciations of the speech also came from sources
which approved of the general foreign policy views of the
America First Committee. The executive director of the
Keep America Out of War Congress wrote that the speech
had "done more to fan the flames of Anti-Semitism and
push 'on-the-fence' Jews into the war camp than Mr. Lindbergh can possibly imagine." [90] The governing committee of the Keep America Out of War Congress announced
its "deep disagreement" with the "implications" of the Des
Moines address. However, this statement also criticized
the interventionists for concealing Lindbergh's denunciation of the treatment of Jews in Germany in their attacks
on the speech. All of the twenty-five persons at the meeting
which authorized this statement, including four Jews,
agreed that the Des Moines speech was not anti-Semitic.[91]
The national executive committee of the Socialist Party
labeled the speech a "serious blow to democracy and to
the movement to keep America out of war." [92] Norman
Thomas said Lindbergh was "not as anti-Semitic as some
who seize the opportunity to criticize him." But he denounced the speech as "amazingly hurtful" and an "over
simplification." [93] He declined to speak at America First

147

meetings after this time.[94] The Hearst newspapers strongly criticized Lindbergh's speech.[95] Even the *Chicago Tribune* refused to go along with its hero. Its headline on the following day told of Lindbergh's attack on the Roosevelt administration, but a careful examination of the news columns was necessary to learn of his references to the Jews.[96] On September 13, the *Tribune* carried an editorial designed to explain that the newspaper was not anti-Semitic.[97] A feature page with pictures of some of Lindbergh's medals had already been printed for the September 21 issue. On September 20, 1941, the *Tribune* carried an editorial which denounced the "impropriety" of Lindbergh's reference to the Jews and stated hopefully, "We are confident that none of our readers will assume that the publication of this page at this time is to be regarded as in any sense an evidence of approval of the Des Moines speech." [98]

Many America First leaders and local members expressed disapproval. Merle H. Miller, chairman of the Indianapolis chapter; Herbert K. Hyde, Oklahoma state chairman; Irvin S. Cobb, General Hugh S. Johnson, and Al Williams, national committee members, all criticized the address. John T. Flynn, chairman of the New York chapter, protested to America First headquarters against the "stupid" speech. He expressed a fear that it would give the interventionists an opportunity to launch an "all-out smear" campaign against noninterventionists.[99] Some members of local chapters resigned in protest.[100]

Most America First leaders and members, however, gave Lindbergh at least qualified support. Eighty-five to

90 per cent of the letters received by national head-quarters supported Lindbergh.[101] Most of them did not believe Lindbergh was anti-Semitic. They believed the references to the Jews might have been phrased more tactfully and accurately. Or, better still, not have been voiced at all. Most of the Committee's supporters believed Lindbergh's statements concerning the Jews were largely correct and the overwhelming majority opposed repudiation of Lindbergh. Most of them, however, hoped America First would make a clear statement that it was not anti-Semitic. The secretary of the Cleveland chapter, Dorothy Thum, wrote:

I happen to be very far from anti-Semitic myself. . . . However, I would not dcndemn [*sic*] Mr. Lindbergh's speech as anti-Semitic. . . . That the Jews are almost without exception keen for war, or at least intimidated by their brethren into not talking peace, seems irrefutably a fact. Statement of fact doesn't necessarily entail condemnation, and surely his remarks about the Germans' treatment of the Jews showed that he sympathizes with the Jews. I think I'd be for war myself if I were a Jew. But I do think it was unfortunate to mention the fact. It encouraged our anti-Semitic members to be more outspoken. . . . I would be much happier to see an official statement that Mr. Lindbergh did not mean to damn the Jews, and thereafter see America First pretend the name Jew was never invented. I would like to see representatives of both Jewish and negro races occupying platform seats at America First rallies.[102]

This general point of view was expressed in dozens of letters from America First national and chapter leaders.[103] Gregory Mason, chairman of the Stamford-Greenwich-Norwalk America First chapter in Connecticut and later a national committee member, turned the charge of anti-Semitism back on the interventionists. Professor Mason wrote:

A great deal of hypocrisy has been evidenced by smug citizens in our midst who sounded off to condemn Lindbergh on the basis of a hasty reading of two or three sentences lifted from his Des Moines address. Many such citizens *practice* anti-Semitism every day of their lives. Many of the individual supporters of the Committee to Defend America by Aiding the Allies and of the Fight for Freedom Committee . . . belong to exclusive social clubs from which Jews are strictly barred . . . . the Greenwich Real Estate Board opposes renting or selling houses to Jews in the "exclusive" part of Greenwich from which was subscribed in a few weeks enough money to buy England six ambulances . . . and from which comes the loudest local denunciation of Lindbergh.[104]

Most America First leaders and members tried to take a moderate position in defending the Committee. But many anti-Semites within America First ranks and on its fringes interpreted the address as an invitation to use the Committee as a vehicle for spreading their anti-Semitic ideas. Many chapters were faced with this problem. It was especially critical in New York where many of the less desirable elements had long been agitating for the removal of John T. Flynn.[105] One leader of a West Coast unit wrote that "for the first time hundreds will come in that otherwise have felt we were evading the truth as to who is largely responsible for the War push." [106] There are dozens of letters in America First files commending Lindbergh's speech in such extreme anti-Semitic terms that the headquarters staff stamped them "Crank-Ignore." [107]

150

Anti-Semitism and America First

America First leaders had not read Lindbergh's Des Moines speech before it was delivered.[108] Such an outburst of criticism, however, could not be ignored without serious consequences to the Committee. National headquarters admonished local chapters to withhold comment on the speech until after the national committee met.[109] The course which the Committee should follow with regard to the Des Moines speech was discussed at length at a national committee meeting on September 18, 1941. In the discussion it was pointed out that Lindbergh had sacrificed a great deal for America First. Further, most of them were inclined to feel that what Lindbergh had said was actually quite true. Thus the decision was made not to repudiate Lindbergh or his speech.[110] A letter by Amos R. E. Pinchot, a national committee member present at the meeting, throws light on the view taken in the discussion. Pinchot wrote:

We did not consider the Lindbergh speech anti-Semitic. . . . It did not criticize . . . the Jewish people on the ground of race or religion. It did, however, state plainly what I think you will agree is true namely that, as a group, the Jews of America are for intervention, and that they constitute one of the main forces for intervention . . . in view of this, I see no more impropriety in expressing the opinion, provided it is sincere and well founded, that the Jews are interventionists, than in saying for example, the people of Polish or Dutch descent in this country are, as a group, interventionist. . . . I think the Lindbergh statement was true. And so far I have met no Jewish man or woman who doesn't admit it's true. . . . Needless to say I'm thoroughly opposed to anti-Semitism in any form. . . . I am personally grateful to Colonel Lindbergh for helping to keep America patriotic and sane.[111]

151

Anti-Semitism and America First

On September 24, 1941, after those national committee members not at the meeting had been consulted, the America First Committee issued its official statement on the Des Moines speech. In this statement the national committee declared the attack on Lindbergh was merely one of many attempts on the part of the interventionists "to hide the real issues by flinging false charges at" noninterventionist spokesmen. The statement declared:

Colonel Lindbergh and his fellow members of the America First Committee are not anti-Semitic. We deplore the injection of the race issue into the discussion of war or peace. It is the interventionists who have done this. America First, on the other hand, has invited men and women of every race, religion and national origin to join this committee, provided only that they are patriotic citizens who put the interests of their country ahead of those of any other nation. We repeat that invitation. ... There is but one real issue—the issue of war. From this issue we will not be diverted.[112]

At the same time Stuart sent a letter to all chapter chairmen admonishing them to redouble their efforts "to keep our membership rolls clear of those who seek to promote racial and religious intolerance." [113]

A few days later America First released a letter from Dr. Hyman Lischner, a San Diego physician and former president of B'nai B'rith in San Diego. In this letter Dr. Lischner, a Russian-born Jew, defended Lindbergh and insisted that there was no race prejudice in any of Lindbergh's talks. He agreed that the Jewish group was one of the most important pressing America toward war.[114]

The national committee statement, a product of compromise, was not completely satisfactory to all Committee leaders.[115] Dr. Charles Fleischer, a prominent Jew, resigned from the executive committee of the New York chapter of America First in protest.[116] At least three members of the America First national committee resigned after the statement was published.[117] Even Senator Wheeler felt it necessary to point out that he was not actually a member of the committee.[118]

The Des Moines speech was the only major foreign policy address by Lindbergh in the two years before Pearl Harbor in which he specifically placed the interventionist label on the Jews. In neither of his two major addresses which followed the Des Moines speech did he directly mention the Jews. However, without referring to the Des Moines speech or the Jews, he did attempt to defend himself at an America First rally at Fort Wayne, Indiana, on October 3, 1941. In this address he stated that in all his speeches he had only said what he believed to be the truth. He maintained that his statements had been distorted and that his motives and meanings had been "falsely ascribed." Obviously answering the charge of anti-Semitism, he said that he did not "speak out of hate for any individuals or any people." Finally, he expressed a fear that he might be giving his last speech because "there is no way of telling how long we will be able to hold meetings of this kind." [119] His fears proved groundless, however, and approximately twenty thousand persons attended his last major America First rally in New York later in October, 1941.[120]

There can be little doubt that, however sincere and well

meaning he may have been, Lindbergh's Des Moines speech was an extremely serious political blunder and dealt the America First Committee a staggering blow.[121] It complicated the problem of preventing anti-Semites and pro-fascists from working through the Committee. It gave the interventionists their best opportunity to discredit America First. The deluge of criticism which the Des Moines speech and the grand jury hearings precipitated was so all-encompassing that it dwarfed the Committee's major effort to prevent repeal of the vital provisions of the Neutrality Act in the fall of 1941.

9　　　Shoot on Sight

AFTER LEND-LEASE became law on March 11, 1941, America's role in delivering war materials to England became a key issue in the foreign policy debate. Lend-Lease resolved the problem of financing and allocating aid to Great Britain. But there still remained the problem of assuring that the goods actually reached their intended destination. The Lend-Lease Act would be futile as a measure to aid Britain against the Axis if German submarines sent the war materials to the bottom of the Atlantic Ocean. Consequently, in the spring of 1941 Secretary of War Henry L. Stimson and other interventionists urged the President to use the American Navy to convoy goods to Great Britain.

America First leaders were convinced the use of the American Navy for convoys would put the United States into the European war. The America First Principles released in December, 1940, declared: "We oppose any change in the law which would permit American vessels to enter the combat zone or which would permit the American Navy to convoy merchant ships through that zone, as any such course would inevitably plunge this country into Europe's war." [1] The revised statement of America First Principles released in March, 1941, after Lend-Lease was passed, insisted: "In 1917 we sent our American ships into the war zone and this led us to war. In 1941 we must keep our naval convoys and merchant vessels on this side of the Atlantic." [2] An America First pamphlet flatly asserted: "Convoys mean war—a shooting, bloody war." [3] Speakers such as Senators Burton K. Wheeler and Gerald P. Nye who addressed America First rallies in the spring of 1941 expressed opposition to convoying by the American Navy. America First leaders quoted President Roosevelt's statement that convoys would mean shooting and "shooting comes awfully close to war." [4]

In April, 1941, the America First Committee endorsed an anti-convoy resolution introduced in the Senate by Senator Charles W. Tobey of New Hampshire. Members of local chapters were urged to swamp the Senate Foreign Relations Committee with letters supporting the resolution. [5] On April 30, 1941, the Foreign Relations Committee voted thirteen to ten against reporting out the anti-convoy resolution. [6] In May Senator Tobey, who had been waging almost a one-man battle in the Senate against convoys, wanted to press for a vote on the measure. Though America First had endorsed the Tobey resolution, General Wood, at the suggestion of Senator Robert A. Taft and others, urged Tobey not to offer his measure as an amendment to pending legislation. It was feared the Administration might interpret a Senate vote against the anti-convoy amendment as permission to convoy. General Wood's telegram was an influential factor in persuading Tobey not to press for a vote on the measure.[7]

Actually, President Roosevelt had decided at least as early as April 10, 1941, not to seek Congressional authorization for convoying. He feared he would be defeated in a vote on the question. Instead, President Roosevelt ordered naval "patrols" designed to render the maximum aid to Britain against Axis raiders short of actual convoys. Late in April, 1941, American warships began to trail German submarines in areas outside the war zones and report their positions to British convoys and airplanes.[8]

President Roosevelt in an address on May 27, 1941, declared: "The delivery of needed supplies to Britain is imperative. This can be done; it must be done; it will be done." He announced the extension of American patrols but did not call specifically for convoys. In his address the President re-asserted the doctrine of freedom of the seas and proclaimed a state of unlimited national emergency.[9] America First officials denied that the declaration of unlimited national emergency necessitated any curtailment of the Committee's battle against intervention. They insisted that the declaration did not authorize convoys. General Wood called President Roosevelt's speech "the least war-like of any of his utterances since election." [10] Other America First supporters, however, were less optimistic in their appraisals.[11]

Early in July, 1941, the United States took over the defense of Iceland. Subsequently the American Navy extended its patrols and convoyed American and Icelandic ships as far as Iceland.[12] An America First Research Bureau bulletin insisted that "the occupation of Iceland is another evasion of the convoy issue. By keeping open the sea route to Iceland, the U.S. Navy, in effect will be convoying British shipping . . . up to Iceland." It said the waters around Iceland were actually in the war zone.[13] John T. Flynn was even more explicit in his denunciation of the move: "This is a plan to stick our neck out in the hope that someone will hack at it . . . . the Iceland incident now puts us right in the middle of the war zone. Only a miracle can save us from an incident or a series of incidents which is what the war-bund here wants." [14]

On July 13, 1941, a meeting of America First chapter chairmen in Chicago passed a resolution calling for the removal of Secretary of the Navy Frank Knox. The resolution accused Knox of advocating that the American Navy intervene in the Atlantic war. It reasoned that such activities would be "actual and open war without consent of Congress." The resolution interpreted this as a violation of the Constitution which the Secretary had sworn to uphold.[15]

The policies of the American and German governments combined to prevent incidents involving American ships on the Atlantic Ocean during the first twenty months of the European war. No ship flying the American flag was sunk by a German submarine until May 21, 1941. On that date the *Robin Moor,* an American merchant vessel, was sent to the bottom of the South Atlantic with no loss of life.

However, during the last half of 1941 the number of incidents increased. On August 17, 1941, the *Sessa*, an American-owned merchant ship under Panamanian registry, was torpedoed near Iceland. One of the casualties was an American. September 4, 1941, the *Greer*, an American destroyer, was missed by two torpedoes fired by a German submarine. The *Steel Seafarer* flying the American flag was bombed in the Red Sea on September 5, 1941, with no loss of life. Three other American-owned ships flying the flag of Panama were torpedoed later in September, 1941. And on October 17, 1941, the *Kearny*, an American destroyer, was torpedoed near Iceland with the loss of eleven lives.[16]

As a consequence of the attacks on American ships, President Franklin D. Roosevelt on September 11, 1941, delivered his famous "shoot-on-sight" address. He accused the German submarine of firing on the *Greer* first "without warning, and with deliberate design to sink her." He labeled this "piracy—legally and morally." He denounced the sinking of the *Sessa* and the *Steel Seafarer* and described Hitler's plan to control the oceans. The President ordered the American Navy to attack German and Italian war ships wherever found within the patrol zone without waiting for them to attack first.[17]

The America First Committee did not condone the sinking of American ships. But Committee leaders insisted that the attacks were being invited and provoked by American tactics. They gravely feared these incidents would ultimately put the United States into war. As the months of 1941 passed, many America First leaders became convinced that the Administration and the interventionists were hoping for incidents to arouse support for a declaration of war. Consequently when crises occurred the Committee tried to "calm" the American people by explaining the circumstances surrounding the incidents as they viewed them.

Though it deemed the treatment of the passengers and the crew unjustifiable, the America First Research Bureau contended that the cargo of the *Robin Moor* was 70 per cent contraband. The Research Bureau also denounced the practice of transferring American merchant ships to Panamanian registry to avoid the restrictions of the Neutrality Act. The Bureau pointed out that the *Steel Seafarer* was sunk in the Red Sea after President Roosevelt revoked his earlier proclamation which declared the Red Sea a war zone.[18] Committee leaders accused President Roosevelt of giving a misleading account of the *Greer* incident in his address on September 11, 1941. They based their accusation upon a statement by Admiral Harold R. Stark. Stark wrote that the *Greer* trailed the submarine for more than three hours in co-operation with an English war plane before the submarine finally fired upon its pursuer.[19] The Research Bureau on September 13, 1941, pointed out that up to that time no American lives had been lost on any ship flying the American flag.[20]

President Roosevelt's "shoot-on-sight" speech was met with a storm of protest from the America First Committee. The executive committee of the New York chapter labeled the speech "an amazing move to arouse hysteria and plunge us into a foreign war, unwanted by the people ... and needless for national defense." [21] The Research Bureau accused the President of circumventing the spirit of the Neutrality and Lend-Lease Acts. The Bureau described President Roosevelt's interpretation of "freedom of the seas" as "freedom to aid one country at war without interference from that country's enemies." [22] General Wood released a statement endorsed by fifty-eight prominent Americans denouncing the speech. This statement made no mention of America First but the "independent group" of endorsers included most of the America First national committee members and its principal advisors. The "independent group" also included Philip C. Jessup, Edwin M. Borchard, Edwin S. Corwin, Charles Clayton Morrison, Ray Lyman Wilbur, Charles A. Beard, Igor Sikorsky, and others. This statement described the President's speech as

a grave threat to the constitutional powers of Congress and to the democratic principle of majority rule.... The President has decreed that shooting shall begin. His edict is supported neither by Congressional sanction nor by the popular will. It is authorized by no statute and undermines the Constitutional provision which gives the war power to Congress alone.[23]

When the *Kearny* was torpedoed General Wood urged Americans to "withhold judgment" until all the facts were disclosed.[24] Speaking at an America First rally, Senator Nye said the *Greer* and *Kearny* incidents were "very largely of our own making and our own inviting. We cannot order our ships to shoot to destroy the vessels of certain belligerent nations and hope at the same time that the ships of those nations are not going to seek to destroy our ships." [25] John T. Flynn insisted that the incidents were "being manufactured for war-making purposes." [26]

In October and November, 1941, in its final major campaign the America First Committee fought against the repeal of the vital provisions of the Neutrality Act. This campaign compared in intensity with the Committee's battle against Lend-Lease. The effort in the fall of 1941 was made more powerful because of the Committee's more extensive organization and increased membership. But the persistent attacks on America First reduced its effectiveness. The organization never recovered in the eyes of a large segment of the American people from the blow given it by Lindbergh's Des Moines speech. Nevertheless, the America First battle against repeal of the vital provisions of the Neutrality Act was conducted with immense fervor, conviction, and drama.

President Roosevelt on October 9, 1941, urged Congress to repeal the "crippling provisions" of the Neutrality Act. Specifically, he proposed that the Act be revised to permit the arming of American merchant ships and to allow them to enter the combat zones. He insisted that the revision of the Act would "not leave the United States any less neutral than we are today, but will make it possible for us to defend the Americas far more successfully, and to give aid far more effectively against the tremendous forces now marching toward conquest of the world." [27]

General Wood opened the America First Committee's campaign against the Administration's proposals the same day they were presented to Congress. He declared that President Roosevelt was "asking Congress to issue an engraved drowning license to American seamen." His statement continued:

It will mean that American ships will be sunk, American lives lost—and that the country will be led into war on a wave of hysteria just as it was in 1917. . . . Now the President and all those who advocate our immediate involvement, realize that we will never go to war while this law stands. They seek its repeal, although there is less practical need for repeal today than at any time since the war began. . . . The only reason for the repeal of the Combat Zone prohibition is the war party's need for a series of incendiary incidents.

General Wood then pledged the America First Committee's full power to fight against repeal of the provisions of the Act.[28]

The central theme in the Committee's campaign was the conviction that repeal of the vital provisions of the Act would put the United States into the war. Before the Senate Foreign Relations Committee John T. Flynn objected to the move as perhaps the final step to war.[29] Stuart wrote:

For the first time they cannot argue that it's a peace measure. No one can deny that sending vessels into the war zone tends to promote war. The obvious war-like intentions of such a course are made all the clearer by the fact that the goods could be delivered to England just as effectively by merely transferring the registry of the ships. The only objective of the Administration's policy is to get the American flag ships into the war zone.[30]

General Wood's letter to President Roosevelt late in October, 1941, urging a vote in Congress on the issue of war or peace was part of the Committee's campaign. Stuart insisted that if President Roosevelt refused to "put the question honestly before Congress" the Committee would "treat the Neutrality repeal for what it is—a war vote. We will fight it as we would fight a declaration of war." [31] The Committee credited the Neutrality Act with keeping the nation out of war up to that time.[32]

The America First Committee also insisted that there was less need for revision of the Neutrality Act at that time than the preceding year. It cited British and American sources which indicated that England had "more shipping today than she had when the war began." It quoted Churchill's statement that losses during July, August, and September, 1941, were only one-third of those during the preceding quarter of the year. The Committee quoted the chairman of the United States Maritime Commission to show that less than 4 per cent of the cargoes leaving America failed to reach England. Contrary to the contentions of the interventionists, the America First Committee insisted that American and British shipyards were producing new ships at a much faster rate than Germany was destroying them. The Committee held that, if necessary, ships could be transferred to England under the provisions of Lend-Lease without risking war for the United States.[33]

The America First Committee mobilized its maximum strength and used every proved method to make its strength felt in Washington, D.C., Flynn testified before the Senate Foreign Relations Committee. America First distributed thousands of pamphlets and staged dozens of meetings.[34] Officers of the Committee were in close consultation with Congressional leaders.[35] America First national headquarters marshaled local chapters in the battle. A meeting of chapter leaders was held in Washington, D.C., to plan the campaign. This meeting passed a resolution pledging support in the 1942 elections for those Congressmen and Senators who voted against revision of the Neutrality Act.[36] *Emergency Bulletin #1* outlined a plan for "mail brigades" in local chapters. This bulletin declared:

Bear in mind none of these letter writers are just to write letters. They are to follow instructions. National Headquarters will decide when, to whom, and, in general, what to write, and notify the state and chapter chairmen. . . . Remember this is not a problem of writing every day, it is a problem of getting a specific number of letters to a specific person on a specific subject.[37]

Stuart and other top staff members of the Committee went to Washington, D.C., to direct the Committee's campaign.[38] As the final vote drew near in Congress, fervent and dramatic telegrams were sent to direct the efforts of chapters in all parts of the nation.[39] And chapter members worked feverishly in the attempt to flood legislators with letters and telegrams opposing repeal of the vital provisions of the Neutrality Act.[40]

But all the Committee's efforts were of no avail. The vital provisions of the Act were repealed on November 13, 1941. This defeat greatly discouraged many America First members.[41] The results, however, were not without their encouraging aspects for the Committee. The vote against

165

the Administration in both houses of Congress was larger than it had been on Lend-Lease. A shift of ten votes in the House of Representatives would have defeated the Administration measure. Those Congressmen who voted against the Administration represented approximately 50 per cent of the American voters. Among Representatives of twenty states a majority of those voting cast their votes against the President's proposal. The Administration even lost the votes of a few Southern Congressmen.[42] The margin of the Administration's victory was much too narrow to encourage any move for a declaration of war. Perhaps, even without the Japanese raid on Pearl Harbor, attacks on armed American merchant ships in the war zones would have resulted in an American declaration of war. But the closeness of the vote on revision of the Neutrality Act encouraged America First leaders to hope that the 1942 elections might give them sufficient strength in the House of Representatives to stop Administration steps toward war.

10 Politics and the Battle Against Intervention

FOR MANY the America First Committee was identified with opposition to President Roosevelt and the Democratic Party. A writer in the *New Republic* gave vent to a widely held view when he asserted: "The America First Committee was established at such a strategic preelection moment and backed by such an impressive list of anti-New Dealers that it gave the impression of having been organized not so much to oppose Roosevelt's foreign policy as to oppose Roosevelt on the basis of his foreign policy." [1] There is ample evidence to indicate that political motives were important in the strength of the Committee. It is significant that R. Douglas Stuart, Jr., visited the Republican National Convention in Philadelphia in June, 1940, in his early efforts to expand his college group into a national noninterventionist organization. While at Philadelphia he consulted with Senator Robert A. Taft and others and found them sympathetic with his plans.[2]

A majority of those with political affiliations on the executive committee of America First were Republicans. Hanford MacNider, vice-chairman of America First and a

167

member of the executive committee, had long been active in the Republican Party. He was a delegate to the Republican National Convention of 1924. He was endorsed for presidential nomination by the Republican State Convention in Iowa in 1940. His services to the Republican Party were rewarded with political appointments by both President Calvin Coolidge and President Herbert Hoover.[3] General Thomas S. Hammond took an active part in the unsuccessful campaign to elect Wendell Willkie in 1940.[4] General Wood supported President Roosevelt in 1932 and approved much of the early New Deal. In 1936 he again voted for Roosevelt. Nevertheless, a competent article in *Fortune* in 1938 declared that General Wood was a Republican. By 1936 his ardor for the New Deal had begun to cool and his vote for Roosevelt in that year was cast "doubtfully." It is significant that his opposition to aspects of the Roosevelt administration began to develop *before* there were substantial foreign policy bases for his opposition.[5] In 1940 he supported Wendell Willkie—ostensibly in opposition to the third term and the President's foreign policy. Indeed, one reason General Wood in August, 1940, temporarily reversed his decision to serve as chairman of the Committee appears to have been his fear that the organization might handicap Willkie's chances for election.[6] Mrs. Janet Ayer Fairbank, vice-chairman of America First and member of the executive committee, had been a member of the executive committee of the Democratic National Committee in 1919. She was an Illinois Democratic National Committeewoman from 1924 to 1928.[7] She still considered herself a Democrat in 1941.[8] Nevertheless, she campaigned for Alfred M. Landon against President Roosevelt in 1936 and supported Willkie in 1940.[9] Again, it is significant that she began opposition to the Roosevelt administration *before* the real clash with the Administration on foreign policy issues developed. In contrast, Stuart appears to have approved the New Deal and voted for Willkie in 1940 largely on the basis of the foreign policy issue.[10]

A majority of the members of the national committee of America First with political affiliations also were Republicans. Alice Roosevelt Longworth, daughter of Theodore Roosevelt, was a member of the Board of Counsellors of the Women's Division of the Republican National Committee in 1932. In 1936 she was a delegate from Ohio to the Republican National Convention.[11] Mrs. Ruth Hanna Simms had been a Republican National Committeewoman from 1924 to 1928, a Republican member of Congress from Illinois from 1929 to 1931, and a Republican nominee for the United States Senate in 1930.[12] Mrs. Ellen French Vanderbilt Fitz Simons was a member of the Republican National Committee from 1930 to 1944 and a member of the Republican National Executive Committee from 1936 to 1944. She was also Eastern vice-chairman of the Republican National Committee from 1940 to 1944.[13] William L. Hutcheson was in charge of the Labor Division of the National Republican Party in 1932 and 1936.[14] Among other members of the America First national committee who were active in the Republican Party were William R. Castle, Frank O. Lowden, Louis J. Taber, Mrs.

Florence Kahn, Thomas N. McCarter, Isaac Pennypacker, H. L. Stuart, Sterling Morton, Edward L. Ryerson, Jr., and Charles Francis Adams.[15]

In addition there were on the national committee members of the Democratic Party who had been dropped by the wayside by the Roosevelt administration. Notable in this category were General Hugh S. Johnson, former head of the National Recovery Administration of the early New Deal, and George N. Peek, former head of the original Agricultural Adjustment Administration.[16] Whatever influence their political demise may have had upon their position in the foreign policy debate of 1940–1941, it is not likely that it inhibited any desires they had to oppose the Roosevelt administration on the basis of its foreign policy.

Among the multitude of Republicans who served as speakers or advisors for the America First Committee were Philip La Follette, Gerald P. Nye, Karl Mundt, Hamilton Fish, and Dewey Short.

Abundant evidence suggesting partisan bases for America First strength was also to be found in local chapters throughout the country. Indeed, Earl Jeffrey, the leading field representative of America First, had been a former campaign worker for Hoover in 1928 and for Landon in 1936.[17] In referring to his efforts to organize America First in Indianapolis early in 1941 he wrote: "Am bearing in mind non-partisan aspect, but lacking any detailed lists of backers must work thru sources generally against FDR to find proper 'non-partisan friends.' " [18]

Lansing Hoyt, chairman of America First in Milwaukee

and later for the whole state of Wisconsin, was at the same time Milwaukee County Republican chairman. Indeed, much to the dismay of Stuart, Hoyt even used the same office and telephone number for both groups.[19] Monte Appel, head of America First in St. Paul, had been state chairman for Robert A. Taft in Minnesota.[20] J. D. Holtzermann, preconvention campaign manager for Thomas E. Dewey in Minnesota in 1940, was the sparkplug of the America First chapter in Minneapolis.[21] D. C. MacDonald, executive secretary of the America First chapter at Grand Forks, North Dakota, was also chairman of the Republican Party Central Committee for the county.[22] Frederic A. Chase, who became executive secretary of America First in Southern California in August, 1941, had been active in the Republican Party and did publicity work for Hiram Johnson's campaign in 1940.[23] John B. Gordon, executive vice-chairman of the chapter in Pittsburgh, Pennsylvania, was a member of the county Republican committee.[24] Perry W. Howard, head of the Charles A. Young Division of America First for Negroes, was very active in Republican politics and had been an organizer for Robert A. Taft in 1940.[25] C. C. Crowe, who tried unsuccessfully to organize a chapter in Birmingham, Alabama, was active in the Republican Party in that state.[26] J. Stanley Collins, chairman of the chapter in Richmond, Virginia, had connections with the Republican Party.[27] Herbert K. Hyde, who made a brief attempt to head the Committee in Oklahoma, was Republican candidate for the United States Senate in 1936.[28] His wife was an officer in the Republican Women's Club of Oklahoma City—as was Mrs. W. A. McKeever, treasurer of the America First chapter.[29] A multitude of other illustrations of Republican strength in the local America First organization could easily be cited.

Much of the criticism of President Roosevelt and his Administration by America First spokesmen was directed specifically against his foreign policy. But many speakers directed attacks upon Roosevelt himself, upon the New Deal, and upon the Democratic Party. Just when criticism degenerates into petty partisan politics is not always easily determined. But political partisanship was clearly evident in many speeches at America First meetings.

DESPITE EVIDENCE of political bases for its strength, the national leaders of America First did exert genuine efforts to make the Committee nonpartisan. In letters which he wrote in the summer of 1940 to garner support for the proposed organization, R. Douglas Stuart, Jr., repeatedly indicated his desire that the organization should be nonpartisan.[30] In this early period they purposely refrained from inviting political office holders to become members of the sponsoring committee.[31] Late in 1940 Stuart asserted: "I quit when this becomes a purely anti-Roosevelt organization." [32]

Though in a minority, there were numerous Democrats associated with the America First Committee. Mrs. Fairbank had been a Democrat and General Wood had voted for Roosevelt twice.[33] Chester Bowles, an important member of the national committee, was a Democrat and later became a Democratic Governor of Connecticut.[34] Otto Case, a member of the national committee, was a Democratic office holder—the only member of the national committee to hold a political office at that time. He was State Treasurer in the state of Washington. Mrs. Burton K. Wheeler and Mrs. Bennett Champ Clark, wives of Democratic United States Senators, were both on the national committee. Other Democrats on the national committee included Irvin S. Cobb, Samuel Hopkins Adams, Clarence E. Manion, General Hugh S. Johnson, and George N. Peek.[35]

Prominent among Democrats who served as advisors or speakers for America First were Samuel B. Pettengill, former Democratic Congressman from Indiana; Rush Holt, former United States Senator from West Virginia; and Senators Burton K. Wheeler, Bennett Champ Clark, and D. Worth Clark.[36]

Nor was it impossible to find Democrats among leaders of local chapters. Both the chairman and the secretary of the Albuquerque chapter were Democrats.[37] Mrs. Fairbank was head of America First in Illinois and Iowa.[38] Otto Case was active as chairman of America First in the state of Washington.[39] Mrs. Bennett Champ Clark was chairman of the chapter in Washington, D.C., and Mrs. Wheeler was treasurer.[40] Mrs. Katrina McCormick Barnes, an active worker in the Washington, D.C., chapter, had supported the New Deal.[41] Additional illustrations of Democratic leaders of local chapters of America First could also be cited.

The Republican Party was by no means everywhere eager to join hands with America First. There is some evidence indicating Republican Party coolness toward America First in Maine, Indiana, and even Illinois.[42]

While many individual members played active roles in the campaign, the America First Committee as an organization endeavored to be nonpartisan in the campaign of 1940. General Wood, however, did hope that the Committee's full-page newspaper advertisements in October, 1940, would help to inject the foreign policy issue into the campaign.[43] Some of the Committee's advertisements, while reasserting the nonpartisan character of America First, urged voters to support candidates in the election, "regardless of party, who stand for defense at home, and, by their acts as well as by their words oppose war in Europe or Asia." [44]

John T. Flynn asked the America First Committee to sponsor a national radio broadcast in which he proposed to oppose the election of President Roosevelt but would not advocate the election of Wendell Willkie.[45] At the executive committee meeting on November 1, 1940, Clay Judson strongly objected to America First sponsorship of the broadcast. As a consequence the executive committee unanimously adopted a resolution declining to sponsor Flynn's broadcast and declaring: "It shall be the policy of this Committee to avoid influencing or furthering the success of any political party, or the election of any candidate for office, including presidential and vice-presidential electors." [46] Clay Judson further elaborated upon his position in a letter to Stuart:

174

Politics

The particular questions with which it [America First Committee] has been most concerned, such as the furnishing of aid to Great Britain (short of war), have not been partisan questions. In fact, there is little to choose between the declarations of the two candidates for President on this particular subject. I am advised that the officers and Directors of the Committee feel that its greatest influence may be exercised after the election. By reason of the developments in the European war and public opinion in this country during the past summer, the Committee was organized and became immediately active in September. It was only a coincidence that this activity happened to coincide with the last days of a presidential election. Actually the Committee is concerned with the establishment of a principle and not with the election of candidates.[47]

After the election the Committee staff continued its endeavors to make the America First Committee nonpartisan. The initial America First efforts to organize local chapters began after the November, 1940, elections. Robert L. Bliss, national director of the organization of new chapters, and Joseph R. Boldt, Jr., assistant director of organization and later responsible for forming America First chapters in the East, both insisted that chapters be nonpartisan. They urged new chapters to secure their leaders, sponsors, and members from both political parties.[48] Frequently special efforts were made to have both major parties represented on speaking platforms at America First rallies.[49]

THERE WAS increasing agitation within America First chapters during 1941 for more positive action in the fight against intervention than merely writing letters to the President and Congressmen. As the Committee suffered defeat after defeat in its campaign, there was increased support for new

175

and different methods for making America First strength felt in Washington, D.C.

There was, for example, considerable agitation for a "March on Washington" which would be of such imposing proportions as to impress government officials with the strength of noninterventionist sentiment. Small groups made trips to Washington, D.C., from chapters in the East.[50] Even the national organization toyed with the idea and variations of it. However, after consultation with noninterventionist Congressmen, Committee representatives in Washington, D.C., and chapter leaders, the idea for a mass march was dropped. They believed that such a venture would have to be of truly gigantic proportions to be effective. They feared such a large group might actually discredit the Committee rather than advance its principles.[51] A plan for a Peoples' Lobby proposed by Andrae Nordskog was considered by the executive committee in the summer of 1941. This proposal called for representatives from each chapter to go to Washington, D.C., as an organized lobby. This plan was also rejected—in part because of lack of confidence in Nordskog's qualities.[52] The Committee did, however, decide to stage a gigantic rally in Washington, D.C., as a substitute for a march on Washington. Lindbergh was slated to be the main speaker. The rally was tentatively scheduled for the last week in September, 1941. Even this plan was canceled when the seriousness of the repercussions from Lindbergh's Des Moines speech became apparent.[53]

There were some followers of America First who believed President Roosevelt should have been impeached. The South Shore unit of America First in New York and the Yonkers, New York, chapter both passed resolutions in October, 1941, urging America First support for the impeachment of the President.[54] A youth group in the America First Committee of Southern California agitated for impeachment despite the objections of officers of the Committee.[55] Norman H. Wilson, one of the leaders in a concerted drive to stimulate support for the impeachment of the President, was one of the signers of the application to establish an America First chapter at Yonkers, New York.[56] Other chapter leaders and staff members wished the President could have been impeached.[57] Even Stuart was interested enough to request a report from the New York chapter on the response which Wilson got to his petition for the impeachment of the President.[58] A meeting of 118 chapter representatives called by national headquarters in Chicago on July 12, 1941, passed a resolution urging the removal of Secretary of the Navy Frank Knox. They urged this course on the grounds that Secretary Knox had defied the Constitution by advocating an undeclared naval war.[59]

Nevertheless, the America First national headquarters staff and most chapter leaders consistently discouraged talk of impeachment of President Roosevelt by followers of the Committee. In most instances this policy appears to have been based upon the conviction that political conditions and the legal requirements of the Constitution made impeachment a practical impossibility. In their view it

Politics

would have been poor strategy for the Committee to sponsor the movement.[60] One report quoted Wilson to the effect that America First opposition was an important factor
in preventing the movement for impeachment of the President from gaining ground.[61]

Despite local agitation, the America First Committee
rejected the "March on Washington" and the movement
for impeachment of the President as positive courses of
action in the battle against intervention. Instead, the Committee decided late in 1941 to fight intervention by taking
an active part in the elections of 1942.

THE ANNOUNCEMENT on December 1, 1941, that the America First Committee would play an active role in the 1942
elections was the culmination of a slowly developing trend
in the views of leaders, members, and supporters of the
Committee. America First advertisements in October, 1940,
urged voters to support candidates who favored building
defenses and who opposed involvement in war in Europe
and Asia.[62] After his election defeat Wendell Willkie gave
his support to President Roosevelt's foreign policy. Early
in 1941 Willkie asserted that his prediction in the 1940
campaign that America might be at war by April, 1941, if
Roosevelt were elected had been merely "a bit of campaign oratory." This candid statement (frequently distorted by his critics) infuriated noninterventionists. Many
felt that they had been tricked in that election. They believed the election of 1940 had not given the American

178

people an opportunity to express their views clearly on American foreign policy.[63]

Jay C. Hormel, then a member of the executive committee of America First, as early as January, 1941, urged that the Committee organize in every Congressional district to re-elect noninterventionist Congressmen regardless of political affiliations.[64] At the same time Philip La Follette was beginning to refer to the "War Party" and speculate on the possibility of a breakdown of old party alinements.[65] Senator Burton K. Wheeler in May, 1941, predicted that in 1944 "a new party will have to spring up, composed of Democrats and Republicans—one that will not break faith with the American people after election." [66] Both Senator Wheeler and Chester Bowles believed that a new political party would have to be developed in the postwar period to provide a democratic alternative to the twin threats of communism and fascism in America. They viewed Lindbergh as an excellent leader for such a postwar group. Bowles suggested that Lindbergh should run for the Senate in Minnesota in 1942 so that he would be in an important position for the future.[67]

Colonel Lindbergh created a furor by an address at an America First rally in Philadelphia on May 29, 1941, when he called for "new leadership" for America. He explained later that neither he nor the America First Committee wanted to change the leadership "by anything but constitutional methods." [68]

General Robert E. Wood in a radio address on July 7,

179

1941, gave a concrete preview of the course America First policy was to follow:

I believe with Colonel Lindbergh that we must change our policies and our leadership. And when I say that, I mean in a strictly constitutional way. We have a Congressional election in 1942. Regardless of party, every interventionist in the House and every interventionist senator who comes up for election should be defeated. And while our President remains in office until 1944, if the will of the people in this matter of an European war is expressed strongly enough in the election of 1942, he may see fit to remove some of the leading war mongers in his cabinet.[69]

General Wood again expressed this view at a meeting of America First chapter chairmen in Chicago a few days later.[70] The *Chicago Tribune* promptly took up the cry and urged the America First Committee to begin at once to prepare for the 1942 elections.[71]

At the meeting of the America First executive committee on August 11, 1941, General Wood raised the issue of whether the Committee should make "non-political endorsements of non-interventionist candidates" in elections. The question was referred to a subcommittee for further study. The subcommittee consisted of General Wood, Clay Judson, Samuel B. Pettengill, and Richard A. Moore.[72]

As the weeks passed the conviction that America First should take an active part in elections continued to spread. Ruth Sarles, America First representative in Washington, D.C., urged the Committee to take such a course. She viewed political action as the only remaining effective means of stopping the increasing strength of the interventionists.[73] Without specifically naming the America First Committee, the New York *Daily News* called for the formation of an America First Party to oppose an interventionist World First Party.[74] An America First bulletin in October, 1941, denied that America First was interested in partisan politics. However, it urged members to vote in the primary elections and the general elections of 1942.[75]

In the midst of the battle against repeal of the Neutrality Act, the America First Committee took a major official step in the direction of political action. A meeting of representatives of America First chapters was held in Washington, D.C., on November 1, 1941. At this meeting Isaac A. Pennypacker introduced a resolution which was passed unanimously. This resolution declared:

We, the Chairmen and delegates of one hundred nineteen chapters of the America First Committee . . . do *individually* pledge ourselves to work and vote in the 1942 primaries and general election for every member of the Senate and House of Representatives, irrespective of Party, who votes [to] retain provisions of the present Neutrality Act which prohibit the entry of American flag ships into combat areas or belligerent ports; and

We do further pledge ourselves to work and vote against the renomination and re-election in 1942 of every member of the Senate and House of Representatives who votes to repeal the provisions of the present Neutrality Act, which prohibit the entry of American flag ships into combat areas or belligerent ports.[76]

It is significant that this resolution declared that the vote on repeal of the Neutrality Act was to be the determining criterion for America First support or opposition in the

181

1942 elections. Coming while the debate on the Neutrality Act was still in progress, the Committee obviously hoped in this manner to bolster opposition in Congress to repeal of the vital provisions of the Neutrality Act. The keynote speaker at this Washington meeting of chapter representatives was, appropriately enough, an unemployed politician, Philip La Follette. In his address he made frequent use of the terms "War Party" and "American Party." He closed his oration with a burst of histrionics reminiscent of many political convention addresses: "We leave this hall tonight with our coats off, our sleeves rolled up. We are headed for the 1942 elections. We have only two planks in our platform: The Declaration of Independence and the Constitution. Our motto: 'I am an American.' " [77]

Later in November, 1941, General Wood sent a letter to all chapter chairmen to learn their views on the proposed program of nonpartisan political support for noninterventionist candidates.[78] There was disagreement on the subject among members of a few chapters.[79] However, there appear to have been no America First chapters which flatly opposed political action by America First. The overwhelming majority of the chapters gave their approval to the proposed plan.[80]

A meeting of the national committee to discuss the future program of America First was called for November 28, 1941. National committee members who were unable to attend were requested to express their views in letters to Wood.[81] General Wood also secured the advice of Congressional leaders on the matter. At the meeting on November 28, the national committee unanimously approved a motion that "a non-partisan political program should be undertaken as soon as those adjustments which are made necessary by law have been effected." General Wood was authorized to appoint a political advisory board to assist the Committee in carrying out the political program. This board was to include Congressmen and Senators from both parties and political leaders outside of Congress.[82] On December 1, 1941, the America First Committee made a public announcement of its decision to take an active part in the 1942 elections. In this announcement the Committee declared:

This program will be undertaken in a spirit free from partisanship and without regard to the political affiliations of the candidates. It will not be used as an attempt to build a third political party. . . . The America First Committee . . . now feels it to be its duty to enable its members in any state or district to . . . mobilize their supporters behind those public officials who oppose further steps to involve us in war. . . . It is a step which has been made necessary and inevitable by the President's persistent efforts to deny to the American people any voice in the gravest issue which has ever confronted them. This program will be undertaken in accordance with the best traditions of American democracy and with the knowledge that it will contribute to the preservation of representative government and the cause of freedom in America.[83]

In spite of discussion by individuals of re-forming party lines under new banners, all available Committee sources indicate that there were no immediate plans in America First to form a third party.[84]

Though the overwhelming majority of leaders of the

America First Committee approved the decision, important members of the national committee seriously questioned the wisdom of the move. William R. Castle expressed his disapproval of the policy early in November, 1941.[85] Mrs. Bennett Champ Clark viewed the fanfare given the decision as "an unseasoned and brash procedure." [86] General Hugh S. Johnson had been an inactive and not always contented member of the national committee of America First. He had remained in the organization in part because of his personal friendship with General Wood. But upon the announcement of the decision to enter the elections of 1942 General Johnson resigned from the Committee.[87] Mrs. Fitz Simons also resigned from the national committee. She believed that as vice-chairman of the Republican national committee she could not be a member of an organization engaged in nonpartisan political activity which conceivably would be directed against some Republican candidates. However in her resignation she reaffirmed her approval of the America First Committee and its views. She gave no publicity to her resignation at the time.[88] More serious was the resignation of Hanford MacNider, a member of the executive and national committees of America First and a vice-chairman of the Committee until October, 1941. He based his resignation upon his unwillingness to support Democratic candidates even if they were noninterventionists. He wrote:

I am a Republican, a rabid Republican, and I don't know how to be non-partisan politically. Those members of Congress who have supported the domestic policies of the New Deal—and

184

they are what have led us into our present desperate situation—
are just as undesirable and obnoxious to me as those who have
supported the foreign policies of this Administration. I believe
that the only hope for the nation's future lies in the Republican
party.[89]

This partisanship in his letter of resignation is so extreme
that it encourages the suspicion that he may have been
using this more as an excuse than as a reason for his resignation. This disaffection re-emphasized the fact that the
heterogeneity of Committee membership made it extremely difficult for America First to shift from a negative
to a more positive course of action.

Committee leaders began late in August, 1941, to study
the legal problems involved if America First engaged in
political activity. During November increased attention
was given to this matter. After the decision by the national
committee on November 28, the full attention of the national headquarters was given to the problem. Clay Judson, an attorney and legal advisor in the executive committee; Richard A. Moore, a lawyer and assistant national
director of America First; and Earl Jeffrey, America First
field representative and former Republican campaign
worker—all prepared memoranda on the problem.[90] Ruth
Sarles, head of the America First Research Bureau, had
had experience in the political activities of pacifist organizations. She drew upon this experience to make recommendations to America First.[91] James Lipsig, a worker in
the Research Bureau, had been on the Committee on Election Laws and Minority Parties of the American Civil Liberties Union and was law secretary for the American Labor

Party in 1940. He claimed to have handled over sixty election cases in New York and to have defeated both Tammany Hall and the Republicans.[92] His advice was sought by America First national headquarters and early in December, 1941, he was brought to Chicago to help work out plans for the reorganization of the Committee.[93] Noninterventionist politicians both in and out of Congress were consulted for advice.[94] General Wood announced that the Committee would probably "dissolve as a corporation and become an unincorporated association." He thought the reorganization would be completed by the first part of 1942.[95]

Plans were initiated to mobilize local chapters in the political effort. They intended to divide the organization into congressional districts. A Club Plan was developed to provide small units in districts where it was not possible to organize more elaborately.[96] Actually some chapters had begun to organize by political units before the decision to enter the 1942 elections was made. The chapters at Boston, Massachusetts, and Buffalo, New York, began to organize by wards and voting districts early in the summer of 1941.[97] Other chapters and units in New York began reorganization by wards by November, 1941.[98] The executive secretary of America First in Southern California planned reorganization.[99] Lansing Hoyt, chairman of America First in Wisconsin, and Milwaukee County Republican chairman, worked vigorously to insure noninterventionist control of the Republican Party in Wisconsin.[100] When he announced his intention to run for Congress he was assured of America First support.[101] In Colorado, America First national headquarters supplied both personnel and money to help elect a noninterventionist candidate for Congress in a special election. The leaders of the efficient Colorado America First organization entered the fourth district and actively worked for the election of a noninterventionist candidate, Robert F. Rockwell. America First representatives ceased their efforts as soon as the Japanese attacked Pearl Harbor, but the candidate they had backed was elected later in December, 1941.[102] General Wood announced that the America First Committee would give its support to Senator C. Wayland Brooks of Illinois for reelection.[103]

It is not possible to determine just what effect the America First Committee might have had if it had participated in the election campaigns of 1942. General Wood expressed the opinion that if America First could unseat only a few interventionists, the noninterventionists would have control of a majority in the House of Representatives.[104] A shift of ten votes in the House would have prevented repeal of the vital provisions of the Neutrality Act in November, 1941.[105] According to a Gallup poll in the fall of 1941, 16 per cent of American voters would have supported candidates of a hypothetical "keep-out-of-war party" led by Lindbergh, Wheeler, Nye, and others. This would have been a larger vote than any third party had secured since 1924.[106] America First, however, did not intend to form a third party. Since it proposed to give nonpartisan support to the candidates of the established political parties, America First strength might have been sufficient to swing some close elections.

Whatever might have been the results, the Japanese attack on Pearl Harbor on December 7, 1941, took the decision of war or peace out of American hands. By the time the 1942 elections were held, the United States was engaged in an all-out war against the Axis. The America First Committee had long since been dissolved. In subsequent elections many noninterventionists fell by the wayside in election defeats. These casualties included Senators Burton K. Wheeler, Gerald P. Nye, Robert La Follette, and C. Wayland Brooks; Representative Hamilton Fish, and others. Noninterventionist efforts did not prove politically fatal for some. Chester Bowles became head of the Office of Price Administration and was later elected Governor of Connecticut.[107] Clare Hoffman continued in office. Representative Karl Mundt moved up to the United States Senate. Other noninterventionists in Congress managed to hold on. Philip C. Jessup, a sponsor of the Norfolk, Connecticut, and New York America First chapters,[108] later became American Ambassador at Large. Gerald L. K. Smith (never a member of the America First Committee) formed an America First Party in 1943. Though it undoubtedly secured support from some former followers of the America First Committee, it had no direct connection with the Committee and was completely ineffective.[109] The America First Committee as an organization was prevented by the attack on Pearl Harbor from ever testing its political strength at the polls.

188

II   Pearl Harbor

THOUGH America First opposed participation in war with Japan before Pearl Harbor, this possibility received relatively little attention from the Committee and its spokesmen. Nearly all of the America First Committee's energies were focused against intervention in the European war. During its history America First leaders, like most Americans, gave only secondary attention to the Far Eastern situation.

A few statements by America First spokesmen endorsed a "get-tough" policy for the United States in the Far East—but these were isolated exceptions. One writer said that Charles A. Lindbergh would have had no serious misgivings about a war with Japan providing Europe was not involved. Lindbergh thought America could easily win such a war.[1] He criticized the government's failure to construct adequate bases in the Pacific and said America should either have fortified the Philippines or evacuated them.[2] In July, 1941, Senator Burton K. Wheeler approved freezing Japanese assets in the United States to "slow up Japan from an economic standpoint and call their bluff so

189

they will not start anything." [3] The chairman of the chapter in Columbus, Ohio, believed the United States should fight a war with Japan.[4] These, however, were exceptions to the general views of America First supporters. And both Wheeler and Lindbergh opposed a war with Japan before Pearl Harbor.[5]

Virtually all the America First Committee leaders and members opposed American participation in a war in the Pacific before the Japanese attack on Pearl Harbor. They were convinced that the interests of the United States in the Far East were not of sufficient importance to justify a war with Japan. A few expressed the opinion that Japan had as much right to dominance in Asia as the United States had to dominance in the Western Hemisphere. Many America First leaders insisted that war with Japan would only be to preserve Britain's imperialistic and undemocratic domination of Asia. Some America First spokesmen in the last half of 1941 feared that the Roosevelt administration was seeking to get the United States into the war through the Asiatic back door. An America First advertisement in December, 1940, declared:

We have no real quarrel with Japan. We have no conceivable stake in Asia worth the terrific cost of a long-distance struggle with Japan.

We sympathize with China. But we must not plunge America in war across 6,000 miles of the Pacific for sentimental reasons. And it is certainly not our mission to act as a knight-errant in Asia.

There will be no "emergencies" that necessitate war with Japan unless we make them ourselves. For peace with the United States is a stark necessity for Japan.[6]

Opposition to war in the Pacific was often combined with denunciations of British imperialism. A writer in the New York chapter publication wrote:

The battle in Asia is Britain's battle—and a battle not for democracy, but to continue her hold on 300,000,000 people in India, millions more in Malay and other territories of Asia, to say nothing of a hundred million in Africa. She is parked there for the gold, the oil, the rubber, the silver, the diamonds, the rich supplies which her capitalists own there—which belong to the peoples of those countries, but which Britain has stolen. Yet ... America ... will send our sons to Asia ... to enable the British empire to perpetuate its hold upon Asia.

Before any American blood is spent for democracy in Asia and the four freedoms there, we might ask when Britain is going to release the 30,000 political prisoners in India, and particularly the leader of the parliamentary party who is at this moment in jail.[7]

Sterling Morton reasoned that "after all, we want 'America for the Americans,' so perhaps they want 'Asia for the Asiatics.'"[8] Many America First spokesmen viewed America's trade with Japan as a basis for satisfactory relations.[9]

As relations with Japan grew more strained late in the summer of 1941 the America First Committee directed more attention to the Far Eastern question. The Committee expressed the fear that the Atlantic Charter released by President Roosevelt and Prime Minister Churchill in August, 1941, was a cover for secret agreements.[10] A writer in the New York chapter publication insisted that: "It was beyond a doubt, about this mess in the Orient that Roosevelt and Churchill met in the Atlantic. . . . They were unquestionably conferring about the manner in which Amer-

191

ica will take up Britain's battle to save her dictatorship over India in Asia and the manner in which Britain will 'come to our aid.' " [11]

On August 11, 1941, General Wood raised the question of the position of America First on the Far Eastern issue at an America First executive committee meeting. The executive committee expressed unanimous opposition to war in the Pacific by the United States except in case of attack. It adopted the following resolution:

RESOLVED, that the America First Committee opposes war with Japan as it has consistently opposed our entry into the war with Germany. This Committee believes in adequate defense of our own nation, a defense so strong that no attack would ever be made upon us. Involvement in war on the Atlantic would make more difficult adequate defense on the Pacific. Involvement in war on the Pacific would make more difficult adequate defense on the Atlantic. In the absence of attack on this country we should maintain peace. [12]

The possibility of a complete Nazi victory over the Soviet Union in 1941 raised the question of the effect of a Russian defeat upon the balance of power in the Far East. The chairman of a San Francisco chapter insisted that "if Great Britain can substitute us in the place of Russia to offset any threat from Japan then her Oriental treasure chest will be safe at our expense." [13]

When relations between the United States and Japan neared the breaking point late in November, 1941, America First again focused attention on the issue. The day before the Japanese attacked Pearl Harbor the New York chapter under John T. Flynn asserted:

The Administration, and the Administration alone, will be completely responsible for any breakdown in relations with Japan. The Administration has taken it upon itself to demand actions from Japan that in no way concern the national interests of the United States. None of our territorial possessions are in any way involved.[14]

Specific plans for opposing war in the Pacific, however, never got beyond the talking stage in America First national headquarters.[15] The America First Committee did not conduct any concerted campaign to prevent war with Japan. Its main attention was still primarily directed toward the Atlantic when Japanese bombers on December 7, 1941, wiped out the Committee's *raison d'être*. As Professor Thomas A. Bailey correctly asserted: "The torpedoes that sank the American battleships in Pearl Harbor also sank 'America Firstism.' "[16]

TRUE TO ITS pledges, the America First Committee ceased all noninterventionist activity after the Japanese attack.[17] America First national headquarters released the following statement on the evening of December 7, 1941:

The America First Committee urges all those who have subscribed to its principles to give their support to the war effort of this country until the conflict *with Japan* is brought to a successful conclusion. In this war the America First Committee pledges its aid to the President as commander in chief of the armed forces of the United States.[18]

Chapters were advised to postpone all scheduled rallies.[19] The Committee ceased distribution of noninterventionist literature.[20]

But the national headquarters statement was deliberately phrased to leave the door open for possible continued opposition to participation in the European war.[21] Chapter leaders were admonished to make no statements concerning the future of America First until after the national committee met.[22] Chapter leaders and noninterventionist Congressmen and Senators were consulted for their views concerning the Committee's course. The overwhelming majority of chapter leaders believed America First should not dissolve completely. Most of them recommended that the organization be kept intact for use later on some other public issue.[23] The Congressmen and Senators consulted advised against a hasty decision. Most of them, including Senators Robert M. La Follette, Jr., Hiram Johnson, and D. Worth Clark, and Congressmen Karl Mundt and Paul Shafer, believed the Committee should continue in some form. Their views were probably influenced in part by hope for support at the polls. Senator Robert A. Taft believed the Committee should dissolve.[24]

The America First national committee met in Chicago on December 11, 1941. A minority of the members present at the meeting—including Edwin S. Webster, Jr., Amos R. E. Pinchot, and Robert R. Young—believed "some method of adjourning was preferable to complete liquidation." [25] But the majority of those present favored complete dissolution. Those who took this stand included General Wood, Clay Judson, John T. Flynn, Mrs. Fairbank, Sterling Morton, and others. They reasoned that the Committee had been identified with opposition to participation in the war and continued activity even on different issues would be subject to suspicion and criticism.[26] The majority at this meeting approved the following public statement:

Our principles were right. Had they been followed, war could have been avoided. No good purpose can now be served by considering what might have been, had our objectives been attained. . . . We are at war. Today, though there may be many important subsidiary considerations, the primary objective is . . . victory.

While the executive branch of the government will take charge of the prosecution of the war, the fundamental rights of American citizens under our Constitution and Bill of Rights must be respected. The long range aims and policies of our country must be determined by the people through Congress. We hope that secret treaties committing America to imperial-istic aims or vast burdens in other parts of the world shall be scrupulously avoided to the end that this nation shall become the champion of a just and lasting peace.

The period of democratic debate on the issue of entering the war is over; the time for military action is here. Therefore, the America First Committee has determined immediately to cease all functions and to dissolve as soon as that can legally be done. And finally, it urges all those who have followed its lead to give their full support to the war effort of the nation, until peace is attained.[27]

Then the dreary task of dismantling the organization began. Because of the expensive campaign against repeal of the Neutrality Act, the Japanese attack caught national headquarters with a deficit of approximately twelve thousand dollars. But contributions, receipts from local chapters, and the willingness of William H. Regnery to write off the unpaid portion of his advance enabled the Committee to close its books free of debt.[28] Local chapters were directed to terminate all activities and send their records and membership files to national headquarters.[29] A few groups were reluctant to dismantle their units but these were the exceptions.[30] By February, 1942, the process of dissolution was essentially complete.[31] The America First corporation, however, was not dissolved legally until April 22, 1942,[32] to prevent use of the Committee's name by other groups.[33]

America First leaders actively supported the nation's war effort. General Wood and General Hammond served during the war with Army Ordnance in Chicago. General Wood later served overseas with the Air Force. Both Stuart and MacNider volunteered and served with distinction overseas in the Army. When Lindbergh's offer to serve was rejected, he was hired by Henry Ford and, as a civilian, tested aircraft under combat conditions in the Southwest Pacific. Many young men who had been on the headquarters staff or leaders of local chapters volunteered their services to the armed forces.[34] Here and there former local members continued anti-war activities [35] but they were the exceptions.

IT IS NOT possible to determine with complete accuracy the effects of the efforts of the America First Committee upon the history of the United States. America's course in 1940–1941 was the product of a complex maze of forces and influences inside and outside of the nation. Undoubtedly events in Europe and Asia had far greater influence upon the subsequent course of the United States than the efforts of mass pressure groups on either side of the foreign policy debate. The effect of its efforts cannot be separated with accuracy from the effects of noninterventionist efforts not channeled through America First. The historian cannot conduct controlled experiments to determine what would have happened if America First had never been formed.

The America First Committee obviously failed to achieve its primary objective of keeping the United States out of the European war. The Committee was not even able to defeat any major Administration foreign policy proposals actually put to the test in Congress. During the last third of 1941 the attacks on America First and its leaders received much more publicity than the Committee's noninterventionist efforts.

Nevertheless, the America First Committee did mobilize noninterventionist strength and help make that strength felt in Washington, D.C. Opposition in Congress to the Administration's foreign policy not only remained strong but increased during 1941. The arms embargo was repealed in the fall of 1939 by a vote of 63 to 30 in the Senate and 243 to 172 in the House of Representatives.[36] But draft extension was passed in the summer of 1941 by the House of Representatives by a margin of only one vote. And less than a month before the attack on Pearl Harbor the vital provisions of the Neutrality Act were repealed by a vote of only 50 to 37 in the Senate and 212 to 194 in the House of Representatives.[37]

More important, the noninterventionist strength, which the America First Committee and other groups repre-

sented, definitely affected the strategy of President Franklin D. Roosevelt. The accounts of Roosevelt's conduct of
American foreign relations are replete with references to
his sensitivity to noninterventionist strength. He was determined to avoid an "irrevocable act" which would give the
noninterventionists an opportunity to defeat him.[38] Robert E. Sherwood wrote: "The isolationists' long and savage
campaign against the President . . . had failed to blind
American public opinion to the huge accumulation of
events, but it certainly had exerted an important effect on
Roosevelt himself; whatever the peril, he was not going to
lead the country into war—he was going to wait to be
pushed in." [39] President Roosevelt decided not to seek
Congressional authorization for convoying in the spring of
1941 because he feared defeat at the hands of noninterventionists.[40] He did not press for authority to send selectees
outside of the Western Hemisphere when Congressional
leaders informed him he would be defeated on the question. A witness at this conference reported that this information evoked from the President a verbal lashing of
America First and its activities.[41] Despite pressure from
Secretary of War Stimson and others, President Roosevelt's
fear of noninterventionist strength was at least one factor
which prevented him from putting the issue of war or peace
squarely before Congress.[42] The President's general strategy was established before the America First Committee
was formed. But the efforts of the America First Committee undoubtedly helped to discourage him from moving
further and faster to help Britain defeat Hitler.

198

Persons close to Roosevelt felt the noninterventionists had fought the President very nearly to a standstill late in 1941. Sherwood wrote:

The truth was that, as the world situation became more desperately critical, and as the limitless peril came closer and closer to the United States, isolationist sentiment became ever more strident in expression and aggressive in action, and Roosevelt was relatively powerless to combat it. He had said everything "short of war" that could be said. He had no more tricks left. The hat from which he had pulled so many rabbits was empty.[43]

Secretary of War Stimson wrote that "the impasse into which America had thought herself in 1941 might have continued indefinitely if that had been the will of the Axis." Stimson wrote that if that had happened "the President would have had to shoulder a large share of the blame." [44] But a part of the "blame" would have to have been shared by the noninterventionists whose strength forced the President into his dilemma. And the America First Committee provided the most powerful vehicle for the expression, mobilization, and focusing of that noninterventionist strength.

NOTES

Notes

CHAPTER 1—THE GENESIS

1   Henry L. Stimson and McGeorge Bundy, *On Active Service: In Peace and War* (New York, 1947, 1948), 374–75; and *The Public Papers and Addresses of Franklin D. Roosevelt* (9 vols., New York, 1938–1941), VIII and IX.

2   Walter Johnson, *The Battle Against Isolation* (Chicago, 1944), 32, 41–42, and 56–57.

3   *Ibid.*, 63–71.

4   *Ibid.*, 59–60, 91–92.

5   *Ibid.*, 180–94.

6   *Ibid.*, 223–25.

7   Robert Edwin Bowers, "The American Peace Movement, 1933–41" (Unpublished Ph.D. dissertation, Department of History, University of Wisconsin, 1949), iv, 342–43.

8   Samuel Lubell, "Who Votes Isolationist and Why," *Harper's Magazine*, 202 (April, 1951), 30–31.

9   *Daily Worker* (New York), December 26, 1940; and Albert Horlings, "Who Are the Appeasers?," *New Republic*, 104 (January 27, 1941), 111.

10   *Future: The Magazine for Young Men* (March, 1941), 6; and interview with Stuart, April 6, 1949.

11   Undated draft of unaddressed telegram from Stuart to Potter Stewart, and telegram from G. P. Nye to Stuart, October 26, 1939, General Wood Papers, Chicago, Illinois; and letter to the author from Stuart, August 31, 1950.

12   R. D. Stuart, Jr., to the author, February 16, 1948; *St. Louis Post-Dispatch,* October 27, 1940; *Time,* 36 (December 23, 1940), 13; and a typewritten, undated, and unpublished confidential report on America First which was prepared—probably late in 1940—by Friends of Democracy, Inc., and loaned to the author. A petition circulated by the Yale Christian Association in the spring of 1940 appears to have arisen out of the discussions of the group of students of which Stuart was a member. Stuart had, however, little or nothing to do with the Yale Christian Association petition. *Yale Daily News,* May 25, 1940; and letter from Stuart to the author, August 31, 1950.

13   Stuart to author, February 16, 1948, and August 31, 1950; an unsigned, unaddressed mimeographed form letter sent from Stuart's address in New Haven, June 16, 1940, Wood MSS; and mimeographed form letter from W. W. Brown, G. W. Humphrey, Philip Peltz, R. S. Shriver, Potter Stewart, and R. D. Stuart, Jr., June 20, 1940, America First Papers, Hoover Library, Stanford, California.

14   Form letter from Stuart, Stewart, Bill Krebs, and Eugene Locke, June 22, 1940, and enclosed petitions, Wood MSS.

15   Stuart to the author, February 16, 1948; Kingman Brewster, Jr., to the author, March 28, 1948; *Future* (March, 1941), 6; Michael Sayers and Albert E. Kahn, *Sabotage! The Secret War Against America* (New York and London, 1942), 199; and Friends of Democracy confidential report on America First.

16   "General Robert E. Wood, President," *Fortune,* 17 (May, 1948), 104–8; *Current Biography,* 2 (May, 1941), 88–90; *St. Louis Post-Dispatch,* October 27, 1940; and *Who's Who in America,* 1948–1949, 2735.

17   Philip La Follette to Wood, June 22, 1940, Wood to La Follette, July 15, 1940, Wood to W. H. Regnery, July 15, 1940, Wood MSS; and *St. Louis Post-Dispatch,* October 27, 1940.

18   Wood to Philip La Follette, July 19, 1940, Wood MSS.

19   Stuart to author, February 16, 1948.

20   Wood to Stuart, June 20, 1940, Wood MSS.

21   Wood to J. T. McCutcheon, July 22, 1940, Wood MSS.

22   *St. Louis Post-Dispatch,* October 27, 1940; Wood to Stuart,

July 23, 1940, Stuart to Kingman Brewster, Jr., July 26, 1940, and W. H. Regnery to Wood, August 13, 1940, America First MSS.

23 *Future* (March, 1941), 6; and Stuart to B. K. Wheeler, July 20, 1940, America First MSS.
24 Edward Rickenbacker to Wood, July 29, 1940, Mrs. B. K. Wheeler to Wood, August 2, 1940, General H. S. Johnson to Wood, August 2, 1940, and Stuart to Wood, August 3, 1940, America First MSS.
25 Stuart to Wood, August 23, 1940, America First MSS.
26 Stuart to Wood, August 14, 1940, and Stuart to Brewster, August 19, 1940, America First MSS.
27 Stuart to Wood, August 23, 1940, and unsigned memo, August 24, 1940, America First MSS.
28 Stuart to E. L. Ryerson, Jr., September 6, 1940, America First MSS.
29 *Chicago Tribune,* September 5, 1940.
30 *Ibid.*
31 General Robert E. Wood, *Our Foreign Policy* (Chicago, October 4, 1940), 2. These are paraphrased in *Chicago Tribune,* September 5, 1940.
32 *Chicago Tribune,* September 6, 1940.

CHAPTER 2—LEADERSHIP, ORGANIZATION AND FINANCES

1 Stuart to Wood, August 23, 1940, America First MSS.
2 Minutes of America First Board of Directors Meeting, September 21, 1940, Wood MSS; and *Chicago Herald-American,* January 5, 1941.
3 Telegram Wood to Stuart, August 28, 1940, Wood to W. R. Castle, December 14, 1940, and Stuart to MacNider, December 18, 1940, Wood MSS; Stuart to MacNider, August 30, 1940, Stuart to J. C. Hormel, August 30, 1940, Stuart to Mrs. B. C. Clark, January 4, 1941, Stuart to O. G. Villard, December 11, 1940, and Kennedy to Mrs. M. P. Weedy, December 31, 1940, America First MSS; *Chicago Herald-American,* Decem-

ber 13, 1940; and interviews with Stuart, April 6, 1949, and May 6, 1949.
4 Minutes of America First Board of Directors, March 28, 1941, Wood MSS.
5 *Ibid.*, April 10, 1941.
6 *New York Times,* April 18, 1941.
7 "General Robert E. Wood, President," *Fortune,* 17 (May, 1938), 66–69, 104–10; and *Chicago Herald-American,* January 5, 1941.
8 Interviews with Stuart, April 6, 1949, and May 6, 1949, and with Harry Schnibbe, June 21, 1949.
9 Stuart to Clay Judson, September 11, 1940, Stuart to T. S. Hammond, September 20, 1940, Judson to Wood, April 11, 1941, America First MSS and Certificate of Incorporation, September 19, 1940, Wood MSS.
10 Judson to Wood, April 11, 1941, Wood to Hormel, April 15, 1941, Hormel to Wood, April 16, 1941, Judson to Stuart, April 24, 1941, America First MSS; and Minutes of America First Board of Directors Meeting, May 28, 1941, Wood MSS.
11 Minutes of America First Board of Directors Meeting, September 26, 1940, Wood MSS; and Judson to Stuart, October 10, 1940, America First MSS.
12 America First Committee Corporate Records Book, Wood MSS.
13 Interview with H. C. Schnibbe, June 21, 1949.
14 *Ibid.*, and interviews with Stuart, April 6, 1949, and May 6, 1949.
15 For lists of national committee members see: *Congressional Digest,* 20 (1941), 167; *Chicago Tribune,* September 5, 1940; *New York Times,* October 14, 1941; America First Committee Bulletin, #647, October 23, 1941, America First MSS; and notebook in R. Douglas Stuart, Jr., Papers, San Francisco, California.
16 America First Committee Corporate Records Book, Wood MSS.
17 Interviews with General Wood, December 23, 1947, and with Stuart, April 6, 1949; and Stuart to Wood, August 3, 1940, America First MSS.

206

18 For data on the national committee members see: *Who's Who in America; St. Louis Post-Dispatch,* October 27, 1940; and an unidentified memo on military records of members in America First MSS. Many lists of Committee members include brief identifying sketches.

19 The generalizations in this and the following paragraph are based upon interviews with General Wood, December 23, 1947, and Stuart, April 6, 1949, and May 6, 1949; and hundreds of letters from, to, and about these national committee members in the America First MSS and Wood MSS.

20 See footnote #19. Also, letterhead stationery in America First MSS lists chapter officers. A notebook in Stuart MSS contains a convenient list of speakers for America First. See also Large Contributor Files, America First MSS.

21 Interviews with Stuart, April 6, 1949, and May 6, 1949, and with H. C. Schnibbe, June 21, 1949. The statements on this matter in these interviews were verified by hundreds of letters to, from and about these individuals in the America First MSS and Wood MSS.

22 *Congressional Record,* 77 Congress, 1 session (1941), A3491; and *Washington Post,* November 3, 1941.

23 For two examples see below, Chapter 10, pp. 175–78.

24 Interview with H. C. Schnibbe, June 21, 1949.

25 *Capital Times* (Madison, Wisconsin), December 14, 1940.

26 Stuart to E. L. Ryerson, Jr., December 17, 1940, and Katrina McCormick to Page Hufty, August 4, 1941, America First MSS; Chester Bowles to William Benton, November 28, 1940, Stuart to MacNider, December 18, 1940, Wood to Pettengill, May 1, 1941, and Minutes of America First Board of Directors Meeting, March 28, 1941, Wood MSS.

27 Wood to I. A. Pennypacker, July 15, 1941, America First MSS; and interview with H. C. Schnibbe, June 21, 1949.

28 Wood to Pettengill, May 1, 1941, Wood MSS; J. C. Bayley, Jr., to J. R. Boldt, Jr., July 11, 1941, Wood to Pennypacker, July 15, 1941, Stuart to J. A. Gwyer, July 17, 1941, Katrina McCormick to Page Hufty, July 28, 1941, Katrina McCormick to Page Hufty, August 4, 1941, America First MSS.

29 For examples see: Wood to Mrs. Fairbank, September 18, 1940, Wood MSS; and Stuart to H. S. Richardson, December 23, 1940, America First MSS.

30 Stuart to Chester Bowles, December 20, 1940, Stuart to H. S. Richardson, December 23, 1940, Stuart to J. P. Selvage, April 16, 1941, Wood to Stuart, July 16, 1941, and Wood to Stuart, July 17, 1941, America First MSS; Minutes of the America First Board of Directors Meeting, April 10, 1941, and Wood to Pettengill, May 1, 1941, Wood MSS.

31 Minutes of America First Board of Directors Meeting, March 28, 1941, Wood MSS; and *Chicago Tribune,* March 30, 1941.

32 Minutes of America First Board of Directors Meeting, April 10, 1941, Wood MSS.

33 Interviews with Stuart, April 6, 1949, and with Schnibbe, June 21, 1949; Wood to Stuart, July 16, 1941, Wood to Stuart, July 17, 1941, America First MSS; and Wood to Pettengill, May 1, 1941, Wood MSS.

34 Agenda of meeting of national committee, October 20, 1941, America First MSS.

35 Barbara McDonald to H. E. MacGibbon, May 15, 1941, America First MSS; and interview with Schnibbe, June 21, 1949.

36 William Benton to Stuart, September 4, 1941, and Stuart to Benton, September 16, 1941, America First MSS.

37 Minutes of America First Executive Committee Meeting, September 21, 1940, September 26, 1940, October 7, 1940, and Minutes of National Committee Meetings, October 25, 1940, and November 12, 1940, Wood MSS.

38 Stuart to all members of the younger committee, August 2, 1940, and Stuart to Avery Brundage, September 24, 1940, America First MSS.

39 Stuart to Richardson, December 10, 1940, Wood MSS.

40 Minutes of America First National Committee Meeting, November 12, 1940, Wood MSS.

41 Walter Johnson, *The Battle Against Isolation* (Chicago, 1944), 73–75; and a typewritten, undated, and unpublished confidential report on America First prepared—probably late in 1940

—by Friends of Democracy, Inc., and loaned to the author.

42 America First Committee, "Chapter Manual" (undated mimeographed pamphlet), America First MSS; and "Application to Establish a Chapter of the America First Committee" (undated printed application blank), America First MSS.

43 Stuart to Mrs. C. E. Saltzman, November 5, 1940, Stuart to R. L. Lambert, December 11, 1940, America First MSS; and *Chicago Herald-American,* December 11, 1940.

44 "Application to Establish a Chapter of the America First Committee" (undated printed application blank), America First MSS.

45 America First Committee, "Chapter Manual" (undated mimeographed pamphlet), America First MSS.

46 R. E. Wood to J. T. Flynn, February 25, 1941, America First Committee Bulletin, #126, March 13, 1941, #203, April 16, 1941, #239, May 7, 1941, America First MSS.

47 Memo from R. L. Bliss to all field men, February 14, 1941, America First MSS; and Earl Jeffrey to Bliss, April 19, 1941, America First MSS.

48 Barbara McDonald to H. E. MacGibbon, May 15, 1941, R. L. Bliss to Margaret Muldoon, January 24, 1941, Otto A. Case to H. C. Schnibbe, August 26, 1941, A. A. Brooks, Jr., to R. D. Platt, March 5, 1941, R. D. Stuart, Jr., to S. B. Pettengill, February 5, 1941, B. W. Croxdale to E. S. Webster, Jr., and R. L. Bliss, May 5, 1941, America First MSS; and *Chicago Tribune,* November 10, 1941.

49 Earl Jeffrey to R. A. Moore, June 19, 1941, W. T. Dodson to Mrs. E. N. Jordan, July 2, 1941, J. L. Wheeler to Jeffrey, July 9, 1941, R. B. Wurlitzer to R. E. Wood, August 29, 1941, America First MSS.

50 Memo Stuart to Bliss, January 29, 1941, Bliss to Wood, May 19, 1941, W. S. Foulis to Hufty, July 26, 1941, Wood to Edgar Palmer, October 21, 1941, and memo signed by R. H. Emerson, February 1, 1941, America First MSS.

51 *Chicago Tribune,* January 28, 1941; N. Doll to H. D. Swim, March 5, 1941, Hufty to Mrs. C. D. Barnes, June 18, 1941, Hufty to P. W. Howard, August 7, 1941, Mrs. E. W. Kimbark

to G. A. Paddock, August 22, 1941, R. H. Emerson to Mrs. C. De Hueck, November 14, 1941, America First MSS.

52 Form letter Page Hufty to all chapter chairmen, August 20, 1941, America First MSS.

53 H. C. Schnibbe to John Gordon, December 1, 1941, Schnibbe to R. H. Emerson, August 7, 1941, and America First Committee, "The America First Club" (mimeographed undated pamphlet), America First MSS.

54 Interviews with H. C. Schnibbe, June 21, 1949, and with General Wood, December 23, 1947.

55 Douglas Dobson to Page Hufty, June 19, 1941, and Stuart to D. P. Ferris, February 19, 1941, America First MSS.

56 For examples see: S. E. Aiken to Mrs. F. F. Van Derveer, May 22, 1941, A. A. Brooks, Jr., to Bliss, January 16, 1941, telegram Bliss to Brooks, January 17, 1941, America First MSS.

57 For one example see: C. C. Crowe to H. C. Schnibbe, June 5, 1941, telegram Wood to Crowe, June 13, 1941, Schnibbe to Crowe, June 21, 1941, Ursula Little to Mrs. Pierce, August 24, 1941, Little to Schnibbe, September 3, 1941, Mrs. L. P. Munger to Stuart, Hufty, and Schnibbe, November 6, 1941, and Schnibbe to Crowe, September 12, 1941, America First MSS.

58 Interview with H. C. Schnibbe, June 21, 1949; and confirmed by countless letters by members of the America First staff in America First MSS.

59 For illustrations see: Earl Jeffrey to R. L. Bliss, April 3, 1941, memo by Dorothy Thum, June 25, 1941, Earl Jeffrey to R. A. Moore, June 12, 1941, J. W. Bissell to America First Committee, September 24, 1941, James Bayley to J. R. Boldt, Jr., March 28, 1941, America First MSS.

60 Most contemporary published estimates of membership and chapter totals were much higher than the figures given in this paragraph. These figures and generalizations are based upon an analysis of the Chapter Dissolution Files, America First MSS; a notebook in Stuart MSS; and data from countless letters and clippings. General Wood told the author on December 23, 1947 that he did not believe the Committee's membership exceeded one million.

61 Chapter Dissolution Files, America First MSS.
62 Mrs. L. D. Jolly to America First Committee, August 7, 1941, E. V. Kluge to H. C. Schnibbe, December 6, 1941, Mrs. I. R. Tweed to R. L. Bliss, February 2, 1941, Mrs. Tweed to H. C. Schnibbe, July 23, 1941, Mrs. Tweed to Schnibbe, July 28, 1941, Granger Hansell to Bliss, April 25, 1941, Clyde Pharr to Stuart, May 21, 1941, America First MSS.
63 For General Wood's description of the situation in the East see: *Chicago Tribune,* March 7, 1941.
64 Chapter Dissolution Files, America First MSS.
65 Minutes of America First Board of Directors Meetings, September 26, 1940, and November 1, 1940, Stuart to J. C. Hormel, November 15, 1940, Wood MSS; and Wood to E. S. Webster, Jr., February 12, 1941, America First MSS.
66 Minutes of Board of Directors Meeting, September 26, 1940, Wood MSS.
67 *Ibid.,* December 27, 1940, Wood MSS.
68 *Ibid.,* October 7, 1940, Wood MSS.
69 America First Audit Reports, July 29, 1940 to February 7, 1942, and memo Wood to M. B. Stanley, April 27, 1942, Wood MSS.
70 Memo F. H. Camphausen to Miss Matz, December 11, 1941, General Contributor Correspondence Files, America First MSS; and lists of small contributors, Wood MSS.
71 Files of Contributors of Larger Amounts, and General Contributor Correspondence Files, America First MSS. *New York Herald Tribune,* March 12, 1941, lists the names of sixty-nine persons who had contributed one hundred dollars or more to the national organization by February 20, 1941.
72 Mrs. J. W. Nichols to America First Committee, n.d., America First MSS.
73 "America First Committee, New York Chapter, Inc. Daily Treasurer's Report," December 8, 1941, and "Preliminary America First Committee, New York Chapter, Inc. Statement of Receipts and Disbursements from Inception to March 26, 1942," America First MSS.
74 Chapter Dissolution Files, America First MSS.

CHAPTER 3—THE GREAT ARSENAL OF DEMOCRACY?

1 For a few illustrations see: R. L. Bliss to R. F. Moseley, January 9, 1941, H. G. Swann to Bliss, February 21, 1941, Clay Pugh to Page Hufty, October 17, 1941, Earl Jeffrey to R. L. Bliss, March 12, 1941, Russell Thompson to Editor of *Miami Herald*, November 19, 1941, America First Committee Research Bureau, "America First Digest" (mimeographed pamphlet prepared for national legislators, n.d.), America First MSS.

2 *Shield America* (Kansas City), September 27, 1941, and November 11, 1941.

3 America First Committee Bulletin, #523, August 26, 1941, America First MSS.

4 J. A. Mayer to Stuart, December 20, 1941, America First MSS.

5 S. B. Pettengill to R. E. Wood, April 25, 1941, Wood MSS.

6 H. G. Swann to Barbara McDonald, May 10, 1941, America First MSS.

7 H. C. Schnibbe to Ray Moseley, June 7, 1941, America First MSS.

8 Walter Johnson, *The Battle Against Isolation* (Chicago, 1944), 113–14, 136–37, 171–73; Committee to Defend America by Aiding the Allies, *Official Statement of Policy* (New York, November 26, 1940); Fight for Freedom Committee, *A "Negotiated Peace"* (New York, n.d.); and a mimeographed copy of address by Adlai E. Stevenson to League of Women Voters, October 14, 1940, America First MSS.

9 *Chicago News*, December 23, 1940, and December 18, 1940; *New York Times*, April 18, 1941, and April 24, 1941; *Chicago Tribune*, September 6, 1940; Stuart to J. J. Lelis, December 2, 1940, America First MSS; and *Hearings before the Committee on Foreign Affairs, House of Representatives* (77 Congress, 1 session, on H.R. 1776; Washington, 1941), 350, 488.

10 *Chicago Times*, February 2, 1941; *New York Times*, October 31, 1940, and April 24, 1941; *Chicago Tribune*, December 19, 1940, and May 18, 1941; *Chicago Herald-American*, January

30, 1941; *Seattle Times,* June 27, 1941; Ralph Ingersoll, Burton K. Wheeler, and Louis Wirth, *Is This Our War?* (University of Chicago Round Table Pamphlet, Chicago, January 12, 1941), 10; and mimeographed copies of addresses by General Wood, February 3, 1941, Senator Wheeler, August 28, 1941, G. P. Nye, May 3, 1941, J. T. Flynn, April 3, 1941, and H. S. Johnson, February 6, 1941, America First MSS.

11 Robert E. Wood, *Our Foreign Policy* (Chicago, October 4, 1940), 6–8, 13–14; *House Hearings,* H.R. 1776, 353; *San Francisco Chronicle,* June 25, 1941; *Chicago Tribune,* December 19, 1940, and January 20, 1941; Clay Judson, *Is This Our War?* (Chicago, November 30, 1940), 5, 9, 13; and Stuart to Wood, April 26, 1941, Judson to Wood, September 24, 1940, mimeographed text of address by G. P. Nye, February 20, 1941, and J. T. Flynn, April 3, 1941, and September 27, 1941, America First MSS; and also *Chicago News,* December 18, 1940.

12 Wood, *Foreign Policy,* 13; *Chicago Tribune,* December 12, 1940; *New York Times,* December 14, 1940; *Chicago Times,* February 2, 1941; and mimeographed text of address by Wood, July 7, 1941, and Wood to R. A. Moore, August 29, 1941, America First MSS.

13 For illustrations see: *New York Post,* January 11, 1941; *San Francisco Chronicle,* June 25, 1941; *Buffalo Courier-Express,* January 28, 1941; *Milwaukee Sentinel,* January 18, 1941; *A. F. C. Bulletin* (New York), May 31, 1941, and June 7, 1941; Chester Bowles to Stuart, April 25, 1941, and Judson to R. M. Hutchins, May 19, 1941, Wood MSS; and W. R. Castle to Stuart, March 11, 1941, and G. P. Nye, "No Further Without War," May 3, 1941, America First MSS.

14 *House Hearings,* H.R. 1776, 378. General Wood even took this position in one statement. *Chicago Times,* February 2, 1941.

15 Wood to Mrs. E. W. Kimbark, May 28, 1941, America First MSS. This may have been due in part to Stuart's fear that it would bring the "appeasement" label on America First. F. J. Libby to Lindbergh, July 29, 1941, America First MSS.

16 Mimeographed text of address by General Wood, January 29,

1941, and form letter Stuart to J. J. Nelis, December 2, 1940, America First MSS.

17 *Chicago Tribune,* December 12, 1940; *New York Times,* October 31, 1940; *America First Bulletin* (New York), June 21, 1941; Bennett Champ Clark, "Union Now? No," in *Rotarian,* 57 (October, 1940), 57; mimeographed text of address by Stuart, August 1, 1941, America First MSS; and *News* (New York), May 2, 1941.

18 For illustrations see: *Congressional Record,* 76 Congress, 2nd session (1939), A553, A228, A83–4, and 249; *Hearings before the Committee on Foreign Relations, United States Senate* (77 Congress, 1 session, on S. 275; Washington, 1941), 494; and Philip La Follette and Frank Knox, *Should the Arms Embargo Be Lifted* (Bulletin of America's Town Meeting of the Air, New York, October 16, 1939), 14.

19 Wood to J. T. McCutcheon, July 22, 1940, Wood MSS.

20 *Chicago Tribune,* September 5, 1940.

21 *Des Moines Tribune,* October 15, 1940; *Chicago Tribune,* November 13, 1940; and form letter Stuart to J. J. Nelis, December 2, 1940, America First MSS.

22 Minutes of America First Board of Directors Meeting, December 27, 1940, Wood MSS.

23 *Chicago Tribune,* April 18, 1941.

24 Wood to A. E. Arnstein, January 21, 1941, Wood MSS.

25 For examples see: *Chicago Tribune,* January 23, 1941; *Chicago Daily News,* December 23, 1940; *Senate Hearings,* S. 275, 499, 526; mimeographed address by J. T. Flynn, March 8, 1941, America First MSS; and *Chicago Herald-American,* March 20, 1941, and January 30, 1941.

26 For examples see: *Chicago Tribune,* December 12, 1940; B. K. Wheeler, "America's Present Emergency," *Vital Speeches of the Day,* 7 (January 15, 1941), 204; Stuart to Wood, April 26, 1941, mimeographed text of address by G. P. Nye, February 20, 1941, America First MSS; and *New York Times,* April 17, 1941, and January 6, 1941.

27 *Chicago Tribune,* January 23, 1941.

28 Minutes of America First Board of Directors Meeting, December 17, 1940, and Stuart to Hanford MacNider, December 18, 1940, Wood MSS.

29 Minutes of America First Board of Directors Meeting, December 27, 1940, Wood MSS.

30 *Chicago News,* December 23, 1940; mimeographed text of address by General Wood, January 29, 1941, and February 3, 1941, America First MSS; *Chicago Times,* February 2, 1941; and *Senate Hearings,* S. 275, 347–49, 391–92.

31 Basil Rauch, *Roosevelt From Munich to Pearl Harbor* (New York, 1950), 295–96; and Robert E. Sherwood, *Roosevelt and Hopkins: An Intimate History* (New York, 1948), 225.

32 Rauch, *Roosevelt,* 297–300; and Sherwood, *Roosevelt and Hopkins,* 226–28.

33 Mimeographed America First News Release, December 30, 1940, America First MSS.

34 *Chicago Tribune,* January 12, 1941.

35 Minutes of America First National Committee Meeting, January 14, 1941, Wood MSS.

36 *House Hearings,* H.R. 1776, 350–58.

37 *Ibid.,* 481.

38 *Senate Hearings,* S. 275, 342–49, 355, 361, 379, 397.

39 *New York Times,* February 13, 1941.

40 Mimeographed memo to all America First speakers, February 13, 1941, America First MSS.

41 *Buffalo Courier-Express,* January 28, 1941.

42 Mimeographed text of address by G. P. Nye at an America First rally on February 20, 1941, America First MSS.

43 B. K. Wheeler, J. T. Flynn, Herbert Agar, and Josh Lee, *Should Congress Adopt the Lend-Lease Program?* (Pamphlet of the American Forum of the Air, Washington, 1941), 9; and *New York Times,* January 15, 1941.

44 Stuart, "Rough Outline of Projects Completed During Past Month," February 25, 1941, America First MSS.

45 *Ibid.; Congressional Record,* 77 Congress, 1 session (1941), A901–2; and *Chicago Tribune,* February 8, 1941.

46 *Fox Lake Representative* (Fox Lake, Wisconsin), February 13, 1941, and clippings from dozens of rural newspapers, America First MSS.

47 Stuart, "Rough Outline," F. H. Camphausen unaddressed memo, February 4, 1941, and Stuart to Fellow American, February 6, 1941, America First MSS.

48 For example see: "Highlights of Interviews with Senators and Representatives," February 25, 1941, America First MSS.

49 America First Committee Bulletin, #33, January 29, 1941, America First MSS.

50 *Chicago Tribune,* February 12, 1941, and February 17, 1941.

51 *Ibid.,* January 15, 1941.

52 *Ibid.,* January 18, 1941, and February 6, 1941.

53 *Ibid.,* January 19, 1941.

54 *Ibid.,* January 10, 1941.

55 *Ibid.,* January 21, 1941.

56 *Ibid.,* February 6, 1941, and February 11, 1941.

57 Stuart, "Rough Outline," February 25, 1941, America First MSS; and Stuart to A. L. Dodge, January 24, 1941, Wood MSS.

58 Drew Pearson and Robert S. Allen, "The Washington Merry-Go-Round," *Chicago Herald-American,* February 24, 1941.

59 *Chicago News,* February 28, 1941; and *Chicago Tribune,* March 4, 1941. Mrs. Bennett Champ Clark believed this was a mistake. She said it was a meaningless amendment to try and make the vote for the bill larger. Mrs. Clark to Wood, February 28, 1941, America First MSS.

60 *Chicago Tribune,* March 10, 1941.

61 *Public Opinion Quarterly,* 5 (1941), 323.

62 America First Committee Bulletin, #122, March 10, 1941, #192, April 10, 1941, #246, May 7, 1941, America First MSS.

CHAPTER 4—WAR OR PEACE?

1 Judson to Wood, September 24, 1940, America First MSS.

2 Judson to Wood, March 24, 1941, and Wood to Mrs. A. G. Simms, May 21, 1941, Wood MSS; and Castle to Stuart, March

11, 1941, Regnery to Stuart, March 17, 1941, Mrs. Fairbank to Mrs. E. W. Kimbark, June 5, 1941, and enclosure to Hormel to Stuart, October 20, 1941, America First MSS.

3 *Public Opinion Quarterly,* 6 (1942), 161–62, 5 (1941), 485, 323–25.

4 *Ibid.,* 6 (1942), 151, 5 (1941), 481, and Hadley Cantril, "Opinion Trends in World War II: Some Guides to Interpretation," *Ibid.,* 12 (1948), 37.

5 For examples see: telegrams Ulric Bell to Wood, May 29, 1941, and June 6, 1941, Wood MSS.

6 Philip La Follette, "With Malice Toward None" (mimeographed text of address, February 12, 1941), America First MSS. See also: Stuart, "A is for America" (mimeographed text of radio address, August 1, 1941), America First MSS.

7 Cantril, "Opinion Trends," *Public Opinion,* 37.

8 For illustrations see: *Hearings before the Committee on Foreign Relations, United States Senate* (77 Congress, 1 session, on S. 275), 342–45; America First Committee, *Convoy: A Funeral Train* (Chicago, n.d.); America First Committee Bulletin, #389, July 7, 1941; *New York Times,* September 13, 1941; and America First Research Bureau, *Did You Know,* #28, 32–33.

9 *Chicago Tribune,* December 15, 1940.

10 R. E. Wood, "Our Foreign Policy Today" (mimeographed text of radio address, July 7, 1941), America First MSS.

11 *Chicago Times,* June 4, 1941; and Stuart to all chapter chairmen, June 4, 1941, America First MSS.

12 Stuart, "A is for America" (mimeographed text of radio address, August 1, 1941), America First MSS.

13 C. A. Lindbergh, "Government by Representation or Subterfuge" (mimeographed text of address delivered at Cleveland, Ohio, August 9, 1941), America First MSS.

14 Mimeographed text of address delivered in Washington, D.C., November 1, 1941, America First MSS.

15 Copy of address by B. K. Wheeler, August 28, 1941, America First MSS.

16 Wood to Mrs. A. G. Simms, May 21, 1941, Wood MSS; Bowles

to Stuart, July 30, 1941, and Transcript of Remarks at National Meeting of Chapter Heads at Chicago, July 12, 1941, 19, America First MSS.

17 Ken Lee to Stuart, n.d., Mrs. Barbara McDonald to Mrs. F. B. Boeckel, February 26, 1941, W. R. Castle to Stuart, March 29, 1941, mimeographed press release from Keep America Out of War Congress, March 11, 1941, mimeographed press release from Keep America Out of War Congress, National Council for the Prevention of War, and other peace organizations, March 29, 1941, and Keep America Out of War Congress, et al., "Anti-War News Service," April 5, 1941, America First MSS; and *A.F.C.* (New York), June 7, 1941.

18 Minutes of America First Board of Directors Meeting, February 7, 1941, Wood MSS.

19 *Ibid.,* March 28, 1941, Wood MSS.

20 *Chicago Tribune,* June 19, 1941; and W. H. Regnery to Stuart, June 13, 1941, America First MSS.

21 Minutes of America First Board of Directors Meeting, June 23, 1941, Wood MSS; America First Committee Bulletin, #374, June 30, 1941, and #379, July 1, 1941, America First MSS.

22 Ken Lee to Stuart, n.d., S. B. Pettingill to Stuart, March 27, 1941, W. R. Castle to Stuart, March 29, 1941, Ruth Sarles to Stuart, June 13, 1941, H. C. Schnibbe to Wood, June 14, 1941, Hufty to Stuart, June 24, 1941, and Sarles to R. A. Moore, July 3, 1941, America First MSS; and Minutes of America First Board of Directors Meeting, March 28, 1941, Wood MSS.

23 Minutes of America First Board of Directors Meeting, June 23, 1941, Wood MSS.

24 Ruth Sarles to Stuart, June 27, 1941, and Sarles to R. A. Moore, July 3, 1941, America First MSS.

25 *Chicago Tribune,* June 30, 1941; and mimeographed America First news release, June 28, 1941, America First MSS.

26 America First Committee Bulletins, #374, #375, #376, #377, June 30, 1941, #379, #380, July 1, 1941, #400, July 9, 1941, America First MSS.

27 *Chicago Tribune,* July 8, 1941.
28 Minutes of America First National Committee Meeting, November 28, 1941, Wood MSS.
29 Stuart to R. A. Moore, June 2, 1941, America First Committee Bulletin, #315, June 13, 1941, Moore to F. J. Libby, June 23, 1941, [Stuart?] to R. R. McCormick, June 28, 1941, America First Committee Bulletin, #381, July 1, 1941, Stuart to R. M. Hutchins, July 2, 1941, Knute Hill to Donald Despain, July 25, 1941, R. A. Moore to Knute Hill, December 6, 1941, Moore to Paul Shafer, December 6, 1941, Moore to Harry Sauthoff, December 6, 1941, America First MSS.
30 Ruth Sarles to R. A. Moore, September 22, 1941, America First MSS.
31 *Life,* 11 (July 7, 1941), 2; *America First Committee* (St. Louis), July, 1941; and Stuart to Sarles, June 21, 1941, America First MSS.
32 *America First Committee* (St. Louis), July, 1941; *Chicago Tribune,* July 15, 1941; *America First Bulletin* (New York), July 19, 1941; [Stuart?] to MacNider, July 23, 1941, America First MSS.
33 Stuart to Chester Bowles, April 29, 1941, Wood MSS; Stuart to R. M. Hutchins, May 3, 1941, and [Stuart?] to R. R. McCormick, June 28, 1941, America First MSS.
34 Samuel E. Gill, "American Public Opinion Regarding the European War June 28–July 3, 1941" (mimeographed report on the results of the Hutchins committee survey, New York, 1941), America First MSS.
35 Stuart to Hormel, September 19, 1941, America First MSS; and MacNider to Wood, September 20, 1941, Wood MSS.
36 Ruth Sarles to Stuart, June 13, 1941, and Schnibbe to Wood, June 14, 1941, America First MSS.
37 S. B. Pettengill to Wood, October 9, 1941, and draft proposed by Pettengill for an open letter to the President and sent to Stuart, October 9, 1941, America First MSS.
38 Minutes of America First National Committee Meeting, October 20, 1941, Wood MSS.

39 Mimeographed text of open letter from Wood to the President, October 22, 1941, America First MSS; *New York Times,* October 23, 1941; and *Chicago Tribune,* October 23, 1941.

40 Robert E. Sherwood, *Roosevelt and Hopkins: An Intimate History* (New York, 1948), 382.

41 Livingston Hartley, "Washington Office Information Letter" (Committee to Defend America by Aiding the Allies release, Washington, August 15, 1941), America First MSS.

42 Stuart to Chester Bowles, April 29, 1941, Wood MSS.

43 Gill, "American Public Opinion," America First MSS.

44 Sherwood, *Roosevelt and Hopkins,* 132–33; and Henry L. Stimson and McGeorge Bundy, *On Active Service In Peace and War* (New York, 1947, 1948), 370.

45 Sherwood, *Roosevelt and Hopkins,* 382–83, 429–30; and Stimson and Bundy, *On Active Service,* 376.

46 *The Memoirs of Cordell Hull* (2 vols., New York, 1948), 943; Sherwood, *Roosevelt and Hopkins,* 132–33, 299, 382; and Stimson and Bundy, *On Active Service,* 368, 370–73, 376. See also Chapter 11 below.

47 For examples see: *The Public Papers and Addresses of Franklin D. Roosevelt: 1939 Volume: War—And Neutrality* (New York, 1941), 515–19; and Basil Rauch, *Roosevelt: From Munich to Pearl Harbor* (New York, 1950), 6, 13, 138–40.

CHAPTER 5—CAPITALISM, COMMUNISM AND CATHOLICISM

1 Basil Rauch, *Roosevelt: From Munich to Pearl Harbor* (New York, 1950), 10.

2 "Socialists and Planners Must be Isolationists: Why Is That News?" *Saturday Evening Post,* 223 (July 22, 1950), 12.

3 *Public Opinion Quarterly,* 6 (1942), 151.

4 *Daily Worker* (New York), June 23, 1941.

5 For example see: *Public Opinion,* 5 (1941), 161–62.

6 *Washington News,* March 12, 1941.

7 Stuart to Wood, August 3, 1940, America First MSS.

8   Albert Horlings, "Who Are the Appeasers?" *New Republic*, 104 (January 27, 1941), 111.

9   "General Robert E. Wood, President," *Fortune*, 17 (May, 1938), 104–10; Stuart to Wood, December 9, 1940, America First MSS; and Wood to L. R. Reed, February 17, 1941, Wood MSS.

10   *New York Times*, October 10, 1946, and October 16, 1946; and George Seldes, *One Thousand Americans* (New York, 1947), 223–28.

11   *Capital Times* (Madison), March 30, 1948.

12   *Ibid.*, June 13, 1950.

13   *Chicago News*, May 23, 1941.

14   *Capital Times*, June 13, 1950; and Seldes, *One Thousand Americans*, 226.

15   MacNider to Wood, May 1, 1941, America First MSS.

16   *Chicago News*, May 23, 1941.

17   Stuart to Sidney Hertzberg, October 28, 1940, and telegram Stuart to S. Don, November 1, 1940, Wood MSS; and *PM* (New York), October 4, 1940.

18   Basil Rauch, *The History of the New Deal 1933–1938* (New York, 1944), 66–67, 94–99.

19   *Ibid.*, 11; Samuel Grafton, "The Appeasement Tropism," *New Republic*, 104 (January 6, 1941), 18; *Washington Times*, December 19, 1940; and John T. Flynn, *The Road Ahead: America's Creeping Revolution* (New York, 1949).

20   *Capital Times* (Madison), March 30, 1948.

21   Files of Contributors of Larger Amounts, America First MSS.

22   O. G. Villard to Stuart, August 21, 1940, Villard to Stuart, September 24, 1940, Villard to Stuart, October 5, 1940, Wood MSS.

23   Stuart to H. S. Richardson, December 10, 1940, Sidney Hertzberg to Stuart Chase, December 27, 1940, America First MSS; and Minutes of Board of Directors Meeting, March 28, 1941, Wood MSS.

24   Katrina McCormick Barnes to Mrs. C. A. Beard, July 23, 1941, and memo attached to Stuart to S. B. Pettengill, July 30, 1941, America First MSS. Included on this staff in 1941 were Ruth

Sarles, Kendrick Lee, James Lipsig, and Cushman Reynolds.

25 C. A. Beard to Wood, July 27, 1940, Wood MSS; telegram Stuart to Kingman Brewster, Jr., August 2, 1940, and Wood to Beard, February 10, 1941, America First MSS; and *New York Times,* September 9, 1940.

26 Stuart to Stuart Chase, August 16, 1940, Stuart to Chase, October 25, 1940, Chase to Stuart, November 12, 1940, Sidney Hertzberg to Chase, December 27, 1940, America First MSS; and Stuart Chase, *Four Assumptions About the War* (America First pamphlet, Chicago, January 6, 1941).

27 Stuart to Lindbergh, April 15, 1941, and J. R. Boldt, Jr., to H. H. Smith, August 12, 1941, America First MSS; Stuart to E. S. Webster, Jr., April 22, 1941, Thomas to Stuart, May 1, 1941, Wood to Thomas, May 2, 1941, Thomas to Wood, May 12, 1941, Wood MSS.

28 Notebook in Stuart MSS; *Chicago Tribune,* September 5, 1940; *New York Times,* October 10, 1941; and Minutes of National Committee Meeting, October 20, 1941, Wood MSS. Professor Carlson said in 1950: "The three W's and three D's of living are work, work, work from diaper days to death. The goal of the current philosophy of the welfare state—security from cradle to grave whether you work or not—is both unscientific and unobtainable." *Time,* 55 (February 6, 1950), 32.

29 Memo by Sidney Hertzberg, January 13, 1941, Wood to Edwin Borchard, September 22, 1941, Borchard to Wood, September 24, 1941, Borchard to Mrs. P. Palmer, October 25, 1941, R. M. Hutchins to Wood, July 25, 1940, Wood to Philip C. Jessup, September 22, 1941, New York and Norfolk, Connecticut, chapter letterhead stationery, and Chapter Dissolution Files, America First MSS; and *America First Bulletin* (New York), August 16, 1941.

30 Mrs. Barbara McDonald to Mrs. E. Coleman, May 9, 1941, and G. B. Baldwin to J. A. Bruhn, August 22, 1941, America First MSS.

31 McDonald to A. A. Eastman, March 12, 1941, America First MSS.

32 Stuart to Wood, August 3, 1940, and copy of telegram from Stuart to Kathryn Lewis, September 13, 1940, America First MSS.

33 Telegram Stuart to Kathryn Lewis, September 16, 1940, and America First Committee Bulletin, #12, January 18, 1941, America First MSS; and Miss Lewis to Stuart, December 5, 1940, and Kathryn Lewis to Wood, September 29, 1941, Wood MSS.

34 *New York Times,* October 14, 1941.

35 America First Committee Bulletin, #12, January 18, 1941, and #29, January 28, 1941, W. R. Castle to Wood, January 22, 1941, Wood to O. L. Sprague, January 28, 1941, America First MSS.

36 *Chicago Tribune,* February 26, 1941; J. R. Boldt, Jr., to Edward McMahon, July 20, 1941, America First MSS.

37 *Chicago Herald-American,* January 30, 1941; and *Chicago News,* January 31, 1941.

38 Sidney Hertzberg to Stuart and Bliss, March 25, 1941, A. L. Dodge to Wood, January 15, 1941, F. J. Libby to Stuart, February 11, 1941, Wood MSS; and Stuart, "Rough Outline of Projects Completed During Past Month," February 25, 1941, America First MSS.

39 For example see: *Fox Lake Representative* (Fox Lake, Wisconsin), February 13, 1941.

40 For examples see: J. B. Gordon to Mrs. S. Meyer, September 5, 1941, America First Committee Bulletin, #519, August 25, 1941, and Minutes of Sioux Falls, South Dakota America First Chapter Meeting, August 29, 1941, America First MSS.

41 Stuart to MacNider, June 20, 1941, Clay Pugh to Stuart, June 26, 1941, J. Jontry to Stuart, June 26, 1941, Hufty to J. A. White, July 24, 1941, America First MSS; *Chicago Tribune,* June 30, 1941; and *Milwaukee News-Sentinel,* July 13, 1941. Though these meetings were the product of America First efforts, no mention was made of the Committee in publicity concerning the meetings.

42 G. N. Peek to Wood, January 14, 1941, Minutes of the America

223

First Board of Directors Meeting, February 7, 1941, Wood MSS; and F. H. Camphausen to Peek, March 24, 1941, America First MSS.

43 Grange and Farm mailing folders in America First MSS. See also: George Baldwin to Stuart, July 23, 1941, America First MSS.

44 Norman Thomas to Stuart, September 23, 1941, America First MSS.

45 Minutes of America First National Committee Meeting, October 25, 1940, Wood MSS; and Robert M. La Follette, *Are We On the Road to War?* (America First Pamphlet, Chicago, September 11, 1940).

46 The last evidence in America First MSS of speeches at America First meetings by Barnes was in a letter from Barnes to Mrs. Barbara McDonald, March 28, 1941, America First MSS.

47 Minutes of America First Board of Directors Meeting, March 28, 1941, Wood MSS; telegram Barbara McDonald to Mrs. E. S. Welch, March 29, 1941, Bertha Tallman to Mrs. K. Johnson, February 11, 1941, G. B. Baldwin to Rush Holt, August 4, 1941, Baldwin to C. O. Mitchell, September 2, 1941, America First MSS; and *Chicago Herald-American,* December 22, 1940.

48 See below Chapter 8.

49 W. S. Foulis to V. Anderson, December 5, 1941, America First MSS; and *Nation,* 154 (February 21, 1942), 206.

50 Stuart to Kingman Brewster, Jr., October 7, 1940, and Minutes of Board of Directors Meeting, December 3, 1940, Wood MSS; and memo Stuart to F. H. Camphausen, October 11, 1941, America First MSS; and *Newsweek,* 18 (November 10, 1941), 15.

51 For example see: Committee to Defend America by Aiding the Allies, *Organized Labor's Stake in the War* (New York, n.d.); and *Trade War—Or, War of Freedom?* (Chicago, n.d.); and Elisabeth Christman, *Labor and the Totalitarian Threat* (Committee to Defend America by Aiding the Allies pamphlet, New York, August 30, 1940).

52 *New York Herald Tribune,* December 21, 1940.

53 For example see: Stuart to Wood, April 26, 1941, America First MSS.

54 *Ibid.;* and Transcript of Remarks at Meeting of America First Chapter Leaders in Chicago, July 12, 1941, America First MSS; and Wood to Mrs. A. G. Simms, May 21, 1941, Wood MSS.

55 For example see: R. E. Wood, *Our Foreign Policy* (Chicago, October 4, 1940), 9–10; Sterling Morton, *Let's Think This Matter Through* (Chicago, December 15, 1940), 3–4; B. M. Baruch, Raymond Moley, and G. N. Peek, *Can Hitler Cripple America's Economy?* (Chicago, n.d.); and J. T. Flynn and R. Niebuhr, *Should Our Ships Convoy Materials to Britain?* (Bulletin of America's Town Meeting of the Air, New York, May 12, 1941), 14–15, 26.

56 For examples see: *Des Moines Tribune,* October 15, 1940; *Automotive News* (Detroit), December 9, 1940; *News* (New York), May 2, 1941; *America First Bulletin* (New York), July 26, 1941; and mimeographed news release of address by G. P. Nye, Brooklyn, New York, on September 22, 1941, America First MSS.

57 For examples see: *Des Moines Tribune,* October 15, 1940; and *Automotive News,* December 9, 1940; Stuart to C. U. Gorden, October 30, 1941, America First MSS; and Wood to Edgar Queeny, August 13, 1941, Wood MSS.

58 Mimeographed text of radio address by J. T. Flynn, March 8, 1941, America First MSS. See also: Flynn, *War: What is it?* (New York, February 28, 1941).

59 Wood, *Foreign Policy,* 14.

60 Wood to Edgar Queeny, August 13, 1941, Wood MSS.

61 Stuart to C. U. Gorden, October 30, 1941, America First MSS. See also: Stuart to J. P. Donahue, March 25, 1941, Wood MSS.

62 Certificate of Incorporation of America First Committee, New York Chapter, Inc., February 28, 1941, America First MSS.

63 For illustrations see: *Chicago Tribune,* July 2, 1941; *North Park Press* (San Diego), September 15, 1941; and Bowles to Stuart, July 15, 1941, America First MSS.

64 *Daily Worker* (New York), December 26, 1940, January 12,

1941, and May 20, 1941; and *New Masses,* 38 (January 7, 1941), 3–4.

65 *Daily Worker,* June 23, 1941.
66 Minutes of Board of Directors Meeting, June 23, 1941, Wood MSS; and America First Committee Bulletin, #350, June 23, 1941, America First MSS.
67 *Chicago Tribune,* June 25, 1941.
68 *Time,* 37 (June 30, 1941), 69.
69 *Chicago Tribune,* July 2, 1941.
70 *Newsweek,* 18 (July 7, 1941), 12.
71 America First Committee Research Bureau, *Did You Know,* #4, June 27, 1941.
72 *Ibid.,* America First Committee Bulletin, #390, July 7, 1941, H. Lamont to S. A. Day, August 2, 1941, and America First Committee Bulletin, #533, August 29, 1941, America First MSS.
73 *Chicago Tribune,* June 23, 1941.
74 J. T. Flynn, "Understudy for Russia" (mimeographed text of radio address, September 27, 1941), America First MSS.
75 T.R.B. "The War Issue Sharpens," *New Republic,* 104 (May 12, 1941), 663.
76 America First Committee Bulletin, #417, July 16, 1941, America First MSS.
77 Form letter Page Hufty to all Chapter Chairmen, September 2, 1941, America First MSS.
78 *Catholic Review* (Baltimore), July 11, 1941; and *New York Times,* October 3, 1941; and Research Bureau, "Freedom (?) of Religion in Communist Russia," October 8, 1941.
79 America First Committee Bulletin, #634, October 15, 1941, America First MSS; and Wood to Flynn, October 30, 1941, Wood MSS.
80 Research Bureau, *Did You Know,* #5, July 1, 1941.
81 *Ibid.,* #15, August 1, 1941.
82 *Public Opinion Quarterly,* 5 (1941), 675, 679.

CHAPTER 6—MILITARY DEFENSE

1 *Chicago Tribune,* September 5, 1940.
2 R. Douglas Stuart, Jr., to O. G. Villard, September 26, 1940, Wood MSS; and Stuart to A. W. Palmer, November 1, 1940, America First MSS.
3 *Chicago Tribune,* September 5, 1940.
4 Stuart to O. G. Villard, September 26, 1940, Wood MSS.
5 *Washington Times,* December 19, 1940.
6 Telegram Dorothy Detzer to Mrs. Barbara McDonald, April 24, 1941, America First MSS.
7 Mrs. Barbara McDonald to C. A. Braden, December 6, 1940, America First MSS.
8 Ruth Sarles to Page Hufty, December 5, 1941, Ken Lee to Stuart, July 9, 1941, Edwin Schell to Bliss, May 24, 1941, E. O. Newby to Douglas Gregory, September 29, 1941, Walter Hamill to Joseph Boldt, Jr., February 27, 1941, Boldt to Hamill, March 1, 1941, Mrs. D. B. Armstrong to Mrs. M. E. De La Mater, February 17, 1941, and letterhead stationery of Keep America Out of War Congress, America First MSS.
9 Stuart to F. J. Libby, October 11, 1940, Stuart to A. L. Dodge, January 24, 1941, Wood MSS; America First Committee Bulletin, #40, January 31, 1941, and #180, April 3, 1941, Stuart to Libby, October 30, 1941, Katrina McCormick to Hufty, November 25, 1941, Stuart to Mrs. Fairbank, February 15, 1941, Stuart to M. W. Hillyer, October 30, 1941, Dorothy Detzer to Wood, February 14, 1941, Stuart to Fay Bennett, March 12, 1941, and C. F. Boss, Jr., to B. S. Stuart, February 11, 1941, America First MSS. During the first quarter of 1941 the Committee supplied the following organizations with the sums indicated: National Council for the Prevention of War, $1,000.00; Keep America Out of War Congress, $500.00; Youth Committee Against War, $500.00; Women's International League for Peace and Freedom, $500.00. Through the efforts of Committee leaders at least $2,500.00 was channeled to the Ministers No War Committee.

10 Sidney Hertzberg to Stuart Chase, December 27, 1940, America First MSS.

11 Ruth Sarles to Kendrick Lee, April 12, 1941, America First MSS.

12 For examples see: Stuart to Libby, October 11, 1940, Wood MSS; Libby to America First Speakers Bureau, January 29, 1941, Lee to Stuart, n.d., Stuart to Libby, July 15, 1941, Stuart to Hufty, Moore and Schnibbe, October 10, 1941, America First MSS.

13 Ken Lee to Stuart, n.d., Mrs. Barbara McDonald to Mrs. F. B. Boeckel, February 26, 1941, and W. R. Castle to Stuart, March 29, 1941, America First MSS.

14 Ruth Sarles to Stuart, November 26, 1941, America First MSS; and A. L. Dodge to Wood, January 15, 1941, Wood MSS.

15 O. G. Villard to Stuart, October 5, 1940, and A. W. Palmer to Stuart, October 12, 1940, Wood MSS.

16 Norman Thomas to J. T. Flynn and Stuart, June 25, 1941, Thomas to Stuart, November 19, 1940, America First MSS; and Thomas to Wood, May 12, 1941, Wood MSS.

17 Undated memo on military records of members of the national committee, America First MSS; and *Who's Who in America,* 1948–1949.

18 M. M. Keck to Stuart, November 4, 1939, Wood MSS.

19 Memo on military records, America First MSS; and *Who's Who in America,* 1942–1943, and 1948–1949. President Roosevelt declined to approve the reappointment of Johnson as Brigadier General in the Army Reserve in 1941 because of his health. This decision was made though the War Department in recommending reappointment had waived Johnson's physical fitness. When President Roosevelt compared Lindbergh to the Copperhead, Clement L. Vallandigham, Lindbergh resigned his commission in April, 1941. *Richmond Times-Dispatch,* May 1, 1941; *Chicago Herald-American,* May 16, 1941; and *Chicago Tribune,* April 26, 1941, and April 29, 1941.

20 *Chicago Tribune,* February 9, 1941; and J. R. Boldt, Jr., to Edward McMahon, July 20, 1941, America First MSS.

21 Mrs. B. C. Clark to Private Forbar, March 19, 1941, Mrs. E. Armstrong to J. J. Ledwith, May 22, 1941, J. P. to E. W. Whitney, June 12, 1941, America First MSS.

22 *Congressional Record,* 77 Congress, 1 session (1941–1942), 6332–5; "If This Be Treason," *Time,* 38 (August 4, 1941), 13; *Chicago Tribune,* July 29, 1941; and Henry L. Stimson and McGeorge Bundy, *On Active Service In Peace and War* (New York, 1947, 1948), 378.

23 America First Committee Bulletin, #442, July 25, 1941, America First MSS.

24 For examples see: Stuart to K. E. Brammer, August 8, 1941, Julian Garrett to F. W. Michaelsen, October 15, 1941, Garrett to K. Kiefer, November 10, 1941, America First MSS.

25 *Chicago News,* November 6, 1941; and *Chicago Tribune,* November 6, 1941.

26 Hadley Cantril, Donald Rugg, and Frederick Williams, "America Faces the War: Shifts in Opinion," *Public Opinion Quarterly,* 4 (1940), 656.

27 Even the major pacifist organizations professed to approve defense measures. For example see: *Peace Action of the National Council for Prevention of War* (Washington), March, 1941; and *Washington Times,* December 19, 1940.

28 For statements of the interventionist views see: Committee to Defend America by Aiding the Allies, *Primer of American Defense* (n.p., n.d.), *The Atlantic Is Not 3000 Miles Wide Because* (Chicago, n.d.), *We Reply* (n.p., n.d.), *Hitler's American Ambitions* (Chicago, n.d.), and *How Does America's Defense Program Fit the Facts* (Chicago, n.d.); Pierre van Paassen, *Hitler's Plan Against the United States Exposed* (Pamphlet of Committee to Defend America by Aiding the Allies, n.p., n.d.); Fight for Freedom, Inc., "We Mean 'Fight,' and We Mean 'Freedom,'" n.d.; and Walter Johnson, *The Battle Against Isolation* (Chicago, 1944), 107.

29 For examples of views of America First leaders and spokesmen see: R. E. Wood, *Our Foreign Policy* (Chicago, October 4, 1940), 7–9; J. T. Flynn, *Can Hitler Invade America?* (America First pamphlet, Chicago, n.d.); Clay Judson, *Is This Our War?*

(Chicago, November 30, 1940), 7–12; Sterling Morton, *Let's Think This Matter Through* (Chicago, December 15, 1940), 8–9; *Hearings before the Committee on Foreign Relations, United States Senate* (77 Congress, 1 session, on S. 275; Washington, 1941), 492–93; and Ralph Ingersoll, B. K. Wheeler, and Louis Wirth, *Is This Our War?* (University of Chicago Round Table Pamphlet, Chicago, January 12, 1941), 7–17.

30 *Congressional Digest,* 20 (1941), 167. Some statements of this principle have a slightly different phrasing but the essential idea remained unchanged during the Committee's history.

31 Flynn, *Can Hitler Invade America;* Wood, *Foreign Policy,* 8; Morton, *Let's Think,* 1–2; Judson, *Is This Our War,* 10; Ingersoll, Wheeler and Wirth, *Is This Our War,* 12–17; and copy of address by R. E. Wood in Chicago, February 3, 1941, America First MSS.

32 *New York Times,* October 31, 1940.

33 Wood, *Foreign Policy,* 7–8; and Flynn, *Can Hitler Invade America.*

34 *New York Times,* May 20, 1940; and C. A. Lindbergh, "Air Power" (mimeographed text of address at Oklahoma City, August 29, 1941), America First MSS.

35 Mimeographed America First news release, December 30, 1940, America First MSS.

36 Flynn, *Can Hitler Invade America.*

37 *Ibid.;* and R. E. Wood, "Our Foreign Policy Today" (mimeographed text of radio address, July 7, 1941).

38 For example see: Morton, *Let's Think,* 3.

39 *PM* (New York), May 26, 1941; Wood to Editor of *PM,* May 27, 1941, Wood MSS; and interview with General Wood, December 23, 1947.

40 For illustrations see: Roger Butterfield, "Lindbergh," *Life,* 11 (1941), 67; J. T. Flynn and Reinhold Niebuhr, *Should Our Ships Convoy Materials to Britain?* (Bulletin of America's Town Meeting of the Air, New York, May 12, 1941), 26; and *Senate Foreign Relations Hearings,* S. 275, 281.

41 *New York Times,* May 20, 1940.

42 Wood, *Foreign Policy,* 11.

43   America First Committee Research Bureau, *Did You Know* (Washington, 1941), #12, 3.

44   *New York Times,* October 31, 1940.

45   Butterfield, "Lindbergh," *Life,* 67.

46   Research Bureau, *Did You Know,* #7, 1–4.

47   *Washington Post,* November 3, 1941.

48   *Chicago Tribune,* July 8, 1941.

49   For examples see: *Hearings before the Committee on Military Affairs, United States Senate* (77 Congress, 1 session, S.J. Resolutions 92 and 93; Washington, 1941), 208; and *Chicago Times,* February 2, 1941.

50   *Hearings before the Committee on Foreign Affairs, House of Representatives* (77 Congress, 1 session, H.R. 1776; Washington, 1941), 377.

51   For example see: *Chicago Herald-American,* December 28, 1941; and Morton, *Let's Think,* 12.

52   *Washington Post,* December 12, 1940; and *Chicago Tribune,* January 23, 1941.

53   *Chicago Tribune,* November 13, 1940; and Research Bureau, *Did You Know,* #12, 3.

54   For an example see: *Senate Foreign Relations Hearings, S. 275,* 550.

55   America First Committee Bulletin, #485, August 12, 1941, America First MSS.

56   Douglas Dobson to Hufty, August 14, 1941, America First MSS.

57   Mimeographed memo from R. H. Emerson to chapter and unit chairmen in New York, August 25, 1941, America First MSS.

58   *New York Times,* June 16, 1940; and B. K. Wheeler, "Marching Down the Road to War," *Vital Speeches of the Day,* 6 (1940), 689.

59   Stuart to Kenosha (Wisconsin) Christian Business Men's Committee, August 6, 1940, and William Ford to T. J. Murphy, August 12, 1940, America First MSS. The Committee to Defend America by Aiding the Allies did not take a stand on this measure either. Walter Johnson, *The Battle Against Isolation* (Chicago, 1944), 92.

60 *New York Times,* July 5, 1941; *Chicago Tribune,* July 5, 1941; and America First Committee Bulletin, #389, July 7, 1941, America First MSS.

61 Research Bureau, *Did You Know,* #9, 2.

62 B. K. Wheeler to R. E. Wood, July 17, 1941, America First MSS; and *America First Bulletin* (New York), July 26, 1941. In his letter, Wheeler said that Senator Reynolds was at the White House conference at which President Roosevelt was told they would not be able to get the legislation passed authorizing sending selectees outside of the hemisphere. Reynolds is reported as saying that the President during this conference strongly attacked America First for its activities.

63 Research Bureau, *Did You Know,* #13, 2–3.

64 Telegram Stuart to B. K. Wheeler, July 18, 1941, Wood MSS; Harry Schnibbe to Jane Harig, July 21, 1941, S. B. Pettengill to Stuart, July 22, 1941, and America First Bulletin, #444, July 28, 1941, America First MSS.

65 *Chicago Tribune,* July 20, 1941; S. B. Pettengill to Stuart, July 22, 1941, and Stuart to Flynn, July 31, 1941, America First MSS.

66 Telegram Stuart to B. K. Wheeler, July 18, 1941, Sarles to R. A. Moore, July 21, 1941, America First MSS; and *House Military Affairs Hearings,* S.J. Resolutions 92 and 93, 207–11.

67 Research Bureau, *Did You Know,* #10, and #11.

68 *Ibid.;* and *House Military Affairs Hearings,* S.J. Resolutions 92 and 93, 208–9.

69 America First Committee Bulletin, #477, August 7, 1941, America First MSS.

70 Day letter Stuart to all chapter chairmen, August 11, 1941, America First MSS.

71 D. S. MacKay to Senate Military Affairs Committee, July 15, 1941, Minutes of Executive Board of Boston America First Chapter, August 5, 1941, and August 12, 1941, telegram J. A. Fairbank to Helen Lamont, July 24, 1941, and telegram K. D. Magruder to America First Committee Headquarters, August 11, 1941, America First MSS.

72 *America First Bulletin* (New York), July 26, 1941; and Min-

utes of Meeting of Heads of New York Chapters, August 14, 1941, America First MSS.

73 Stuart to Chester Bowles, August 14, 1941, America First MSS.

74 America First Committee Bulletin, #503, August 20, 1941, America First MSS.

CHAPTER 7—THE NAZI TRANSMISSION BELT?

1 *New York Times,* October 30, 1940; *Chicago News,* December 20, 1940; and *Chicago Times,* December 20, 1940.

2 For examples see: Wood to R. A. Shaw, January 3, 1941, Wood MSS; and telegrams W. A. White to Wood, January 9, 1941, Wood to White, May 2, 1941, and White to Wood, May 5, 1941, America First MSS; and R. E. Wood, *Our Foreign Policy* (Chicago, October 4, 1940).

3 *Chicago Tribune,* December 1, 1940, and December 15, 1940.

4 Walter Johnson, *The Battle Against Isolation* (Chicago, 1944), 165–66, 181–83, 195–99; *New York Times,* December 25, 1940.

5 Letter to America First, October 3, 1940, America First MSS.

6 Unsigned letter to America First from Charlotte, North Carolina, March 9, 1941, America First MSS.

7 Unsigned letter to America First from Portland, Oregon, October 16, 1940, America First MSS.

8 Letter to America First, November 6, 1941, America First MSS. A professor of Political Science in an Eastern college told the author in 1949 that he thought most members of America First were pro-Nazi. It was simply impolitic for them to say so openly. He did not believe it possible for Americans to want to keep out of war for solely American and not pro-Nazi reasons. At best he would call such people "crypto-Nazis."

9 Letter to America First, November 6, 1941, America First MSS. All errors were in the original.

10 *Daily Worker* (New York), January 12, 1941.

11 *Chicago Tribune,* August 20, 1941.

12 *New York Herald-Tribune,* October 22, 1940.

13 *Chicago Herald-American,* April 25, 1941.

14   *Time,* 37 (June 2, 1941), 15; and *Life,* 10 (June 9, 1941), **56.**

15   *PM* (New York), May 25, 1941.

16   *Hearings before the Committee on Foreign Relations, United States Senate* (77 Congress, 1 session, on S. 275; Washington, 1941), 380; and *New York Herald Tribune,* January 25, 1941.

17   *News* (New York), May 23, 1941.

18   Telegram H. W. Hobson to R. E. Wood, October 21, 1941, America First MSS.

19   *Chicago Tribune,* April 14, 1941.

20   Philip S. Foner, ed., *Franklin Delano Roosevelt—Selections from His Writings* (New York, 1947), 49.

21   *New York Times,* January 15, 1941; *Newsweek,* 17 (February 10, 1941), 9; and *Time,* 37 (February 10, 1941), 13.

22   *Chicago Tribune,* April 26, 1941.

23   E. J. Kahn, Jr., "Democracy's Friend," *New Yorker* (July 26, 1947), 28, 37–38, (August 2, 1947), 28; and L. M. Birkhead to Stuart, March 11, 1941, America First MSS.

24   For example see: *Cincinnati Enquirer,* May 4, 1941.

25   Johnson, *Battle Against Isolation,* 251–52.

26   L. M. Birkhead to Stuart, November 8, 1940, America First MSS.

27   Friends of Democracy, Inc., *The America First Committee—The Nazi Transmission Belt* (New York, n.d.).

28   *New York Post,* March 11, 1941.

29   Friends of Democracy, Inc., *Is Lindbergh A Nazi?* (New York, n.d.).

30   Americanism Committee, 17th District, Department of California, American Legion, *Subversive Activities in the America First Committee in California* (Los Angeles, October 10, 1941). These reports were authorized by the District Legion but the funds to cover the costs were raised by the Americanism Committee—not supplied by the Legion itself. R. H. Ensign to the author, August 30, 1949.

31   J. P. Wood to R. C. Hoiles, June 19, 1941, America First MSS.

32   *Summary of Proceedings* (Twenty-Fifth Annual National Convention of the American Legion, Omaha, Nebraska, September 21 and 23, 1943).

33 Michael Sayers and Albert E. Kahn, *Sabotage! The Secret War Against America* (New York and London, 1942), 202–3.

34 J. R. Carlson, "Inside the America First Movement," *American Mercury,* 54 (January, 1942), 7; and E. J. Kahn, Jr., "Democracy's Friend," *New Yorker* (August 2, 1947), 35.

35 J. R. Carlson, *Under Cover* (Cleveland and New York, 1943), 260; and Carlson, "Inside America First," *Mercury,* 7, 9.

36 Henry Hoke, *It's A Secret* (New York, 1946); and Hoke, *Black Mail* (New York, 1944).

37 *Chicago Tribune,* May 3, 1941, May 5, 1941, May 10, 1941, July 10, 1941, July 19, 1941, August 28, 1941, August 29, 1941, May 6, 1941, May 11, 1941, September 12, 1941, and September 18, 1941.

38 *Ibid.,* June 14, 1941.

39 Earl Jeffrey to R. L. Bliss, March 12, 1941, Stuart to Wood, August 14, 1940, Stuart to Kingman Brewster, Jr., August 19, 1940, Mrs. H. Mann to M. Cotter, January 23, 1941, Quincy Howe to Wood, March 24, 1941, P. W. Huntington to Wood, March 27, 1941, Bowles to Stuart, January 23, 1941, R. L. Bliss to Richards Emerson, February 17, 1941, H. W. Beal to Bliss, June 8, 1941, H. M. Crane to Stuart, November 6, 1941, L. A. Boettiger to America First Committee, April 27, 1941, and confidential memo dictated by R. A. Moore, August 28, 1941, America First MSS; Wood to Mrs. E. S. Welch, April 7, 1941; and *Chicago Tribune,* March 7, 1941, and April 5, 1941.

40 *Washington Times-Herald,* December 14, 1940.

41 Interview with General Wood, December 23, 1947.

42 Stuart to W. S. Hart, March 13, 1941, and Stuart to Mrs. F. Chapman, March 13, 1941, America First MSS.

43 Telegram Page Hufty to Stuart, March 27, 1941, America First Committee Bulletin, #98, March 5, 1941, and J. M. Richardson to Hufty, September 15, 1941, America First MSS.

44 Philip La Follette, "With Malice Toward None" (mimeographed text of radio address, February 12, 1941), America First MSS.

45 *New York Post,* March 11, 1941.

46 Judson to Wood, March 20, 1941, America First MSS. For

views of other America First leaders see: Chester Bowles to Stuart, March 13, 1941, Wood MSS; and G. H. Whipple to Birkhead, March 13, 1941, Ray McKaig to Stuart, March 15, 1941, W. R. Castle to Birkhead, March 18, 1941, A. J. Carlson to Birkhead, March 20, 1941, G. N. Peek to Birkhead, March 22, 1941, and J. C. Hormel to Birkhead, March 26, 1941, America First MSS.

47 Sterling Morton to Stuart, March 24, 1941, America First MSS.

48 *New York Times,* March 15, 1941; R. L. Bliss to R. E. Wood, March 13, 1941, and the original telegrams received from Friends of Democracy sponsors, America First MSS.

49 A. J. Carlson to Birkhead, March 20, 1941, America First MSS.

50 Chester Bowles, to Stuart, March 13, 1941, Wood to L. J. Taber, March 29, 1941, Minutes of America First Board of Directors Meeting, March 28, 1941, Wood MSS.

51 Letters from Wood to Hammond, Carlson, Ryerson, Regnery, MacNider, Judson, Hormel, Fairbank, and Otis, April 14, 1941, Otis to Wood, April 16, 1941, Judson to Wood, April 15, 1941, Hormel to Wood, April 16, 1941, Ryerson to Wood, April 18, 1941, Hammond to Wood, April 16, 1941, MacNider to Wood, April 16, 1941, Carlson to Wood, April 16, 1941, and W. F. Regnery to Wood, April 16, 1941, Wood MSS.

52 Memo written on telegram from J. H. Sheldon to Wood, July 16, 1941, memo Wood to Stuart, September 29, 1941, R. A. Moore to K. E. Mundt, October 2, 1941, Wood to W. R. Castle, November 27, 1941, America First MSS. National headquarters did, however, send the telegrams to the Friends of Democracy sponsors which resulted in Flynn's release in March, 1941. This was not released from national headquarters however.

53 For examples see: *Chicago Tribune,* September 2, 1941; mimeographed text of address by B. K. Wheeler at Denver, Colorado, April 16, 1941, mimeographed news release of text of address by C. A. Lindbergh at Philadelphia, May 29, 1941, mimeographed text of address by G. P. Nye, at New York, February 20, 1941, mimeographed press release of text of radio address by Hamilton Fish, on June 30, 1941, America First MSS. See also Chapter 4.

54 America First Committee Bulletin, #417, July 16, 1941, #509,

August 21, 1941, and #575, September 24, 1941, and E. S. Webster, Jr., to Mrs. J. A. Fairbank, August 29, 1941, America First MSS; *America First Bulletin* (New York), August 23, 1941; and *America First Committee* (St. Louis), July, 1941.

55 E. S. Webster, Jr., to R. E. Wood, February 27, 1941, America First MSS. See also: *PM* (New York), December 30, 1940; and *Chicago Herald-American,* January 7, 1941.

56 Wood to Flynn, February 25, 1941, Stuart to H. C. Lodge, Jr., September 28, 1940, Sidney Hertzberg to Stuart and Wood, February 18, 1941, Wood MSS; Wood to Webster, February 25, 1941, Webster to Wood, February 27, 1941, Chester Bowles to Stuart, March 3, 1941, Bowles to Webster, March 3, 1941, America First MSS; and *PM* (New York), May 25, 1941.

57 Interview with General Wood, December 23, 1947; and letter from Stuart to the author, February 16, 1948.

58 Most America First pamphlets, contribution cards, and major advertisements made such declarations.

59 Stuart to Kingman Brewster, Jr., October 7, 1940, and Stuart to Sterling Morton, February 8, 1941, Wood MSS.

60 Minutes of America First Board of Directors Meeting, October 7, 1940, Wood MSS.

61 *St. Louis Post-Dispatch,* October 27, 1940; and J. E. F. Wood to R. E. Wood, November 9, 1940, America First MSS.

62 For illustrations see: F. H. Camphausen to Stuart, August 1, 1941, S. H. Otis to H. H. Sedgwick, July 7, 1941, S. H. Otis to Rachel Sedgwick, July 7, 1941, Camphausen to R. Sedgwick, August 5, 1941, J. S. Broeksmit, Jr., to Mrs. W. W. Shields, July 8, 1941, DS to V. Weitzel, November 12, 1941, Camphausen to G. Leuthold, December 15, 1941, America First MSS.

63 Copies of letters from T. S. Hammond to W. S. Devereaux, January, 1941, and to Martin Dies, January 17, 1941, Wood MSS. No reply was received from Dies at this time.

64 R. L. Bliss to Federal Bureau of Investigation, Chicago, March 13, 1941, and W. S. Devereaux to Bliss, March 27, 1941, Wood MSS.

65 Stuart to Wood, June 6, 1941, Stuart to Mrs. Fairbank, June

6, 1941, America First MSS; and Wood to Grenville Clark, July 15, 1941, and copy of letter T. S. Hammond to J. M. Patterson, November 7, 1941, Wood MSS.

66 *Chicago Tribune,* September 3, 1941.

67 *Ibid.,* November 13, 1941, and November 14, 1941.

68 R. L. Bliss to R. A. Moore, August 13, 1941, and attached memo, Wood to S. H. Hauck, August 20, 1941, Flynn to Hauck, September 4, 1941, Hauck to Flynn, September 29, 1941, and Hauck to Wood, September 29, 1941, America First MSS.

69 Stuart to Sidney Hertzberg, September 30, 1940, America First MSS; and *New York Post,* March 18, 1941.

70 Sayers and Kahn, *Sabotage,* 204–6; America First Committee Bulletin, #257, May 15, 1941; and Americanism Committee, *Subversive Activities in America First,* 1–3.

71 *Chicago Tribune,* May 24, 1941; and *PM* (New York), May 25, 1941.

72 Carlson, *Under Cover,* 253–54.

73 R. H. Emerson to E. S. Welch, December 19, 1940, check from H. D. Sim to German-American Voters League of New Jersey, Inc., June 6, 1941, R. L. Bliss to Harry Schnibbe, June 30, 1941, Bliss to staff, July 18, 1941, Bliss to Mrs. L. I. Jump, August 11, 1941, Minutes of Queens America First Chapter, October 14, 1941, and Requests for payments of bills by New York Chapter to W. J. Burns International Detective Agency, Inc., made by Bliss and signed by Flynn, dated November 7 and November 25, 1941, America First MSS.

74 Wood to Stuart, June 3, 1941, Wood MSS; telegram R. A. Moore to E. C. Jeffrey, June 19, 1941, E. C. Jeffrey to R. A. Moore, June 19, 1941, America First MSS.

75 R. A. Moore to Earl Jeffrey, June 19, 1941, telegram Jeffrey to Moore, June 24, 1941, Jeffrey to Dellmore Lessard, July 19, 1941, Lessard to Moore, August 7, 1941, Stuart to J. W. Blodgett, Jr., August 13, 1941, Page Hufty to Clay Pugh, September 8, 1941, Pugh to Hufty, September 11, 1941, and Lessard to Wood, October 27, 1941, America First MSS; and *Oregonian* (Portland), August 7, 1941.

238

76 F. A. Chase to Richard Hood, August 25, 1941, America First MSS.

77 Leaflet distributed at G. P. Nye America First rally at Denver, Colorado, May, 1941, memorandum dictated by J. B. Gordon, June 6, 1941, H. F. Hamilton to Stuart, June 28, 1941, Dorothy Thum, "Report on Cleveland Activities from August 23 to Sept. 17," mimeographed digest of discussion of meeting of chapter officers in Los Angeles, August 24, 1941, Isabel French to H. E. Weihmiller, November 25, 1941, America First MSS; Clay Judson to E. T. Kiehl, October 9, 1941, Wood MSS; and *Hollywood Citizen News,* June 21, 1941.

78 *Facts in Review,* 2 (August 12, 1940), 378.

79 Sayers and Kahn, *Sabotage,* 204; and Johnson, *Battle Against Isolation,* 164–65.

80 *Chicago Tribune,* March 17, 1941; and *Chicago News,* March 17, 1941.

81 Quoted in Sayers and Kahn, *Sabotage,* 209–15. *New York Times,* February 11, 1942, carries a different version of this quotation but the essential idea is the same. See also: *New York Times,* February 14, 1942, and February 21, 1942; *Nation,* 154 (February 21, 1942), 206; and W. S. Foulis to V. Anderson, December 5, 1941, America First MSS.

82 *New York Times,* September 25, 1941, October 15, 1941, and October 18, 1941; and *Akron Beacon Journal,* July 2, 1941.

83 *New York Times,* January 29, 1942, and March 28, 1942; and *Oakland Post Enquirer,* December 31, 1940; and *San Francisco Chronicle,* March 20, 1941.

84 House of Representatives, Special Committee on Un-American Activities, 78 Congress, 1 session, *Nazi Activities* (Section 1 of *Report on the Axis Front Movement in the United States,* which is Part VII of Appendix to *Investigation of Un-American Propaganda Activities in the United States,* Washington, 1943), 84.

85 G.A.N.A. "Do You Want Peace for America?" (Chicago, n.d).

86 Americanism Committee, *Subversive Activities,* 3.

87 Sayers and Kahn, *Sabotage,* 206–8.

88 For examples see: *Ibid.,* 208, 197–99; Americanism Committee, *Subversive Activities;* Carlson, *Under Cover,* 239; *New York Herald Tribune,* February 24, 1941; *Chicago Herald-American,* April 25, 1941; and miscellaneous copies of reports on America First meetings in New York given to the author by Friends of Democracy, Inc.

89 Lawrence Dennis to America First, November 3, 1940, America First MSS.

90 Mrs. Paul Palmer to R. W. Hebard, February 25, 1941, and R. L. Bliss to D. F. Reid, August 19, 1941, America First MSS.

91 For examples see: R. D. Ross to Barbara McDonald, April 30, 1941, and K. D. Magruder to H. Stockmann, May 16, 1941, America First MSS.

92 Mrs. E. A. Fritz to America First, March 3, 1941, M. M. Woessner to New York America First, May 10, 1941, C. G. Ritter to New York America First, June 3, 1941, C. M. Saul to New York America First, August 14, 1941, America First MSS. National headquarters, however, returned a contribution from a California unit of the Steuben Society of America. Stuart to H. J. W. Klehs, September, 1941, America First MSS.

93 *Time,* 39 (March 2, 1942), 14; Sayers and Kahn, *Sabotage,* 187–89; and *Nation,* 154 (March 7, 1942), 270.

94 R. A. Moore to Hamilton Fish, October 27, 1941, America First MSS.

95 *Washington Post,* September 25, 1941, September 27, 1941, and September 28, 1941; and *Chicago Tribune,* September 26, 1941.

96 *New York Times,* July 24, 1942.

97 W. T. Dodson to R. C. Hoiles, June 23, 1941, America First MSS.

98 W. S. Foulis to C. Bird, November 5, 1941, teletype Foulis to D. Gregory, October 31, 1941, teletype Gregory to Foulis, October 31, 1941, Foulis to Lansing Hoyt, November 11, 1941, telegram Mrs. A. Last to Foulis, November 21, 1941, W. K. Wilsmann to Wood, November 17, 1941, M. A. Simeon to Foulis, November 29, 1941, H. Tumm to Foulis, November 24, 1941, Stuart to Foulis, November 15, 1941, Foulis to

Stuart, November 15, 1941, A. A. Brooks, Jr., to Foulis, November 30, 1941, America First Committee Bulletin, #674, November 5, 1941, R. B. Wood to Foulis, November 26, 1941, America First MSS; and *Gary Post-Tribune,* November 26, 1941. The America First national headquarters financial records show that Miss Ingalls was paid four hundred and twenty-five dollars by the Committee in November and December 1941, Wood MSS.

99   *Akron Beacon Journal,* July 2, 1941, and July 4, 1941; Assistant to Bliss to W. M. Johnston, January 27, 1941, Chapter application blank for the Akron chapter, June 12, 1941, Therese Boczek to H. C. Schnibbe, list of noncontributors to national headquarters from Akron, Ohio, July 2, 1941, and blue notebook in chapter dissolution files, America First MSS. However, the chapter records of the Akron chapter were not sent in to national headquarters after Pearl Harbor so it is possible that he may have made financial contributions to the local chapter which cannot be documented in the America First MSS.

100 Sayers and Kahn, *Sabotage,* 215.

101 *Oakland Post-Enquirer,* December 31, 1940; and *San Francisco Chronicle,* March 20, 1941.

102 A. A. Brooks, Jr. to James Fallon, January 8, 1942, and Schnibbe to M. A. Keith, February 16, 1942, America First MSS; interview with Stuart, April 6, 1949; and *Akron Beacon Journal,* July 4, 1941.

103 *New York Times,* March 15, 1941; and L. M. Birkhead to G. A. Whipple, March 14, 1941, America First MSS.

104 Barbara McDonald to Mrs. E. M. Scott, December 5, 1940, E. J. Smythe to McDonald, December 4, 1940, Scott to McDonald, December 7, 1940, telegram Scott to McDonald, December 9, 1940, Smythe to McDonald, December 11, 1940, Smythe to McDonald, December 14, 1940, Stuart to Smythe, December 18, 1940, Stuart to McDonald, December 18, 1940, J. R. Boldt, Jr., to McDonald, March 15, 1941, E. J. Smythe to Flynn, November 8, 1941, America First MSS.

105 Carlson, *Under Cover,* 251–52.

106 *PM* (New York), May 25, 1941.

107   E. S. Webster, Jr., to Stuart, June 18, 1941, Wood MSS.

108   Hoke, *It's A Secret,* 110–11.

109   For examples see: H. H. Sedgwick to America First, April 16, 1941, H. L. Zinzo to America First, December 8, 1940, T. E. Johnson to America First, n.d., and C. Pelton to America First, August, 1941, General Contributor Correspondence Files, America First MSS.

110   This generalization is based upon an examination of the national headquarters correspondence with large and small contributors and the records of many local chapters in the America First MSS, and the correspondence and auditing and accounting records in Wood MSS. See also: H. L. Trefousse, *Germany and American Neutrality, 1939–1941* (New York, 1951), 133–34.

111   *Newsweek,* 18 (October 20, 1941), 21–22; *Transcript of Laws Relating to the Franking Privilege of Members of Congress,* Post Office Department, Washington, D.C.; *Washington Post,* October 12, 1941, and October 9, 1941; and *Congressional Record,* 77 Congress, 1 session (1941), 6333–6344.

112   *Washington Post,* October 11, 1941.

113   H. W. Fisher to Stuart, March 16, 1941, Ruth Sarles to R. L. Bliss, April 27, 1941, H. W. Fisher to Clay Pugh, June 19, 1941, America First MSS.

114   R. A. Moore to Hamilton Fish, October 27, 1941, H. W. Fisher to Clay Pugh, June 19, 1941, and S. A. Day to K. D. Magruder, July 29, 1941, America First MSS. See also: S. E. Aicken to L. Fife, March 18, 1941, H. W. Fisher to Mrs. E. B. Armstrong, April 2, 1941, Armstrong to Fisher, May 10, 1941, and Mrs. P. Palmer to Fisher, August 8, 1941, America First MSS.

115   *New York Times,* January 4, 1944, and December 1, 1944; and Hoke, *It's A Secret,* 50, 59–61.

116   L. M. Birkhead to G. A. Whipple, March 14, 1941, America First MSS.

117   Hoke, *War in the Mails* (New York, 1941). The extra periods were in the original.

118   A. W. O'Connell, "Report on the Oregon America First Situation to Date of November 21st, 1941," America First MSS.

CHAPTER 8—ANTI-SEMITISM AND AMERICA FIRST

1   Donald S. Strong, *Organized Anti-Semitism in America: The Rise of Group Prejudice During the Decade 1930–1940* (Washington, 1941), 4, 14–15, 61; Michael Sayers and Albert E. Kahn, *Sabotage! The Secret War Against America* (New York and London, 1942), 141–47; and letter from Lyrl Clark Van Hyning to J. C. Granbery in Women's Voice, *Truth is Truth to the End of Reckoning* (Chicago, n.d.).

2   For the views of some Jewish publications see: *Opinion: A Journal of Jewish Life and Letters* (September, 1940), 3–4; *Jewish Frontier* (February, 1941), 13–17; *The American Hebrew* (April 18, 1941), 12; *California Jewish Voice* (Los Angeles), October 24, 1941; and mimeographed form letter from David Aronoff, Los Angeles Secretary of the Jewish People's Committee, October 17, 1941, America First MSS.

3   Stuart to Wood, August 12, 1940, J. M. Richardson to Stuart, September 9, 1940, Stuart to Harry Bennett, September 16, 1940, Stuart to Stuart Chase, October 25, 1940, America First MSS; and *New York Times,* September 25, 1940.

4   Strong, *Organized Anti-Semitism,* 15; *Social Justice* (Royal Oak, Michigan), March 31, 1941; George Seldes, *Facts and Fascism* (New York, 1943), 122–25; I. A. Hirschmann to Stuart, November 1, 1940, Stuart to Rosenwald, December 9, 1940, F. Wehmiller to Sidney Hertzberg, January 1, 1941, America First MSS.

5   Carbon of Minutes of America First Board of Directors Meeting, December 3, 1940, Stuart to Rosenwald, December 9, 1940, Rosenwald to Stuart, December 13, 1940, and Stuart to F. A. Goodhue, January 17, 1941, America First MSS; Confidential report on America First prepared by Friends of Democracy, Inc., late in December, 1940 and loaned to the author; *Washington Post,* December 25, 1940; *New York Herald Tribune,* December 24, 1940; and *Time,* 37 (January 6, 1941), 11.

6   Stuart to MacNider, December 3, 1940, and MacNider to Stuart, December 5, 1940, Wood MSS.

7   Stuart to I. A. Hirschmann, December 11, 1940, Stuart to J. T. Flynn, December 11, 1940, Wood to Julius Miner, January 2, 1941, Wood MSS; and Wood to M. J. Fleischmann, January 21, 1941, America First MSS.

8   Interview with Stuart, June 17, 1949; interview with Harry Schnibbe, June 21, 1949; K. D. Magruder to Mrs. Barbara McDonald, May 13, 1941, Willard E. Fraser to America First, October 1, 1941, and Mrs. Paul Palmer to M. R. Dreyfuss, October 9, 1941, America First MSS.

9   Undated form letter from R. L. Bliss to Fellow American used late in November or early December, 1940, America First MSS.

10 For examples see: S. F. Souder to America First, May 25, 1941, S. H. Otis to Souder, June 9, 1941, R. A. Moore to Mrs. E. A. Skopal, August 15, 1941, Moore to Skopal, October 3, 1941, C. C. Schaup to Wood, October 18, 1941, DS to Schaup, October 24, 1941, and Moore to C. U. Baumgatti, December 18, 1941, America First MSS.

11 Interview with Stuart, June 17, 1949; and Stuart to Wood, December 5, 1940, Mrs. B. C. Clark to K. F. Chalkley, September 8, 1941, Page Hufty to G. P. Mueller, October 23, 1941, America First MSS; and Stuart to Flynn, December 2, 1940, Wood MSS.

12 Hufty to E. J. Garner, October 24, 1941, Katrina McCormick to *Publicity*, September 25, 1941, and Katrina McCormick to Lt. Gen. Count V. Cherep-Spiridovich, August 15, 1941, America First MSS.

13 Donald Shea to Stuart, August 9, 1941, R. A. Moore to Shea, August 16, 1941, Moore to Mrs. J. A. Fairbank, August 16, 1941, Fairbank to Moore, August 18, 1941, and form letter Fairbank to chapter chairmen, August 19, 1941, America First MSS.

14 Louie Fife to R. A. Moore, June 23, 1941, day letter to Mae Fife, July 7, 1941, telegram W. E. Cosgriff to Moore, July 9, 1941, Hufty to Louie Fife, August 4, 1941, telegram E. C. Jeffrey to R. A. Moore, July 4, 1941, America First MSS.

15 Day letter R. L. Bliss to Robert Vietig, March 22, 1941, Bliss to J. W. Gates, May 19, 1941, telegram H. C. Schnibbe to Jane

Harig, July 7, 1941, G. B. Baldwin to Dorothy Thum, July 19, 1941, America First MSS.

16 E. J. Smythe to Mrs. Barbara McDonald, December 14, 1940, Stuart to Smythe, December 18, 1940, and Stuart to McDonald, December 18, 1940, America First MSS.

17 R. A. Moore to E. C. Jeffrey, June 19, 1941, America First MSS.

18 For examples see: undated, unsigned letter to America First postmarked, Chicago, October 10, 1940, Jacob Thorkelson to Wood, June 18, 1941, J. F. Garner to Wood, October 27, 1941, F. H. McCullough and C. C. Von Blarcom to R. L. Bliss, December 11, 1940, America First MSS; E. J. Smythe to Stuart, December 21, 1940, Wood MSS; and J. R. Carlson, *Under Cover* (Cleveland and New York, 1943), 245.

19 Strong, *Organized Anti-Semitism*, 59, 65–67; and *PM* (New York), May 25, 1941.

20 Mrs. B. C. Clark to Cornelia Hutcheson, June 16, 1941, and Isabel French to Ottilia Wadner, June 18, 1941, America First MSS; and *Social Justice* (Royal Oak, Michigan), June 9, 1941.

21 *PM* (New York), May 25, 1941, and June 12, 1941.

22 J. R. Boldt, Jr., to V. A. Cusack, April 21, 1941, America First MSS.

23 R. L. Bliss to K. D. Magruder, May 15, 1941, America First MSS. See also: day letter Bliss to J. C. Bayley, February 10, 1941, America First MSS.

24 For examples see: *Social Justice*, June 9, 1941, July 7, 1941, July 21, 1941, and October 6, 1941.

25 *PM*, May 25, 1941.

26 *Social Justice*, July 7, 1941.

27 For examples see: K. H. Murphy to Boston America First, July 4, 1941, T. L. Bursis, Jr., to New York America First, July 5, 1941, A. J. Mullins to America First, July 6, 1941, R. M. Rhody to Pittsburgh America First, July 20, 1941, and E. V. Mahoney to Boston America First, August 5, 1941, America First MSS.

28 Copy Mrs. Nancy Schoonmaker to Wood, July 17, 1941, America First MSS.

29 For example see: Mrs. E. S. Welch to Mr. Maher, January 4, 1941, America First MSS.

30 Stuart to I. C. Mullins, January 16, 1941, Wood MSS.
31 Wood to E. S. Webster, Jr., February 25, 1941, America First MSS; and Wood to Mrs. B. C. Clark, March 13, 1941, Wood MSS.
32 Wood to R. M. Harriss, May 20, 1941, E. L. Curran to Wood, June 26, 1941, and Wood to Curran, July 7, 1941, Wood MSS.
33 *Social Justice,* October 7, 1940, and May 5, 1941.
34 *Ibid.,* June 16, 1941.
35 *Ibid.,* July 7, 1941.
36 F. T. Fox to R. E. Wood, July 11, 1941, America First MSS.
37 Therese Boczek to H. C. Schnibbe, July 11, 1941, America First MSS.
38 J. C. Bayley, Jr., to Wood, July 8, 1941, America First MSS.
39 Mrs. E. S. Welch to E. V. Mahoney, n.d., America First MSS.
40 J. S. Broeksmit, Jr., to R. C. Hershey, July 19, 1941, America First MSS. See also: L. B. Holland to Agnes Hyland, July 9, 1941, R. A. Moore to C. E. Coughlin, July 9, 1941, and Holland to T. E. Coll, July 15, 1941, America First MSS.
41 *Social Justice,* July 28, 1941.
42 Teletype Bliss to Stuart, August 1, 1941, and Stuart to Wood, August 5, 1941, America First MSS.
43 For example see: R. A. Moore to J. A. Gwyer, August 20, 1941, Wood MSS; and J. R. Boldt, Jr. to J. C. Bayley, July 14, 1941, America First MSS.
44 Mrs. Lou Scott to Wood, August 14, 1941, Clay Pugh to Page Hufty, October 17, 1941, J. B. Gordon to Page Hufty, October 23, 1941, and Gordon to W. S. Foulis, November 5, 1941, America First MSS.
45 Letter to Hufty, October 15, 1941, America First MSS.
46 Letter to Mrs. L. R. Miller, November 11, 1941, America First MSS.
47 Letter to Hufty, August 2, 1941, America First MSS.
48 Letter to America First, June 7, 1941, America First MSS. See also: "Voices of Defeat," *Life,* 12 (April 13, 1942), 94; and Carlson, *Under Cover,* 304–6.
49 Letter to Wood, July 19, 1941, America First MSS. Alderman was indicted in 1942 by a Federal Grand Jury on charges of

sedition and conspiracy to block the execution of American
laws. His trial ended in a mistrial. Sayers and Kahn, *Sabotage,*
215.

50 For examples see: letter to Bliss, April 19, 1941, letter to
Hufty, September 2, 1941, mimeographed text of radio ad-
dress delivered, September 22, 1941, and letter to Cincinnati
America First, n.d., America First MSS.

51 Hufty to Russell Thompson, July 26, 1941, Hufty to Louie
Fife, August 4, 1941, J. L. Fallon to H. S. Hickman, October
24, 1941, Fallon to Mrs. Bossen-Honska, November 25, 1941,
America First MSS.

52 Interview with Dr. Hugh R. Parkinson, May 13, 1949.

53 For examples see: Samuel Kider to Wood, October 13, 1940,
J. H. Connery to America First, July 24, 1941, and C. A. Koch,
Jr., to America First, October 4, 1941, America First MSS.

54 For examples see: Jeffrey to Bliss, March 14, 1941, and March
15, 1941, F. A. Chase to R. C. W. Friday, September 25, 1941,
L. M. Hirshson to J. B. Gordon, September 29, 1941, America
First MSS.

55 *New York Post,* February 6, 1941; *Jewish Day,* February 15,
1941; *Social Justice,* March 31, 1941; and *PM,* March 20, 1941.

56 Telegram Stuart to Donald Stewart, November 11, 1940,
Wood MSS; Bessie Simon to *Scribner's Commentator,* March
21, 1941, telegram W. G. Springer to Bessie Feagin, June 6,
1941, telegram Feagin to Springer, June 6, 1941, Bessie Feagin
to Robert Vietig, October 20, 1941, America First MSS.

57 Minutes of America First Board of Directors Meeting, February 7, 1941, Wood MSS; and Frederick Kister to New York
America First, May 6, 1941, America First MSS.

58 H. C. Schnibbe to Marie Widmer, August 23, 1941, Bessie
Feagin to Robert Vietig, September 25, 1941, and Treasurer's
Report of America First rally in St. Louis, October 16, 1941,
America First MSS.

59 Stuart to James Simpson, Jr., February 19, 1941, Wood MSS.

60 Walter Johnson, *The Battle Against Isolation* (Chicago, 1944),
153; *Washington News,* March 12, 1941; Fight For Freedom,
Inc., *The Freedom Press,* 1 (August, 1941), 4–5; and W. T.

Dodson to Benson Inge, June 2, 1941, America First Committee Bulletin, #466, August 5, 1941, America First MSS. The only actress in the national committee was Lillian Gish who resigned in August in order to secure employment. Confidential memo dictated by R. A. Moore, August 28, 1941, America First MSS. Irvin S. Cobb was on the national committee and Edward Everett Horton contributed ten dollars.

61   Sayers and Kahn, *Sabotage*, 229–30; and G. P. Nye, *Our Madness Increases as Our Emergency Shrinks* (Washington, 1941).

62   *Washington Times Herald,* September 24, 1941; and Wood to J. L. Wheeler, August 11, 1941, Wood MSS.

63   Wood to B. K. Wheeler, August 14, 1941, Wood to Wheeler, August 18, 1941, Wheeler to Wood, August 25, 1941, Wood MSS.

64   America First Committee Bulletin, #496, August 16, 1941, #453, July 30, 1941, #462, August 2, 1941, #466, August 5, 1941, #474, August 7, 1941, #508, August 20, 1941, and #528, August 27, 1941, America First MSS.

65   Strong, *Organized Anti-Semitism,* 19.

66   *Time,* 38 (September 22, 1941), 13; and Minutes of America First Meeting for Heads of Chapters, New York, August 14, 1941, America First MSS.

67   *Washington Post,* September 28, 1941; and Sayers and Kahn, *Sabotage,* 230–32.

68   Mrs. I. R. Tweed to R. L. Bliss, April 25, 1941, Page Hufty to Stuart, April 27, 1941, Bessie Simon to Bliss, May 8, 1941, A. A. Brooks, Jr., to R. A. Moore, July 3, 1941, Stuart to Lindbergh, July 14, 1941, Stuart to Lindbergh, October 14, 1941, R. A. Moore to Fred Allhoff, August 23, 1941, and America First Committee Bulletin, #468, August 5, 1941, America First MSS. See also: M. C. Dorntge to Page Hufty, September 3, 1941, and file of letters and telegrams to national headquarters from members of the Boston chapter, America First MSS.

69   R. A. Moore to Fred Allhoff, August 23, 1941, Dorothy Thum to Jeffrey, August 13, 1941, E. C. Jeffrey to Moore, June 24, 1941, Jeffrey to Stuart, July 3, 1941, America First MSS; *New*

York World-Telegram, April 25, 1941; *Star* (Washington, D.C.), April 26, 1941.

70 *New York Times,* May 20, 1940, August 8, 1940, June 22, 1940, and December 12, 1940. See also: "The Attack on Lindbergh," *Christian Century,* 57 (1940), 1022.

71 *New York Times,* December 12, 1940.

72 *Ibid.,* December 18, 1940.

73 For example see: *Ibid.,* August 6, 1940. According to a defender of Lindbergh this medal "was presented at a stag dinner for Field Marshal Goering, given by Hugh Wilson, the American ambassador to Germany, at the embassy in Berlin— a function for the avowed purpose of bettering relations between Germany and the United States, then the policy of the Roosevelt regime. Lindbergh was there by special request of Ambassador Wilson. Even had he desired, the airman could not have declined the decoration without causing an international incident." C. B. Allen, "The Facts About Lindbergh," *Saturday Evening Post,* 213 (December 28, 1940), 53.

74 Stuart to O. G. Villard, October 5, 1940, Wood MSS; Stuart to Kingman Brewster, Jr., October 25, 1940, Stuart to Page Hufty, April 18, 1941, telegram Stuart to Hanford MacNider, April 10, 1941, America First MSS.

75 *Hearings before the Committee on Foreign Affairs, House of Representatives* (77 Congress, 1 session, on H.R. 1776; Washington, 1941), 378; *New York Times,* April 18, 1941, and April 24, 1941; and "Lindbergh for the Record," *Scribner's Commentator,* 10 (August, 1941), 7.

76 For examples see: *Social Justice,* July 21, 1941, and July 7, 1941; *PM,* June 12, 1941; *Publicity* (Wichita, Kansas), October 30, 1941.

77 For examples see: C. A. Lindbergh, "Our National Safety," *Vital Speeches of the Day,* 6 (1940), 485; Lindbergh, "Our Drift Toward War," *Vital Speeches,* 6 (1940), 549–550; Lindbergh, "An Appeal for Peace," *Vital Speeches,* 6 (1940), 644; Lindbergh, "Strength and Peace," *Vital Speeches,* 7 (1940), 42–3; and Lindbergh, "Time Lies With Us," *Scribner's Commentator,* 11 (November, 1941), 88–9.

78 *Chicago Tribune,* September 12, 1941; and *Des Moines Register,* September 12, 1941.
79 For illustrations see: *Des Moines Register, Washington Post,* and *New York Times,* September 12, 1941.
80 *Des Moines Register,* September 13, 1941.
81 *Ibid.,* September 14, 1941. This article carries editorial comments from a large number of newspapers.
82 *Time,* 38 (September 22, 1941), 17; *Commonweal,* 34 (1941), 532; and George Seldes, *Facts and Fascism* (New York, 1943), 141–45.
83 *New Masses,* 40 (September 30, 1941), 4; and *Daily Worker* (New York), September 16, 1941.
84 *New York Times,* September 13, 1941; telegram H. W. Hobson to Wood, September 16, 1941, and telegram Hugh Moore to Wood, September 22, 1941, America First MSS.
85 Anonymous, *America's Answer to Lindbergh* (n.p., n.d.). The copy in the America First files was stamped with the stamp of the Fight for Freedom Committee of Chicago.
86 Council Against Intolerance in America, *America Answers Lindbergh!* (New York, n.d.).
87 *Chicago Tribune,* September 19, 1941.
88 *Newsweek,* 18 (September 22, 1941), 16–17; and *New York Times,* September 15, 1941.
89 *New York Times,* September 13, 1941.
90 M. W. Hillyer to Stuart, September 17, 1941, America First MSS.
91 *Washington Post,* September 21, 1941; *Chicago Tribune,* September 21, 1941; Keep America Out of War Congress, et al., "Anti-War News Service" (mimeographed release, September 24, 1941), America First MSS; and F. J. Libby to Stuart, September 22, 1941, Wood MSS.
92 *New York Times,* September 23, 1941.
93 *Commonweal,* 34 (1941), 590.
94 Norman Thomas to Stuart, September 23, 1941, and R. A. Moore to O. A. Case, September 29, 1941, America First MSS.
95 *Milwaukee Sentinel,* September 17, 1941; and *Newsweek,* 18 (September 22, 1941), 17.

96 *Chicago Tribune,* September 12, 1941.

97 *Ibid.,* September 13, 1941.

98 *Ibid.,* September 20, 1941. The famous German medal was not one of those which were pictured on the *Chicago Tribune's* feature page.

99 *Newsweek,* 18 (September 22, 1941), 17, and 18 (September 29, 1941), 15–16; and *Chicago Tribune,* September 17, 1941, and September 21, 1941.

100 For examples see: J. B. Bingham and J. R. Bingham to America First, September 14, 1941, Jules Sien to New York America First, September 15, 1941, Jean Bevan to New York America First, September 15, 1941, Edward Strasser to New York America First, September 17, 1941, America First MSS.

101 America First Committee Bulletin, #574, September 22, 1941, and K. E. Nordine to D. H. Carrick, October 8, 1941, America First MSS; and *Time,* 38 (October 6, 1941), 18–20.

102 Dorothy Thum to Clay Pugh, September 24, 1941, America First MSS.

103 For examples see: A. J. Carlson to J. P. Lewis, September 16, 1941, T. S. Hammond to Wood, September 17, 1941, W. R. Castle to Stuart, September 15, 1941, W. E. Hammaker to Stuart, September 22, 1941, Wood MSS; and F. A. Chase to J. L. Wheeler, September 16, 1941, America First MSS.

104 Gregory Mason to T. C. Chubb, September 18, 1941, America First MSS.

105 J. R. Boldt, Jr., to H. C. Schnibbe, September 23, 1941, Wood MSS; telegram W. S. Thomas to Wood, September 17, 1941, J. L. Wheeler to Stuart, September 16, 1941, Dorothy Thum to Clay Pugh, September 24, 1941, A. H. Sturcke to Wood, September 16, 1941, telegram R. H. Emerson to Wood, September 17, 1941, America First MSS.

106 L. M. Cole to Wood, September 15, 1941, America First MSS.

107 For examples see: J. D. Sartor to Lindbergh, September 16, 1941, and G. A. Deatherage to Lindbergh, September 14, 1941, America First MSS.

108 Interviews with General Wood, December 23, 1947, Stuart, June 17, 1949, and Robert J. Bannister, September 15, 1947.

109 America First Committee Bulletin, #553, September 15, 1941, America First MSS.

110 Minutes of America First National Committee Meeting, September 18, 1941, Wood MSS; and interview with General Wood, December 23, 1947. Present at the national committee meeting were Wood, Carlson, Mrs. Clark, Mrs. Fairbank, Flynn, Judson, Mrs. Longworth, Peek, Pinchot, and Stuart. Hufty, Moore, Pennypacker, Pettengill, and Webster were present by invitation.

111 "Two Views on Lindbergh," *Catholic World,* 154 (1941), 206–209.

112 *Chicago Tribune,* September 25, 1941; and *Washington Post,* September 25, 1941.

113 Stuart to all chapter chairmen, September 23, 1941, America First MSS.

114 Hyman Lischner to Wood, September 21, 1941, Wood MSS; J. L. Wheeler to Stuart, n.d., America First MSS; *Washington Post,* September 30, 1941; and *Catholic World,* 154 (1941), 209–10.

115 For example see: Stuart to Norman Thomas, September 26, 1941, Hufty to G. P. Mueller, October 6, 1941, America First MSS; Chester Bowles to Stuart, September 19, 1941, and Mrs. Fairbank to Wood, September 23, 1941, Wood MSS.

116 *New York Times,* October 20, 1941.

117 *Ibid.,* October 23, 1941, and October 29, 1941; *Chicago Tribune,* October 29, 1941; *Washington Post,* November 3, 1941; and *Newsweek,* 18 (November 10, 1941), 15; T. N. McCarter to Wood, September 29, 1941, and Kathryn Lewis to Wood, September 29, 1941, Wood MSS. It is not possible to determine with complete accuracy to what extent the Des Moines speech motivated these resignations but it was obviously a factor.

118 *New York Times,* October 1, 1941.

119 *Chicago Tribune,* October 4, 1941.

120 *Washington Post,* October 31, 1941.

121 General Wood expressed the opinion that Lindbergh was absolutely sincere but politically blind. Interview on December 23, 1947.

CHAPTER 9—SHOOT ON SIGHT

1 Minutes of America First Board of Directors Meeting, December 27, 1940, Wood MSS.
2 America First Committee Bulletin, #140 and #140A, March 20, 1941, America First MSS.
3 America First Committee, *Convoy: A Funeral Train* (Chicago, n.d.).
4 R. E. Wood and E. W. Gibson, "Shall We Convoy War Materials to England?" (mimeographed text of "The American Forum" released by United Feature Syndicate of New York, April 19–20, 1941), America First MSS.
5 America First Committee Bulletin, #192, April 10, 1941, and day letter from Wood to all chapters, April 28, 1941, America First MSS; and *Chicago Tribune,* April 13, 1941.
6 Ruth Sarles to Kendrick Lee, May 4, 1941, America First MSS; Basil Rauch, *Roosevelt From Munich to Pearl Harbor* (New York, 1950), 320; Charles A. Beard, *President Roosevelt and the Coming of the War 1941* (New Haven, 1948), 102.
7 Day letter Stuart to Lindbergh, May 13, 1941, day letter Wood to C. W. Tobey, May 13, 1941, Tobey to Wood, May 15, 1941, Wood MSS; and Ruth Sarles to Stuart, May 18, 1941, America First MSS.
8 Henry L. Stimson and McGeorge Bundy, *On Active Service In Peace and War* (New York, 1947, 1948), 368–69; Rauch, *Roosevelt From Munich to Pearl Harbor,* 318–19, 342.
9 Rauch, *Roosevelt From Munich to Pearl Harbor,* 320–23.
10 Enclosure with America First Committee Bulletin, #287, May 28, 1941, mimeographed news release from New York America First Chapter, May 28, 1941, America First MSS; and Wood to R. F. Moseley, May 29, 1941, Wood MSS.
11 For examples see: Lillian Gish to Stuart, June 4, 1941, and William Benton to Wood, June 3, 1941, America First MSS.
12 Rauch, *Roosevelt,* 354–55.
13 America First Research Bureau, *Did You Know* (Washington, 1941), #7.
14 *America First Bulletin* (New York), July 12, 1941.

15 *Congressional Record,* 77 Congress, 1 session (1941), A3491; *Chicago Tribune,* July 14, 1941; and *America First Bulletin* (New York), July 19, 1941.

16 *New York Times,* October 18, 1941.

17 Rauch, *Roosevelt,* 416–19.

18 Research Bureau, *Did You Know,* #1, #22, and #24.

19 "Statement by General Robert E. Wood, Acting Chairman of the National America First Committee" (mimeographed news release from America First headquarters [October 17, 1941]), America First MSS.

20 Research Bureau, *Did You Know,* #22.

21 *New York Times,* September 13, 1941.

22 Research Bureau, *Did You Know,* #22.

23 Undated news release from R. E. Wood, America First MSS. See also: *New York Times,* September 15, 1941.

24 "Statement by General Robert E. Wood, Acting Chairman of the National America First Committee" (mimeographed news release from America First headquarters [October 17, 1941]), America First MSS.

25 *Washington Post,* October 18, 1941.

26 *New York Times,* October 18, 1941.

27 Rauch, *Roosevelt,* 423; and Beard, *President Roosevelt,* 158.

28 Research Bureau, *Did You Know,* #28, 32–33. See also: *Washington Post,* October 10, 1941; and *Chicago Tribune,* October 10, 1941.

29 *Hearings before the Committee on Foreign Relations, United States Senate* (77 Congress, 1 session, on H.J. 237; Washington, 1941), 213.

30 Stuart to S. B. Pettengill, October 27, 1941, America First MSS.

31 Form letter from Stuart to all chapter chairmen, October 22, 1941, America First MSS.

32 America First Committee, *One Way Passage: Neutrality—or War?* (Chicago, 1941), 4.

33 America First, *One Way Passage,* 5; and Research Bureau, *Did You Know,* #28. For Churchill's later summary of British losses on the Atlantic Ocean in 1941 see: Winston S. Churchill, *The Grand Alliance* (Boston, 1950), 516–23.

34 For example see: *Chicago Tribune,* October 28, 1941.

35 For example see: Stuart to R. A. Taft, October 29, 1941, America First MSS.

36 *Chicago Tribune,* October 31, 1941; and *Washington Post,* November 3, 1941.

37 America First Committee, *Emergency Bulletin #1* (Chicago, October 25, 1941).

38 *Time,* 38 (October 13, 1941), 14; Lee Swanson to W. E. Fraser, November 13, 1941, Bertha Tallman to G. N. Peek, November 17, 1941, and Ruth Sarles to Wood, November 14, 1941, America Press MSS.

39 For example see: book wire H. C. Schnibbe to all chapters, November 12, 1941, America First MSS.

40 R. T. Small to Stuart, November 12, 1941, A. P. Hurt to Stuart, November 15, 1941, F. C. Ward to America First, November 17, 1941, America First MSS.

41 J. R. Boldt, Jr., to Page Hufty, November 15, 1941, A. P. Hurt to Stuart, November 15, 1941, F. C. Ward to America First, November 17, 1941, R. W. Davidson to Wood, November 25, 1941, America First MSS.

42 Undated America First news release, telegram Stuart to E. J. Ryan, November 7, 1941, form letter Wood to all members and friends of America First, November 13, 1941, America First Committee Bulletin, #687, November 14, 1941, and unidentified memo, America First MSS.

CHAPTER 10—POLITICS AND THE BATTLE AGAINST INTERVENTION

1 Albert Horlings, "Who Are the Appeasers," *New Republic,* 104 (1941), 110. For expressions of similar views see: *Capital Times* (Madison, Wisconsin), February 4, 1941; and *New York Post,* October 14, 1941.

2 Letter from R. Douglas Stuart, Jr. to the author, February 16, 1948.

3 *Who's Who in America,* 1948–1949, 1556.

4 T. S. Hammond to R. D. Stuart, Jr., October 15, 1940, America First MSS.

5 "General Robert E. Wood, President," *Fortune*, 17 (May, 1938), 66, 104; and *St. Louis Post-Dispatch*, October 27, 1940.

6 Stuart to Wood, August 14, 1940, America First MSS; Wood to Oren Root, Jr., August 15, 1941, Wood MSS; and *St. Louis Post-Dispatch*, October 27, 1940. In 1948 General Wood at first backed General Douglas MacArthur. Wood was an Illinois delegate to the Republican national convention where he supported Thomas E. Dewey. *Des Moines Register*, January 2, 1949.

7 *Who's Who in America*, 1948–1949, 765.

8 Mrs. Fairbank to Miss Helen Lamont, April 4, 1941, America First MSS.

9 *Chicago Daily News*, January 17, 1941, and May 23, 1941.

10 Stuart to Sidney Hertzberg, October 28, 1940, and telegram Stuart to S. Don, November 1, 1940, Wood MSS.

11 *Who's Who in America*, 1948–1949, 1510.

12 *Ibid.*, 1944–1945, 1941.

13 *Ibid.*, 1948–1949, 810.

14 *Ibid.*, 1225.

15 See relevant items in *Ibid.* See also: *New York Post*, October 14, 1941; and T. S. Hammond to Stuart, October 24, 1941, America First MSS.

16 *Who's Who in America*, 1942–1943, 1727–28, and 1191.

17 *Rochester Times Union* (New York), May 21, 1941.

18 Jeffrey to Robert Bliss, February 6, 1941, America First MSS.

19 Stuart to Elizabeth Wheeler Coleman, June 21, 1941, America First MSS; and *Wisconsin State Journal* (Madison), February 17, 1941.

20 R. L. Bliss to R. E. Wood, May 19, 1941, Wood MSS.

21 Holtzermann to Bliss, December 28, 1940, and C. L. Smith to Bliss, January 7, 1941, America First MSS; and *America First Bulletin* (New York), August 16, 1941.

22 D. C. MacDonald to R. E. Wood, December 27, 1941, America First MSS.

23 Chase to R. A. Taft, September 10, 1941, and Chase to Ward Johnson, September 6, 1941, America First MSS.

24 J. B. Gordon to T. M. Marshall, August 20, 1941, America First MSS.

25 Kathrine McCormick to R. A. Moore, June 9, 1941, and Page Hufty to Robert Vietig, July 21, 1941, America First MSS.

26 C. C. Crowe to Wood, June 15, 1941, America First MSS.

27 Minutes of Richmond, Virginia America First chapter, September 29, 1941, America First MSS.

28 W. S. Foulis to Stuart, July 24, 1941, America First MSS.

29 Chapter Dissolution Files, America First MSS.

30 Form letter from Stuart, Potter Stewart, Bill Krebs, and Eugene Locke, June 22, 1940, Stuart to Lindbergh, August 5, 1940, Stuart to Wood, July 1940, Wood MSS, and Stuart to Wood, August 14, 1940, America First MSS.

31 Wood to J. T. McCutcheon, July 22, 1940, Wood MSS.

32 Stuart to Chester Bowles, December 20, 1940, America First MSS.

33 See footnotes 5 through 8.

34 *Who's Who in America,* 1948–1949, 263–64.

35 Notebook in Stuart MSS; *New York Times,* October 14, 1941; and *Who's Who in America,* 1948–1949.

36 Notebook in Stuart MSS; *Who's Who in America,* 1948–1949; and undated typed biographical memos in America First MSS.

37 Mrs. A. P. Hurt to R. L. Bliss, January 30, 1941, America First MSS.

38 Barbara McDonald to H. E. MacGibbon, May 15, 1941, America First MSS.

39 Otto Case to H. C. Schnibbe, August 26, 1941, America First MSS.

40 *Washington Star,* December 12, 1940; *Washington Post,* January 5, 1941; and interview with General Wood, December 23, 1947.

41 *Washington Star,* December 12, 1940; and *Chicago Herald American,* May 19, 1941.

42 E. Jorgensen to Page Hufty, October 29, 1941, C. L. Smith to Bertha Tallman, February 19, 1941, Helen Lamont to Mrs.

Fairbank, April 3, 1941, and Fairbank to Lamont, April 4, 1941, America First MSS.

43 Stuart to Sidney Hertzberg, October 28, 1940, Wood MSS.

44 *Cincinnati Enquirer,* October 31, 1940.

45 "Memo on proposed broadcast by John T. Flynn," America First MSS.

46 Minutes of Board of Directors Meeting of America First, November 1, 1940, Wood MSS.

47 Judson to Stuart, November 2, 1940, America First MSS.

48 America First Committee, "Chapter Manual" (mimeographed pamphlet, Chicago, n.d.), form letter from R. L. Bliss mailed in November and December, 1940; Bliss to Park Chamberlain, December 28, 1940, J. R. Boldt, Jr. to H. A. Smith, April 3, 1941, Boldt to Elizabeth Borton, April 14, 1941, Boldt to T. H. Vail Motter, April 26, 1941, Bliss to K. D. Magruder, May 19, 1941, Bliss to staff, July 11, 1941, and Bliss to staff, October 2, 1941, America First MSS. See also: form letter from Stuart to E. M. Antrim, November 11, 1940, and Stuart to Mrs. B. C. Clark, December 5, 1940, America First MSS. In his letter of November 11, 1940, Stuart interpreted the election as "a mandate for peace, not for war."

49 For illustrations see: J. B. Gordon to Young Republicans of Allegheny County, May 7, 1941, Gordon to Young Democrats of Allegheny County, May 7, 1941, America First MSS; and *America First News* (Los Angeles), October 2, 1941.

50 *Boston Post,* February 23, 1941; and *America First Bulletin* (New York), July 12, 1941.

51 J. R. Boldt, Jr. to Stuart, May 8, 1941, Page Hufty to Mr. Despain, July 23, 1941, form letter from J. S. Broeksmit, Jr., to chapter chairmen, July 26, 1941, Hufty to Ruth Sarles, August 6, 1941, J. T. Flynn to Stuart, August 13, 1941, H. C. Schnibbe to New Jersey State Chapter of America First, September 10, 1941, and H. C. Schnibbe to Mrs. J. F. Branch, November 3, 1941, America First MSS.

52 Mrs. E. W. Kimbark to R. E. Wood, July 15, 1941, A. B. Nordskog to Wood, July 10, 1941, Stuart to Ruth Sarles, July 19, 1941, Stuart to Wood, August 11, 1941, S. B. Pettengill to

Wood, August 14, 1941, form letter from J. A. Fairbank to chapter chairmen, August 27, 1941, America First MSS; and Minutes of Board of Directors Meeting, August 11, 1941, Wood MSS.

53 R. A. Moore to R. E. Wood, September 8, 1941, H. C. Schnibbe to New Jersey State Chapter of America First, September 10, 1941, telegram Page Hufty to Ruth Sarles, September 13, 1941, America First MSS; and *New York Times,* September 23, 1941.

54 Memo from Yonkers, New York America First chapter, October 7, 1941, and J. H. Melloy to J. T. Flynn, October 18, 1941, America First MSS.

55 F. A. Chase to E. R. Verostek, October 8, 1941, America First MSS.

56 R. H. Emerson to N. H. Wilson, September 4, 1941, America First MSS.

57 For examples see: Mrs. Paul Palmer to Mrs. John Wheeler, July 17, 1941, F. W. Horner to Margaret Weissenberger, August 13, 1941, Russell Thompson to D. R. Vaile, September 2, 1941, and Vera Sessler to Stuart, November 25, 1941, America First MSS.

58 Stuart to Fred Horner, November 21, 1941, America First MSS.

59 *Congressional Record,* 77 Congress, 1 session (1941), A3491.

60 Form letter from Stuart to all chapter chairmen, July 23, 1941, R. A. Moore to Donald Shea, August 16, 1941, F. W. Horner to Margaret Weissenberger, August 13, 1941, form letter from J. A. Fairbank to chapter chairmen, August 19, 1941, F. H. Camphausen to H. A. Bothe, August 20, 1941, Russell Thompson to D. R. Vaile, September 2, 1941, R. H. Emerson to N. H. Wilson, September 4, 1941, R. H. Emerson to J. C. McKim, October 17, 1941, and M. R. Page Hufty to all chapter chairmen, October 25, 1941, America First MSS.

61 Fred Horner to Stuart, December 2, 1941, America First MSS.

62 *Cincinnati Enquirer,* October 31, 1940.

63 Hugh S. Johnson, "On the Move," *Chicago Herald American,* January 15, 1941; mimeographed radio address by H. S. Johnson, February 6, 1941, R. E. Wood to Oren Root, Jr., August

15, 1941, Philip La Follette, "Radio Comment on President Roosevelt's Message to Congress" (mimeographed copy of address, January 6, 1941), R. D. Stuart, Jr., "A is for America" (mimeographed radio address, August 1, 1941), John Cudahy, "Get Back to Majority Rule" (mimeographed press release text of radio address, December 4, 1941), and mimeographed news release on address by Senator G. P. Nye at America First meeting in Brooklyn, New York, September 22, 1941, America First MSS. For Willkie's "campaign oratory" statement see: *Hearings before the Committee on Foreign Relations, United States Senate* (77 Congress, 1 session, on S. 275, Washington, 1941), 905.

64 Telegram J. C. Hormel to R. E. Wood, January 14, 1941, America First MSS.

65 Philip La Follette, "Radio Comment on President Roosevelt's Message to Congress" (mimeographed copy of address, January 6, 1941), America First MSS.

66 *Chicago Herald-American,* May 2, 1941.

67 Chester Bowles to Stuart, July 15, 1941, America First MSS.

68 *America First Bulletin* (New York), June 14, 1941; and mimeographed America First Committee news release, May 30, 1941, America First MSS.

69 R. E. Wood, "Our Foreign Policy Today" (mimeographed copy of address, July 7, 1941), America First MSS.

70 Mimeographed transcript of remarks at National Meeting of Chapter Heads, Chicago, July 12, 1941, 7–8, America First MSS.

71 *Chicago Tribune,* July 20, 1941.

72 Minutes of Meeting of America First Board of Directors, August 11, 1941, Wood MSS.

73 Ruth Sarles to Stuart, September 20, 1941, America First MSS.

74 *Daily News* (New York), October 27, 1941.

75 America First Committee Bulletin, #623, October 10, 1941, America First MSS.

76 Mimeographed copy of "Pennypacker Resolution," America First MSS; and *Washington Post,* November 3, 1941. Italics supplied by the author.

77 Mimeographed America First Committee news release, Washington, D.C., November 1, 1941, America First MSS.

78 Form letter R. E. Wood to John Gordon, November 18, 1941, America First MSS.

79 For one example see: Dorothy Thum to Page Hufty, November 25, 1941, America First MSS.

80 For illustrations see: J. A. White to R. E. Wood, November 25, 1941, R. Vietig to Wood, November 25, 1941, A. E. Furlow to Wood, November 25, 1941, and B. R. Trimble to Wood, November 22, 1941, America First MSS.

81 Stuart to S. H. Adams, November 18, 1941, America First MSS.

82 Minutes of America First National Committee Meeting, November 28, 1941, Wood MSS. The national committee members present at the meeting were General Wood, General Hammond, Mrs. Fairbank, Otto Case, J. S. Otis, Clay Judson, Edwin Webster, Jr., Ray McKaig, W. H. Murray, and Stuart. S. B. Pettengill, Page Hufty, R. A. Moore, and Merle Miller were present by invitation.

83 "Statement Issued by the National Committee of the America First Committee, December 1, 1941" (mimeographed), America First MSS.

84 Stuart to Ruth Sarles, November 25, 1941, America First MSS; Wood to Miss F. M. Robinson, December 2, 1941, Wood MSS; *America First Bulletin* (New York), December 6, 1941; form letter from Mrs. J. A. Fairbank to chapter chairmen, December 4, 1941, America First MSS; *Time,* 38 (December 15, 1941), 28; and personal interviews with General R. E. Wood, December 23, 1947, and with Philip La Follette, January 16, 1948.

85 W. R. Castle to Stuart, November 5, 1941, America First MSS.

86 Mrs. Clark to R. L. Bliss, November 22, 1941, America First MSS.

87 H. S. Johnson, "On the Move," *Chicago Herald-American,* December 4, 1941, and December 28, 1940.

88 Mrs. Paul Fitz Simons to Stuart, November 28, 1941, Wood MSS.

89 Hanford MacNider to Wood, December 4, 1941, Wood MSS.

90 Clay Judson to Wood, August 15, 1941, enclosure to R. A. Moore to James Lipsig, November 18, 1941, memo from E. C. Jeffrey to Clay Pugh and Bailey Irwin, November 19, 1941, and Clay Judson to Wood, December 1, 1941, America First MSS.

91 Ruth Sarles to R. A. Moore, November 21, 1941, Sarles to Edith Ellinger, November 24, 1941, Stuart to Sarles, November 25, 1941, Sarles to Stuart, November 26, 1941, America First MSS.

92 James Lipsig to R. A. Moore, November 27, 1941, America First MSS.

93 R. A. Moore to Lipsig, November 18, 1941, and telegram Stuart to Lipsig, December 2, 1941, America First MSS.

94 R. A. Moore to S. B. Pettengill, November 25, 1941, America First MSS; and Minutes of America First National Committee Meeting, November 28, 1941, Wood MSS.

95 *Chicago Tribune,* December 3, 1941.

96 H. C. Schnibbe to John Gordon, December 1, 1941, America First MSS.

97 James Bayley to J. R. Boldt, Jr., June 9, 1941, and "Chapter Chatter" (mimeographed America First release), July 7, 1941, America First MSS.

98 T. M. Gilmore to R. H. Emerson, November 2, 1941, and D. E. Matturro to Wood, November 25, 1941, America First MSS; and Michael Sayers and Albert E. Kahn, *Sabotage! The Secret War Against America* (New York and London, 1942), 239.

99 Fred Chase to Miss Both, October 15, 1941, America First MSS.

100 Lansing Hoyt to Page Hufty, November 19, 1941, Hoyt to Stuart, November 26, 1941, and Stuart to Hoyt, November 27, 1941, America First MSS.

101 Hufty to Hoyt, November 24, 1941, America First MSS.

102 Interview with Harry C. Schnibbe, June 21, 1949; and form letter from A. A. Brooks, Jr., to America First members, September 27, 1941, America First MSS; and A. A. Brooks, Jr., to William Foulis, December 2, 1941, Wood MSS.

103 *Chicago Tribune,* December 3, 1941.

104 *Ibid.*
105 America First Committee Bulletin, #687, November 14, 1941, and mimeographed America First press release, America First MSS.
106 *Washington Post,* September 21, 1941.
107 Bowles was, however, defeated for re-election in 1950.
108 See the letterhead stationery of these two chapters in America First MSS.
109 Letter to author from Gerald L. K. Smith, December 6, 1947; R. L. Bliss to J. W. Gates, May 19, 1941, and day letter Bliss to Robert Vietig, March 22, 1941, America First MSS; and Walter Johnson, *The Battle Against Isolation* (Chicago, 1944), 236.

CHAPTER 11—PEARL HARBOR

1 Roger Butterfield, "Lindbergh," *Life,* 11 (1941), 67.
2 *New York Times,* October 31, 1940.
3 *Chicago Tribune,* July 27, 1941.
4 Douglas Dobson to Page Hufty, October 17, 1941, and Dobson to J. L. Fallon, January 27, 1942, America First MSS.
5 *America First Bulletin* (New York), December 6, 1941; and *Chicago Tribune,* May 11, 1941.
6 *Automotive News* (Detroit), December 9, 1940.
7 *America First Bulletin* (New York), August 16, 1941.
8 Sterling Morton, *Let's Think This Matter Through* (Chicago, December 15, 1940), 2.
9 *Ibid.; Chicago Tribune,* August 28, 1941; and *America First Bulletin* (New York), August 2, 1941.
10 For examples see: mimeographed America First news release, August 19, 1941, America First MSS; *Chicago Tribune,* August 19, 1941; America First Committee Research Bureau, *Did You Know* (Washington, 1941), #19; and *America First Bulletin* (New York), August 23, 1941.
11 *America First Bulletin* (New York), August 30, 1941.
12 Minutes of America First Board of Directors Meeting, August 11, 1941, Wood MSS; and enclosure to Clay Judson to Stuart,

August 11, 1941, and enclosure to Judson to Wood, August 11, 1941, America First MSS.

13 *The Herald of the America First Committee of Northern California* (San Francisco), September 4, 1941.

14 *America First Bulletin* (New York), December 6, 1941.

15 A. R. E. Pinchot to Stuart, December 3, 1941, Wood MSS; Stuart to Sarles, December 5, 1941, and Sarles to Stuart, December 6, 1941, America First MSS.

16 Thomas A. Bailey, *A Diplomatic History of the American People* (Fourth ed.; New York, 1950), 798.

17 Senator Gerald P. Nye addressed an America First rally at Pittsburgh, Pennsylvania on the afternoon of December 7, 1941, but apparently did not have reliable information about the Japanese attack until he had already begun his address. He then informed the audience of the attack and said that if the information was correct Congress would have to declare war. *Washington Post,* December 8, 1941; M. E. Armbruster to Hufty, December 11, 1941, America First MSS; and undated clipping from *Pittsburgh Press.*

18 *Chicago Tribune,* December 8, 1941. The italics were supplied by this author.

19 Book wire Stuart to all chapter chairmen, December 8, 1941, America First MSS.

20 Memo Stuart to F. H. Camphausen, December 8, 1941, America First MSS.

21 Teletype Stuart to Flynn, December 8, 1941, America First MSS.

22 Book wire Stuart to all chapter chairmen, December 8, 1941, America First MSS.

23 For examples see: E. R. Essig to Stuart, December 11, 1941, J. W. Blodgett, Jr., to Stuart, December 10, 1941, Isabel French to Stuart, December 10, 1941, and other messages in dissolution folder, Wood MSS. A memo on this folder said seventy-three of the eighty-two responses from chapters favored adjournment. Only nine voted for dissolution.

24 Ruth Sarles to Stuart, December 10, 1941, America First MSS.

25 E. S. Webster, Jr., to Wood , December 18, 1941, Wood MSS;

and Drew Pearson and Robert S. Allen, "Washington Merry-go-Round," *Tucson Daily Citizen,* December 17, 1941.

26　Minutes of Special Meeting of America First National Committee, December 11, 1941, Wood to O. A. Case, December 15, 1941, Wood to E. R. Essig, December 31, 1941, Webster to Wood, December 18, 1941, Wood MSS; Stuart to Paul Cotton, December 18, 1941, America First MSS; and *Tucson Daily Citizen,* December 17, 1941.

27　"Statement of the National Committee of the America First Committee December 11, 1941" (mimeographed), America First MSS. See also: Minutes of America First National Committee Meeting, December 11, 1941, Wood MSS; *Chicago Tribune,* December 12, 1941. This final Committee statement was based on a draft submitted by Clay Judson. Because the vote for dissolution on December 11, 1941 was less than a majority of the total national committee, the final official vote for dissolution was not made until January 29, 1942.

28　Stuart to J. W. Blodgett, Jr., January 7, 1942, J. R. Boldt, Jr., to H. C. Schnibbe, December 28, 1941, and Chapter Dissolution Files, America First MSS; and W. H. Regnery to America First Committee, January 12, 1942, Wood MSS.

29　Stuart to all chapter chairmen, December 11, 1941, and December 16, 1941, America First MSS.

30　Flynn to Wood, December 22, 1941, and J. L. Wheeler to J. L. Fallon, January 7, 1942, America First MSS.

31　J. L. Fallon to Robert Vietig, February 3, 1942, America First MSS.

32　E. J. Barrett to the author, July 12, 1949.

33　Interview with General Wood, December 23, 1947.

34　Harry Schnibbe to M. A. Keith, February 16, 1942, A. A. Brooks, Jr., to James Fallon, January 8, 1942, J. B. Gordon to Under Secretary of War, December 10, 1941, America First MSS; *Life,* 12 (April 13, 1942), 99; *Who's Who in America,* 1948–1949, 1204, 1483, 1556, and 2735; *Congressional Record,* 79 Congress, 1 session (1945), A5177–8; and interviews with General Wood, December 23, 1947, Stuart, April 6, 1949, and Schnibbe, June 21, 1949.

35 *Life*, 12 (April 13, 1942), 94, 98–99; Flynn to Wood, December 22, 1941, and J. L. Wheeler to J. L. Fallon, January 7, 1942, America First MSS.

36 *The Memoirs of Cordell Hull* (2 vols., New York, 1948), 697.

37 Foster Rhea Dulles, *Twentieth Century America* (Cambridge, 1945), 506.

38 Robert E. Sherwood, *Roosevelt and Hopkins: An Intimate History* (New York, 1948), 132–33; Henry L. Stimson and McGeorge Bundy, *On Active Service In Peace and War* (New York, 1947, 1948), 370; and *Memoirs of Cordell Hull*, 943.

39 Sherwood, *Roosevelt and Hopkins*, 299.

40 Stimson and Bundy, *On Active Service*, 368.

41 B. K. Wheeler to Wood, July 17, 1941, America First MSS.

42 Sherwood, *Roosevelt and Hopkins*, 382; and Stimson and Bundy, *On Active Service*, 370–73.

43 Sherwood, *Roosevelt and Hopkins*, 382–83.

44 Stimson and Bundy, *On Active Service*, 376.

BIBLIOGRAPHY
AND INDEX

Bibliography

MANUSCRIPTS

This study is based primarily upon an examination of the manuscript records of the America First Committee. Most important were the America First Committee Manuscripts in the Hoover Library on War, Revolution and Peace at Stanford University. This collection includes the files of America First national headquarters and the records of many local chapters. The America First Committee materials in the possession of General Robert E. Wood in Chicago included the minutes of policy meetings, financial records, and many key letters. A few items of value were examined in the personal files of R. Douglas Stuart, Jr., of San Francisco, California.

Friends of Democracy, Inc., supplied the author with several unpublished reports on America First. Letters to the author from the following persons provided factual information, points of view, leads and other suggestions: Edward J. Barrett, Springfield, Illinois; Ben S. Beery, Los Angeles; L. M. Birkhead, New York; Chester Bowles, Essex, Connecticut; Kingman Brewster, Jr., Cambridge, Massachusetts; William R. Castle, Washington, D.C.; Ralph H. Ensign, Los Angeles; Hamilton Fish, New York; John T. Flynn, New York; William T. Ford, Lakeville, Connecticut; E. T. Hall, Southboro, Massachusetts; General Thomas S. Hammond, Harvey, Illinois; Robert M. Huntington, New Haven, Connecticut; Donald F. Keefee, Hamden, Connecticut; Hanford MacNider, Mason City, Iowa; Verne Mar-

Bibliography

shall, Cedar Rapids, Iowa; George K. McClelland, Istanbul, Turkey; Sterling Morton, Chicago; J. Sanford Otis, Chicago; Lawrence K. Pickett, Brookline, Massachusetts; Paul S. Pierson, Milwaukee, Wisconsin; Charles B. Price, Jr., Tupelo, Mississippi; Potter Stewart, Cincinnati, Ohio; R. Douglas Stuart, Jr., San Francisco; Louis J. Tabor, Syracuse, New York; Burton K. Wheeler, Washington, D.C.; and General Robert E. Wood, Chicago.

PERSONAL INTERVIEWS

Robert J. Bannister, Des Moines, Iowa, on September 15, 1947.
Philip La Follette, Madison, Wisconsin, on January 16, 1948.
Hugh R. Parkinson, San Francisco, California, on May 13, 1949.
Harry C. Schnibbe, Denver, Colorado, on June 21, 1949.
R. Douglas Stuart, Jr., San Francisco, California on April 6, 1949, May 6, 1949, and June 17, 1949.
General Robert E. Wood, Chicago, Illinois, on December 23, 1947, and August 11, 1949.

GOVERNMENT DOCUMENTS

Congressional Record, 1941–1945.
Hearings before the Committee on Foreign Affairs House of Representatives. 77 Congress, 1 session, Washington, 1941.
Hearings before the Committee on Foreign Relations United States Senate. 77 Congress, 1 session, Washington, 1941.
Hearings before the Committee on Military Affairs United States Senate. 77 Congress, 1 session, Washington, 1941.
Legislative Reference Service of the Library of Congress. *Fascism in Action—A Documented Study and Analysis of Fascism in Europe.* 80 Congress, 1 session, House Document no. 401, Washington, 1947.
Special Committee on Un-American Activities House of Representatives. *Nazi Activities.* Section 1 of *Report on the Axis Front Movement in the United States,* which is Part VII of Appendix to *Investigation of Un-American Propaganda Ac-*

270

tivities in the United States, 78 Congress, 1 session, Washington, 1943.

Transcript of Laws Relating to the Franking Privilege of Members of Congress. Post Office Department, Washington, n.d.

NEWSPAPERS

Akron Beacon Journal
Automotive News (Detroit)
Birmingham News
Boston Post
Buffalo Courier-Express
Capital Times (Madison, Wisconsin)
Catholic Review (Baltimore)
Chicago Herald-American
Chicago News
Chicago Times
Chicago Tribune
Cincinnati Enquirer
Daily Worker (New York)
Des Moines Register
Des Moines Tribune
Fox Lake Representative (Fox Lake, Wisconsin)
Gary Post-Tribune
Hollywood Citizen News
Miami Herald
Milwaukee Sentinel
News (New York)
New York Herald Tribune
New York Post
New York Times
New York World Telegram
North Park Press (San Diego)
Oakland Post Enquirer
Oregonian (Portland)
Peace Action of the National Council for the Prevention of War (Washington, D.C.)

Bibliography

PM (New York)
Publicity (Wichita, Kansas)
Richmond Times Dispatch
Rochester Times Union (Rochester, New York)
San Francisco Chronicle
Seattle Post-Intelligence
Seattle Times
Star (Washington, D.C.)
St. Louis Post-Dispatch
Wall Street Journal
Washington News
Washington Post
Washington Times-Herald
Wisconsin State Journal (Madison)
Yale Daily News (New Haven)

AMERICA FIRST CHAPTER NEWSPAPERS

America First Bulletin (Cincinnati)
America First Bulletin (New York)
America First Committee (St. Louis)
America First Herald (Pittsburgh)
America First News (Los Angeles)
Herald (San Franciso)
Shield America (Kansas City)
Voice of America First (Philadelphia)

PERIODICALS

American Hebrew
American Mercury
Atlantic Monthly
Catholic World
Christian Century
Christian Science Monitor Weekly Magazine Section
Collier's
Commonweal

Congressional Digest
Current Biography
Current History and Forum
Facts in Review
Fortune
Future: The Magazine for Young Men
Jewish Frontier
Life
Living Age
Nation
New Masses
New Republic
Newsweek
New Yorker
New York Times Magazine
Opinion: A Journal of Jewish Life and Letters
Public Opinion Quarterly
Reader's Digest
Rotarian Magazine
Saturday Evening Post
Scribner's Commentator
Social Justice
Time
Virginia Quarterly Review
Vital Speeches of the Day

PAMPHLETS

This list includes only the published pamphlets and the America First Committee Research Bureau releases useful for this study. The America First Manuscripts in Hoover Library included many other useful mimeographed pamphlets and bulletins. Most important of these were the seven hundred mimeographed bulletins issued by America First national headquarters to direct the activities of local chapters. The mimeographed texts of addresses at America First meetings were also useful.

Bibliography

America First Committee:

Address by Charles A. Lindbergh. Chicago, April 23, 1941.
Address by Charles A. Lindbergh. Chicago, May 10, 1941.
America First Committee Aims and Activities. Chicago, n.d.
Barton, Bruce. *How To Write Your Congressman.* Chicago, n.d.
Beckman, Most Reverend Francis J. L. *Congressmen, Be Warned!* Chicago, July 27, 1941.
———. *A Message for Americans.* Chicago, October 19, 1941.
———. *Mr. President.* Chicago, June 21, 1941.
Carlson, Anton J. *Address.* Chicago, n.d.
Chase, Stuart. *Four Assumptions About the War.* Chicago, January 6, 1941.
Convoy—A Funeral Train. Chicago, n.d.
Did You Know. Washington, June 18, 1941 to October 25, 1941.
>#1. *Memorandum on Contraband Material in the Cargo of the Robin Moor.* (June 18, 1941).
>#2. *Memorandum on Arming United States Merchant Vessels.* (June 21, 1941).
>#3. *"Freedom of the Seas."* (June 26, 1941).
>#4. *Lease-Lend Aid to Russia.* (June 27, 1941).
>#5. *Wings Over Nome?* (July 1, 1941).
>#6. *Buy or Die.* (July 5, 1941).
>#7. *Our Iceland Outpost.* (July 9, 1941).
>#8. *Our African Outpost.* (July 11, 1941).
>#9. *Another A.E.F.?* (July 15, 1941).
>#10. *Soldiers Until . . . ?* (July 17, 1941).
>#11. *Long-Term Conscription.* (July 17, 1941).
>#12. *Nobody Knows the Trouble We're In.* (July 24, 1941).
>#13. *The Shape of Things to Come?* (July 30, 1941).
>#14. *"Say, Is This the USA?"* (July 31, 1941).
>#15. *Swastika Over Sickle.* (August 1, 1941).
>#16. *Union Now?* (August 6, 1941).
>#17. *"The All-American Front."* (August 8, 1941).

274

#18. *Oil-Out for Britain.* (August 11, 1941).

#19. *Eight Points for War or Peace. What Do They Mean?* (August 23, 1941).

#20. *Eight Points for War or Peace. What Legal Effect do They Have?* (August 23, 1941).

#21. *Eight Points for War or Peace. Can They Work?* (September 2, 1941).

#22. *One-Man War.* (September 13, 1941).

#23B. *All-Out Aid for the Western Hemisphere.* (September 22, 1941).

#24. *Jekyll-and-Hyde Ships.* (September 23, 1941).

#25. *Priority Orphans.* (September 30, 1941).

#26. *Lease-Lend for War.* (October 4, 1941).

#27. *Freedom (?) of Religion in Communist Russia.* (October 8, 1941).

#28. *Elimination of the Neutrality Law Combat Zones Means War.* (October 25, 1941).

The Economic Consequences of the Lease-Lend Program. (Chicago, n.d.)

Pledges to Keep America Out of War made by 42 United States Senators during Neutrality Debate, October, 1939. (Chicago, n.d.)

Emergency Bulletin #1. Chicago, October 25, 1941.

Flynn, John T. *Can Hitler Invade America?* Chicago, n.d.

———. *War, What Is It?* New York, February 28, 1941.

Hammond, Thomas. *"We Were There!"* Chicago, 1940.

Hoover, Herbert. *Address.* New York, May 11, 1941.

———. *A Call To American Reason.* Chicago, June 29, 1941.

Hutchins, Robert M. *America and the War.* Chicago, January 23, 1941.

———. *The Proposition Is Peace.* Chicago, March 30, 1941.

"I Hate War." Chicago, n.d.

Judson, Clay. *Is This Our War?* Chicago, November 30, 1941.

Kennedy, Joseph P. *Excerpts from Text of Address.* Chicago, January 18, 1941.

La Follette, Robert M. *Are We on the Road to War?* Chicago, September 11, 1940.

Bibliography

Lodge, Henry Cabot, Jr. *The Drift Toward War*. Chicago, September 25, 1940.

Morton, Sterling. *Let's Think This Matter Through*. Chicago, December 15, 1940.

Must We Fight for Our Foreign Trade? Chicago, n.d.

One Way Passage: Neutrality—or War? Chicago, n.d.

One Year of America First—An Amazing Story of Democracy in Action. Chicago, 1941.

Peek, George N., Baruch, Bernard M., and Moley, Raymond. *Can Hitler Cripple America's Economy?* Chicago, n.d.

We Want You. Chicago, n.d.

Wood, General Robert E. *Our Foreign Policy*. Chicago, October 4, 1940.

Committee to Defend America by Aiding the Allies:

The Atlantic Is Not 3000 Miles Wide Because. Chicago, n.d.

Hitler's American Ambitions. Chicago, n.d.

How Does America's Defense Program Fit the Facts? Chicago, n.d.

Labor and the Totalitarian Threat. New York, August 30, 1940.

Official Statement of Policy. New York, November 26, 1940.

Organized Labor's Stake in the War. New York, n.d.

Perry, Ralph Barton. *Triple-Action Defense*. New York, December, 1940.

Primer of American Defense. n.p., n.d.

Secret Nazi Speech. New York, May, 1940.

Sternberg, Fritz. *In Order to Survive*. New York, 1941.

Trade War–Or, War of Freedom? Chicago, n.d.

Van Paassen, Pierre. *Hitler's Plan Against the United States*. n.p., n.d.

We Reply, n.p., n.d.

When Is A War A War? Chicago, n.d.

Which Road Shall We Take? Chicago, n.d.

Fight for Freedom Committee:

Chicago Fight For Freedom Hits at Hitler. Chicago, 1941.

A "Negotiated Peace." New York, n.d.

We Mean "Fight" and We Mean "Freedom." New York, n.d.

Woollcott, Alexander. *A Voice from the Cracker-Barrel.* New York, n.d.

Americanism Committee, 17th District, American Legion, Department of California:

#1. *Subversive Activities in America First Committee in California.* Los Angeles, October 10, 1941.
#2. *"Since Dec. 7" Enemy Propaganda in Southern California.* Los Angeles, February 20, 1942.
#3. *The Case of Hamilton Fish.* Los Angeles, March 17, 1944.

Friends of Democracy, Inc.:

The America First Committee—The Nazi Transmission Belt. New York, n.d.
Father Coughlin Self-Condemned. Kansas City, n.d.
Friends of Democracy's Battle. New York, June 30, 1947.
Henry Ford Must Choose. Kansas City and New York, n.d.
Is Lindbergh A Nazi? New York, n.d.
The Scourge of Bigotry! New York, n.d.

Miscellaneous:

Beale, Howard K. *Some Fallacies of the Interventionist View.* Washington, 1941.
Flynn, John T.; Agar, Herbert; Lee, Josh; and Wheeler, Burton K. *Should Congress Adopt the Lend-Lease Program?* American Forum of the Air, Washington, January 12, 1941.
Flynn, John T. and Niebuhr, Reinhold. *Should Our Ships Convoy Materials to Britain?* Bulletin of America's Town Meeting of the Air, New York, May 12, 1941.
Flynn, John T. *Uncovering Under Cover: The Real Facts About the Smear Book's Odd Author.* New York, April 23, 1944.
La Follette, Philip and Ickes, Harold L. *Second Session on the President's Lend-Lease Plan.* Bulletin of America's Town Meeting of the Air, New York, February 3, 1941.
La Follette, Philip and Knox, Frank. *Should the Arms Em-*

bargo be Lifted? Bulletin of America's Town Meeting of the Air, New York, October 16, 1939.

Nye, Gerald P. *Our Madness Increases as Our Emergency Shrinks*. Washington, August 4, 1941.

Palmer, Albert W. *A Road Away From War*. n.p., June 19, 1940.

Taber, Louis J. *National Master's Address*. Worchester, November 12, 1941.

Wheeler, Burton K. and Wirth, Louis. *Is This Our War?* University of Chicago Round Table, Chicago, January 12, 1941.

Women's Voice. *Truth Is Truth To The End Of Reckoning*. Chicago, n.d.

BOOKS

Bailey, Thomas A. *A Diplomatic History of the American People*. Fourth ed., New York, 1950.

Beard, Charles A. *A Foreign Policy for America*. New York, 1940.

———. *President Roosevelt and the Coming of the War 1941*. New Haven, 1948.

Benns, F. Lee. *European History Since 1870*. New York, 1942.

Bowers, Robert Edwin. "The American Peace Movement, 1933–41." Unpublished Ph.D. dissertation, University of Wisconsin, 1949.

Carlson, John Roy. *The Plotters*. New York, 1946.

———. *Under Cover*. Cleveland and New York, 1943.

Churchill, Winston S. *Their Finest Hour*. Cambridge, 1949.

———. *The Grand Alliance*. Cambridge, 1950.

Davis, Forrest. *The Atlantic System*. New York, 1941.

Davis, Forrest and Lindley, Ernest K. *How War Came*. New York, 1942.

Detzer, Dorothy. *Appointment on the Hill*. New York, 1948.

Dulles, Foster Rhea. *Twentieth Century America*. Cambridge, 1945.

Flynn, John T. *As We Go Marching*. Garden City, 1944.

———. *Country Squire in the White House*. New York, 1940.

———. *The Road Ahead: America's Creeping Revolution.* New York, 1949.

———. *The Roosevelt Myth.* New York, 1947.

Foner, Philip S. ed. *Franklin Delano Roosevelt: Selections From His Writings.* New York, 1947.

Hoke, Henry. *Black Mail.* New York, 1944.

———. *It's A Secret.* New York, 1946.

Hull, Cordell. *The Memoirs of Cordell Hull.* 2 vols., New York, 1948.

Johnson, Walter. *The Battle Against Isolation.* Chicago, 1944.

Kin, David George. *The Plot Against America.* Missoula, 1946.

Millis, Walter. *This Is Pearl.* New York, 1947.

Morganstern, George E. *Pearl Harbor.* New York, 1947.

Ogden, August Raymond. *The Dies Committee.* 2nd revised ed., Washington, 1945.

Pacific Reporter. 2nd Series, Vol. 158, St. Paul, 1945.

Rauch, Basil. *Roosevelt From Munich to Pearl Harbor.* New York, 1950.

———. *The History of the New Deal, 1933–1938.* New York, 1944.

Riess, Curt. *Total Espionage.* New York, 1941.

Roosevelt, Franklin D. *Public Papers and Addresses: War and Aid to Democracies.* New York, 1941.

Sayers, Michael and Kahn, Albert E. *Sabotage! The Secret War Against America.* New York and London, 1942.

Seldes, George. *Facts and Fascism.* New York, 1943.

———. *One Thousand Americans.* New York, 1947.

Sherwood, Robert E. *Roosevelt and Hopkins: An Intimate History.* New York, 1948.

Stettinius, Edward R., Jr. *Lend-Lease Weapon for Victory.* New York, 1944.

Stimson, Henry L. and Bundy, McGeorge. *On Active Service In Peace and War.* New York, 1947, 1948.

Strong, Donald S. *Organized Anti-Semitism in America: The Rise of Group Prejudice During the Decade 1930–1940.* Washington, 1941.

Bibliography

St. George, Maximilian and Dennis, Lawrence. *A Trial on Trial: The Great Sedition Trial of 1944.* n.p., 1946.

Stowe, Leland. *While Time Remains.* New York, 1947.

Tebbel, John. *An American Dynasty: The Story of the McCormicks, Medills and Pattersons.* Garden City, 1947.

Trefousse, H. L. *Germany and American Neutrality, 1939–1941.* New York, 1951.

Van Alstyne, Richard W. *American Diplomacy in Action.* 2nd ed., London, 1947.

Warburg, James P. *Foreign Policy Begins at Home.* New York, 1944.

Who's Who in America. Vols. 19–25.

Index

ADAMS, Charles Francis, 170
Adams, Samuel Hopkins, 21, 173
Administration, Roosevelt: fears of America First concerning, 53–54; America First efforts to put on defensive, 58; proposals on selective service changes, 100; Stuart's comment on, 102–3; criticizes America First, 106; believed hoping for incidents, 160; margin of victory on Neutrality Act revision, 166; and Peek and Johnson, 170; criticized by MacNider, 184–85; Far Eastern policies of criticized, 190–93; opposition to, 197–99. *See also* Roosevelt, Franklin Delano
Advisory Referendum on War or Peace: pacifist support for, 56–57, 90; America First campaign for, 57–59
Africa: America First opposed to bases in, 61; possibility of attack from, 96
Agricultural Adjustment Administration: and Peek, 74, 78, 170
Air Power: views of Lindbergh

and America First on, 96–99
Akron, Ohio, Chapter of America First: sponsor is German agent, 121; role of Burch in, 124; includes Coughlinites, 137; fails to send in records, 241
Albuquerque, New Mexico, Chapter of America First: leaders of were Democrats, 173
Alderman, Garland L.: indicted, 128, 246–47; views on Jews, 139
Allen, Robert S., 73
Alsop, Joseph, 54
America First Book, 118
America First Committee: after Pearl Harbor, 3, 187–88, 193–96, 264; origins, 10–16, 167; finances and contributors, 13, 22–23, 31–33, 73–74, 117, 126, 195, 240, 248; national committee, 13–15, 17, 20–23, 26, 43, 62–63, 71–72, 74, 76–79, 89–92, 117, 132–33, 148–53, 169–70, 182–84, 194–95, 248, 252, 261; named, 14; public announcement of, 14;

281

Index

Coughlin, Father (*contd.*)
ventionist position, 10; discussed and America First policies toward, 117, 134–38; Alderman comment on, 139; at America First rally, 125–26

Council Against Intolerance in America, 146

Crowe, C. C., 171

Curran, Reverend Edward Lodge, 135–36

Cusick, F. H. Peter, 146

Czechoslovakia, 3

D*AILY WORKER:* criticizes America First, 84; said to have been distributed at interventionist meetings, 116; denounces Lindbergh speech, 146

Day, Congressman Stephan A.: book published by Flanders Hall, 118; loans frank to America First, 127

Dearborn Independent, 132

Declaration of War on Axis: vote on proposed by America First, 61–64

Defense, Military: United States preparations for, 5; America First views on, 15; interventionist views on, 93–94; issue discussed, America First views on, 93–103; Goering quoted on, 120–21; views on pacifist organizations on, 229

Delaware: America First failure in, 31

Democracy: America First views on defense of, 15, 37–39

Democratic Party: opposition to

as basis for noninterventionist strength, 9; convention attended by Stuart, 13; among interventionists, 69; views on foreign policy, 69–71; uses frank, 127; America First identified with opposition to, 167; members of in America First, 168–69, 172–73; America First strength based partly on opposition to, 172

Denmark, 4, 95–96

Dennett, Prescott, 122–23

Denver, Colorado, Chapter of America First, 31, 93. *See also* Colorado State Unit of America First

Derounian, Avedis. *See* Carlson, John Roy

Des Moines, Iowa, Chapter of America First: speech by Lindbergh sponsored by, 143–45

Des Moines Register: comment on Lindbergh speech, 145

Destroyer deal: announced, 5; America First views on, 40, 98–99

Dewey, Thomas E., 147, 256

Dies Committee, 117–18, 122

Draft Extension. *See* Selective Service

Duncan, Colonel Early E. W., 93

Dunkerque, evacuation of, 4

E*ARLY,* Stephen T., 147

Eau Claire, Wisconsin, Chapter of America First, 33

Educators, 46, 76

Eichelberger, Clark, 7

Election of 1940: cited as evidence of support for Adminis-

288

tration foreign policies, 52; America First view of, 53, 178–79, 258; diverts critics from America First, 104; America First advertisements before, 174, 178

Elections of 1942: America First pledges support for noninterventionists in, 165; America First decision to participate in, 181–87

Ellender Amendment to Lend-Lease, 48–49, 216

Emergency Committee to Defend America First, 13

England. *See* Great Britain

English Channel, 96–97

Europe: crises in 1930's, 3; beginning of war in, 5; America First view of, 37; effect of events in, 196

European War: begins, 5; America First views on, 15

FACTS IN REVIEW, 120–21

Fairbank, Mrs. Janet Ayer: on America First national committee, 15; vice-chairman of America First, 17, 25; on executive committee, 19–20; critical of Stuart, 20, 24; leader of Chicago chapter, 22; views on war-peace issue, 51; supports advisory referendum, 57; revises letter to President, 63; opposes election of Roosevelt, 73; warns chapters against Shea, 134; political activities, 168–69, 172; leads Illinois and Iowa units, 173; favors dissolving the Committee, 194;

at national committee meetings, 252, 261

Far East. *See* Asia

Farm Groups: America First appeal to, 46; relations with America First, 77–78; relations with pacifist organizations, 90

Fascism: America First views on, 9, 38, 81–83

Fascist Sympathizers: support noninterventionists, 8, 70; barred from America First, 16, 117; America First leaders accused of being, 107; said to work through America First, 104–13; denounced by Flynn, 119

Federal Bureau of Investigation, 117–18

Fight for Freedom Committee: organized, 8; criticizes America First, 106, 108; supported by Birkhead and Stout, 109; America First policy on criticisms by, 115; accused of having communist support, 116; denounces Lindbergh speech, 146. *See also* Interventionists

Fish, Hamilton: sponsors war-peace referendum, 59–60; speaker for America First, 79, 170; secretary of serves propaganda ring, 122–23; defeated, 188

Fitz Simons, Mrs. Ellen French Vanderbilt, 169, 184

Flanders Hall Publishing Company, 118

Fleischer, Dr. Charles, 153

Fleischmann, Max C., 33

289

Index

Flynn, John T.: on America First national committee, 15; influences America First policies, 22; chairman of New York chapter, 22; views on arms embargo repeal, 39; statement against Lend-Lease, 45; economic views of, 74; views on foreign trade, 81; predicts economic consequences of intervention, 82–83; reaction to Russo-German War, 85–86; criticizes England, 86; relations with pacifists, 89; views on military defense, 97; opposes draft extension, 102; reply to Friends of Democracy, 114, 236; works to bar questionable persons or groups from America First, 116, 118–19, 122, 125–26, 134–35; aids Senate investigation, 141; criticizes Lindbergh speech, 148; agitation for removal of, 150; criticizes occupation of Iceland, 158; comment on ship sinking incidents, 162; opposes revision of Neutrality Act, 163–64; talk opposing Roosevelt, 174; chapter statement on relations with Japan, 192–93; favors dissolving Committee, 194; at national committee meeting, 252. *See also* New York Chapter of America First

Ford, Henry, 21, 132–33, 196

Foreign Affairs Committee, House of Representatives: Lend-Lease hearings, 43–45

Foreign Relations Committee, United States Senate: Lend-Lease hearings, 44–45; hearings on revision of Neutrality Act, 164

Fort Wayne, Indiana, Chapter of America First, 31, 153

Fosdick, Harry Emerson, 48

Foster, William Z., 107

France: conquered by Germany, 4, 95–96

Franking privilege, Congressional: Wheeler's loaned to America First, 92; use of by America First, 92, 126–28; use of to distribute propaganda, 122–23

Free American and Deutscher und Weckruf Beobachter, 119

Freedom: America First views on way to preserve, 38–39; interventionist views of effect of German victory on, 80

Free Enterprise. *See* Capitalism

Friends of Democracy, Inc.: criticizes America First, 106, 109–11; described, 109; J. R. Carlson becomes investigator for, 112; reaction of America First to criticism by, 114–15, 236; Anton Carlson resigns from, 114–15

GALLUP Poll. *See* Polls, Public Opinion

Georgia, 31

German-American Bund: supports noninterventionist position, 10, 71; America First repudiates support of, 119, 122

German-American National Alliance: America First files checked for members of, 118;

290

Index

Index

Index

Socialism: feared and opposed by America First, 9, 72, 84

Socialists: foreign policy views, 70–71; reaction to Des Moines speech, 147. *See also* Thomas, Norman; and Krueger, Maynard

Social Justice: views on America First, 134–38

South: America First failure in, 31; foreign policy views of, 70

Southern California Unit of America First, 171, 177, 186

Soviet Union: nonaggression pact, 3; America First reaction to German attack on, 68, 85–86; Catholics oppose aid to, 87; cheered by interventionists, 116; Far Eastern effects of defeat of, 192

Stamford, Connecticut, Chapter of America First, 22, 149–50

Stark, Admiral Harold R.: account of *Greer* incident cited, 160

Steel Seafarer: bombed, 159–60

Steuben Society of America, 122, 240

Stimson, Henry L.: urges Congressional vote on war, 63, 198; Wheeler incident, 92; urges use of convoys, 155; cited on Roosevelt, 199

Stout, Rex, 109

Streit, Clarence, 8

Stuart, H. L., 22, 32, 170

Stuart, R. Douglas, Jr.: background and education, 10–11; Yale noninterventionist activities, 11; organizes America First, 11–14; role as leader of America First, 14, 17, 19, 22–26; desire to form chapters, 26; views on war-peace issue and public opinion, 51, 54, 61, 64–65; economic views, 72–73, 75, 80, 84; commission, 91; on draft extension vote, 102–3; reply to critic, 113; views on America First membership and leadership policies, 116–17, 119, 132–33, 136, 152; on movie propaganda, 140; opposes Neutrality Act revision, 163–65; political views, 171; desire to make America First nonpartisan, 171–72; inquiry on impeachment movement, 177; during World War II, 196; at Yale, 204; on negotiated peace, 213; at Committee meetings, 252, 261

Swann, Professor Howard G., 36

Swift, Philip T., 33

Tabor, Louis J., 15, 21, 77, 169

Taft, Robert A.: consulted by Stuart, 12, 167; America First distributes speeches of, 46; opposes vote on anti-convoy resolution, 156; supported by America First members, 171; advises Committee to dissolve, 194

Tennessee, 31

Terre Haute, Indiana, Chapter of America First, 138

Texas: resolution against Lindbergh, 146

Thomas, Norman: supports noninterventionists, 70; relations

302

with America First, 75, 78; economic ideas opposed, 82; views on defense, 90–91; reaction to Lindbergh speech, 147–48

Thompson, Dorothy, 107, 113

Thorkelson, Jacob, 134

Thum, Dorothy, 149

Time Magazine, 107

Tobey, Charles W.: campaign against convoys, 156–57

Townsend, Ralph: and America First, 121, 124–25

UIHLEIN, Edgar J., 33

Un-American Affairs Committee, House of Representatives: and America First, 117–18

Uncensored, 75

Under Cover, 112

Union Now, 8

United States of America: foreign policies, 4–5; defense efforts, 5; relation to European war, 37–39; question of declaring war on Axis, 56–67; predicted effects of foreign policies on economy of, 79–84; aids Russia, 86; military defense of, 93–103; policies avoid ship sinkings, 158

United States Maritime Commission, 164

University faculty members: in America First, 21, 76

VALENTINE, Alan, 76

Vallandigham, Clement L., 109, 228

Viereck, George Sylvester: German propaganda activities, 122–23

Villard, Oswald Garrison: on national committee, 15, 75, 89; resigns, 78, 90

WAR PARTY: mentioned by La Follette, 55, 179, 182

War-Peace Issue: discussed, 50–67; and aid to Russia, 86; and revision of Neutrality Act, 163; and election of 1940, 258

Washington, D.C., Chapter of America First: leadership, 22, 173; and grand jury investigation, 123; denies ordering reprints from Fish, 127; bars Coughlinites, 134

Washington State Unit of America First, 22, 28, 30, 173

Webster, Edwin S., Jr.: role in America First, 22–23, 252, 261; on working with other groups, 116; account of America First rally, 126; favors adjourning Committee, 194

Western Hemisphere: sending American troops out of, 48; referendum on action in event of attack on, 59; effects of Nazi victory on economy of, 80; military defense of, 93–103

West Virginia, 31

Wheeler, Burton K.: consulted by America First leaders, 12, 14, 23, 63; on arms embargo repeal, 39; attack on Lend-Lease, 45–46; speeches distributed, 46; on national unity, 55; supports advisory refer-

Index